# JAZZ ODYSSEY

## American Made Music Series

ADVISORY BOARD

David Evans, General Editor
Barry Jean Ancelet
Edward A. Berlin
Joyce J. Bolden
Rob Bowman
Curtis Ellison
William Ferris
John Edward Hasse
Kip Lornell
Bill Malone
Eddie S. Meadows
Manuel H. Peña
Wayne D. Shirley
Robert Walser

# JAZZ ODYSSEY

## THE GLOBAL LIVES OF BOOKER T. PITTMAN

### JASON BORGE

UNIVERSITY PRESS OF MISSISSIPPI / JACKSON

The University Press of Mississippi is the scholarly publishing agency of
the Mississippi Institutions of Higher Learning: Alcorn State University,
Delta State University, Jackson State University, Mississippi State University,
Mississippi University for Women, Mississippi Valley State University,
University of Mississippi, and University of Southern Mississippi.

www.upress.state.ms.us

The University Press of Mississippi is a member
of the Association of University Presses.

Copyright © 2026 by University Press of Mississippi
All rights reserved
Manufactured in the United States of America

∞

**Publisher:** University Press of Mississippi, Jackson, USA
**Authorized GPSR Safety Representative:** Easy Access System Europe - Mustamäe tee 50, 10621 Tallinn, Estonia, gpsr.requests@easproject.com

Library of Congress Cataloging-in-Publication Data

Names: Borge, Jason, 1965– author
Title: Jazz odyssey : the global lives of Booker T. Pittman / Jason Borge.
Other titles: American made music series
Description: Jackson : University Press of Mississippi, 2026. | Series:
American made music series | Includes bibliographical references and
index.
Identifiers: LCCN 2025039219 (print) | LCCN 2025039220 (ebook) | ISBN
9781496860712 hardback | ISBN 9781496860729 trade paperback | ISBN
9781496860736 epub | ISBN 9781496860743 epub | ISBN 9781496860750 pdf |
ISBN 9781496860767 pdf
Subjects: LCSH: Pittman, Booker, 1909–1969 | Pittman, Ophélia, 1922– |
Pittman, Eliana | Jazz musicians—Biography | Saxophonists—Biography |
Clarinetists—Biography | LCGFT: Biographies
Classification: LCC ML419.P58 B67 2026 (print) | LCC ML419.P58 (ebook) |
DDC 781.65092 [B]—dc23/eng/20250926
LC record available at https://lccn.loc.gov/2025039219
LC ebook record available at https://lccn.loc.gov/2025039220

British Library Cataloging-in-Publication Data available

# CONTENTS

ACKNOWLEDGMENTS . . . . . . . . . . . . . . . . . . . . . . . . . . . . . . . . . . . VII
PRELUDE: Teatro Paramount . . . . . . . . . . . . . . . . . . . . . . . . . . . 3
CHAPTER ONE: The Escape Artist . . . . . . . . . . . . . . . . . . . . . . . 12
CHAPTER TWO: Le Jazziste . . . . . . . . . . . . . . . . . . . . . . . . . . . . . 49
CHAPTER THREE: Becoming Carioca . . . . . . . . . . . . . . . . . . . . 65
CHAPTER FOUR: Southern Star . . . . . . . . . . . . . . . . . . . . . . . . . 81
CHAPTER FIVE: Some Neglected Spot . . . . . . . . . . . . . . . . . . . 106
CHAPTER SIX: The Revivalist . . . . . . . . . . . . . . . . . . . . . . . . . . . 131
CHAPTER SEVEN: Saxophone, Microphone, Telephone . . . . . . . . . . 162
CHAPTER EIGHT: The Long *Adeus* . . . . . . . . . . . . . . . . . . . . . . 199
CODA: How to Lay a Saxophone to Rest . . . . . . . . . . . . . . . . . 224
NOTES . . . . . . . . . . . . . . . . . . . . . . . . . . . . . . . . . . . . . . . . . . . . . .235
INDEX . . . . . . . . . . . . . . . . . . . . . . . . . . . . . . . . . . . . . . . . . . . . . 259

# Acknowledgments

THIS BOOK WOULD NOT HAVE BEEN POSSIBLE WITHOUT ELIANA PITTMAN, Booker Pittman's stepdaughter, whom I first met in 2018. I had been given Eliana's email from filmmaker and professor Rodrigo Grota, whose stylish short film on Booker helped to convince me that a book-length biography was not only possible but also necessary. Some months later, as I was traveling to Rio de Janeiro to give a paper on Booker at the annual congress of the Brazilian Studies Association, I reached out to Eliana and, as a courtesy more than anything else, invited her to attend my panel, without any clear expectation that she would answer my email, much less show up to an academic conference. No sooner had I arrived at my hotel in Arpoador than I received a phone call in my room. "Jason, it's Eliana." Her tone was friendly yet direct, almost disarmingly so. She wanted details about the conference and not only promised to be there but also invited me and my partner Sônia to have dinner with her in her Copacabana apartment that very night. When she arrived at the panel, held at the mid-century campus of the Pontifical Catholic University (PUC-Rio) in the Gávea neighborhood some distance from Copacabana, Eliana was regal yet informal. She sat in the front row, graceful, encouraging, and also intent on correcting anything I had gotten wrong about her stepfather.

This same frankness and generosity became clearer the more I spent time with Eliana Pittman. In subsequent meals, conversations, interviews, and phone calls, Eliana invariably proved willing to provide me with all the documents and memories at her disposal. She clearly wished the book to be written as much as I did, not as a hagiography but rather as an honest portrayal of the flawed but talented and dedicated man who had helped to raise her and served as her artistic mentor.

Although the memoirs, photographs, and other artifacts that Eliana held in her apartment would serve as the backbone of my biography, gaps abounded. With the support of a College Research Fellowship from the College of Liberal Arts at the University of Texas, I was able to travel to

Buenos Aires and Montevideo before the COVID-19 pandemic closed down libraries and archives. In Buenos Aires, I consulted the book and magazine holdings of the Biblioteca Nacional Mariano Moreno to complete the narrative of Booker's crucial years in Argentina in the late 1930s and early 1940s. At the Biblioteca Nacional de Uruguay, as well as the archives of the Cinemateca Uruguaya, both in Montevideo, I gathered material on Booker Pittman's short and long stays in Uruguay during this same period.

Fortunately, I was still able to consult collections remotely in 2020, 2021, and beyond, so I relied heavily on the Hemeroteca Digital of the Fundação Biblioteca Nacional in Rio de Janeiro, which has digitized an enormous amount of Brazilian magazine and newspaper collections from the twentieth century. I was also able to conduct remote research at the Bibliothèque de France, which helped me to fill in some of the lacunae of Booker's stay in Paris during 1934 and 1935. For secondary materials, I counted on the stacks and digital collections of several libraries of the University of Texas at Austin, particularly the Benson Latin American Collection.

For their early encouragement, I would like to thank Kathryn Sánchez of the University of Wisconsin-Madison for inviting me to give my first paper on Booker Pittman at BRASA 2018; Bryan McCann of Georgetown University for our fruitful conversation at the same conference; Adriana Cuervo of Rutgers-Newark's Institute of Jazz Studies and Special Collections & University Archives for her general support of the project during my visit to Rutgers in 2018; and Roberto Marques from the Universidade Regional do Cariri (URCA) and Mylene Mizrahi from PUC-Rio for inviting me to present further research on Booker at LASA 2019 and for lending me their valuable feedback on the project during the panel discussion. For an especially inspiring and informative conversation in Buenos Aires in 2019, I would like to thank the incomparably knowledgeable and generous music scholar and cultural historian Sergio Pujol. Finally, for their helpful comments later in the process, I am grateful to the two anonymous readers of the book manuscript, as well as UPM's American Made Music Series editor, David Evans.

Although in many ways *Jazz Odyssey* has been a labor of love, much of my research on Booker consisted of hunting down clues and filling in gaps. In this regard, many thanks to Ruy Castro for his views on Booker from the 1960s from the perspective of a contemporary. Thanks also to my UT colleague and musicologist Robin Moore for his insights into the Cuban musician and bandleader Isidro Benítez. For pointing me in the right directions at different moments, thanks to Cheryl Ferguson from Tuskegee University Archives, Edith A. Sandler from the Manuscript Division of the Library of Congress, Marisa Jefferson at Dolph Briscoe Center for American History at UT Austin, and the journalist and music scholar Mark Holston. For finding an elusive recording of Booker and Eliana's performance on the Jack Paar Show, I am grateful to the director, producer, and archivist extraordinaire Eric Kulberg. Many thanks to Laura Souza for transcribing parts of Booker Pittman's taped interview held at the Centro de Pesquisa e Documentação RCA at the Museu da Imagem e do Som in Rio de Janeiro. In Buenos Aires, some of the most helpful "librarians" are the city's many booksellers. For his assistance in tracking down a few texts that eluded me, credit goes to Enrique Tempone at the Librería El Rufián Melancólico.

Finally, I am very grateful to Nettie Washington Douglass, chairwoman of the Frederick Douglass Family Initiatives and great-granddaughter of Booker T. Washington, and to her son Kenneth Morris, cofounder and president of the same organization and the great-great-grandson of Booker T. Washington, as well as the great-great-great-grandson of Frederick Douglass, on his father's side. My invigorating conversations with Nettie and Ken gave me an invaluable, personal perspective on the complex legacy of Booker T. Washington in the United States.

My project also benefited from informal conversations with a number of friends. In particular, I would like to acknowledge Antônio Dimas from the Universidade de São Paulo (USP), who put me in touch with a number of key people and documents in Brazil; writer Adriana Lisboa for her keen sensitivity to questions of composition and imagination and her husband Paulo Cunha for his vivid memories of Brazilian television from the 1960s; and my UT colleagues and friends Marcelo Paixão, whose wide-ranging knowledge of Brazilian popular music helped me to locate Booker and Eliana Pittman in the musical and political milieu of Rio de Janeiro in the 1960s, and Randolph Lewis, whose thoughtful reading of parts of two of the book's chapters helped me find the right tone and register for the sections on Booker's years in Paraná.

Last but not least, my eternal gratitude goes to my artist mother, Martha Borge, for her wise insights into the creative process and to my wife and colleague, Sônia Roncador: *por tudo, como sempre*.

༄

Fragments of several chapters appeared previously in different form in my essay "Booker T. Pittman and the Mid-Twentieth Century South American Jazz Diaspora" in *The Routledge Companion to Diasporic Jazz Studies* (Routledge, 2024).

# JAZZ ODYSSEY

*Prelude*

# TEATRO PARAMOUNT

[E]very island is an effort of memory; every mind, every racial biography culminating in amnesia and fog.
    —DEREK WALCOTT, "THE ANTILLES: FRAGMENTS OF EPIC MEMORY"[1]

IN THE MIDDLE MONTHS OF 1957, NEWS TRICKLED INTO BRAZIL THAT LOUIS Armstrong was scheduled to play a series of dates in São Paulo and Rio de Janeiro later in the year. Armstrong was soon to be the centerpiece of a Cold War jazz propaganda campaign sponsored by the US State Department, a campaign that sent jazz celebrities from Dave Brubeck and Dizzy Gillespie to Duke Ellington to far-flung nations, securing the music's place at home and abroad as a modern art form and an emblem of American freedom and exceptionalism even as the fight for racial equality and civil rights in the United States raged on.[2] If Armstrong's 1957 trip to South America was still not official, it had all the trappings of a goodwill tour of the first order. By the time he touched down in Brazil, Satchmo had just spent three weeks in Buenos Aires and Montevideo in what can only be described as nonstop jazz hysteria, seemingly being followed wherever he went by mobs of fans who felt they needed a piece of him, presumably as a memento of their brush with musical royalty. Sometimes literally a piece of him: the mouth and lips on which Armstrong depended for his very livelihood were a favorite target of fan affection. After a few scares, Satchmo became so protective of his chops that he could think of nothing better to do than half-jokingly don a catcher's mask he had brought with him on the tour.[3]

    Beyond the hordes of Brazilian jazz fans that greeted him at Congonhas Airport, someone else eagerly awaited Louis Armstrong in São Paulo. But Booker T. Pittman, the maternal grandson of Booker T. Washington, was not just any aficionado. Long forgotten in the United States, Booker had been the single most influential jazz musician working in South America for the better part of two decades. In a sense, he was the Satchmo of another universe, a smaller, more remote, feast-or-famine jazz world where Black American musicians of Booker's talents could dazzle and flourish as local celebrities. Of course, they could just as easily languish for years and even decades, leagues from the international spotlight, and sometimes—as had happened to Booker on two separate occasions—left for dead. Except that now Booker was very much alive, and not just alive: he was the talk of the town once again. If most foreign visitors had never heard of him, the Brazilian press corps saw his meeting with Armstrong as the inevitable reunion of two jazz titans.

On November 24, Louis Armstrong gave his final two performances in São Paulo, the first a televised performance at the Ginásio do Ibirapuera, a brand-new arena located next to the city's main urban park, and the second at the Teatro Paramount, an elegant venue reserved for the biggest stars and the most coveted touring spectacles. When Booker greeted Satchmo in the dressing room of the Paramount, it all came back to him in a flash: Armstrong recognized the graceful if gaunt middle-aged man as the same alto saxophonist and clarinetist who had lit up Paris for a brief few months in the middle 1930s, a stone cold virtuoso whom the jazz critic and tastemaker Hugues Panassié had declared at the time as one of the top talents in the world on alto saxophone. Armstrong was not so much surprised to see Booker after all these years—he had often wondered what had happened to him—as he was shocked to bump into him in *Brazil*, of all places. It was as though Satch had miraculously stumbled across a long-lost cousin from New Orleans on the streets of São Paulo.[4]

When Louis Armstrong invited him to jam with the orchestra, it would prove to be Booker Pittman's long-awaited rechristening. Suddenly materializing stage left, holding his clarinet gingerly as though it were a small antique, the wisp of a man glided into the spotlight fully self-assured, energetic, and resplendent. Sonically, it was as though no time had passed at all. Sensing the unusual drama of the moment, Armstrong dedicated to Booker a performance of "La Vie en Rose," a thoughtful tribute to the two musicians' nights performing together twenty-three years earlier at the venerable Parisian concert hall, la Salle Pleyel.[5] Booker rose to the moment just as he had so often in the halcyon days of the interwar jazz scene. Paramount's well-dressed spectators, seemingly half asleep up till this point, were jolted awake by Booker's verve and electricity. With his piercing cascades of hot notes and blue notes, his style meshed perfectly with the band's. The crowd began to sway, then to stand, then to dance. For a brief moment, rather improbably, Booker upstaged Satchmo himself. And more than that, he *rescued* the orchestra, injecting life into an otherwise desultory final performance by the King of Jazz and his road-weary entourage. Far from being a mere novelty item, Booker drove the All Stars to a reenactment of their glory years. According to one spectator, it was more than just a performance; it was an apotheosis.[6]

Booker Taliaferro Pittman's improbable journey to South America began in the 1910s in the still provincial city of Dallas, Texas. The second son of Portia Washington and William Sidney Pittman, the first major Black architect in Texas and a protégé of Booker Taliaferro Washington, the younger Pittman was at once privileged and cursed. His manacles were many: the insidious pressure to carry on his grandfather's legacy, his mother Portia's lofty expectations for him to study classical music just as she had, and his own father's anger, alcoholism, and imperiousness, not to mention the routine injustices of growing up Black in the Jim Crow South. It was in the streets of East Dallas, echoing with the strains of jazz and blues, where Booker found his own private respite from family life, the inspiration for his musical path, and ample reasons to flee Texas just as soon as he was able.

Booker Pittman left home not all at once but gradually over the course of decades, his meanders rippling outward in concentric circles ever farther from Dallas and the hopes and demons that plagued him. His struggles to adjust to life in countless locales on three different continents placed him in rarefied company. Booker's most immediate community was the scores of Black American musicians and performers who lived and worked in Kansas City and Harlem in the late 1920s and early 1930s and abroad in Europe during the interwar and postwar eras. During his two years in Paris in this same period, Booker Pittman would encounter, play with, and occasionally befriend a wide range of performers, among them Louis Armstrong and Josephine Baker, but also less illustrious names such as Cozy Cole and Freddy Johnson, Frank Goudie and Bibi Miranda. Booker's impulse to leave home was not unique to him, of course. For many Black American expatriates of the 1930s, as Tyler Stovall has noted, Paris symbolized a kind of American dream in reverse, whereas the United States "loomed as an obstacle to freedom, not its attainment."[7] For Black performers like Booker Pittman, the escape to Paris from a divided, vicious America amid the Great Depression was a siren song like no other.

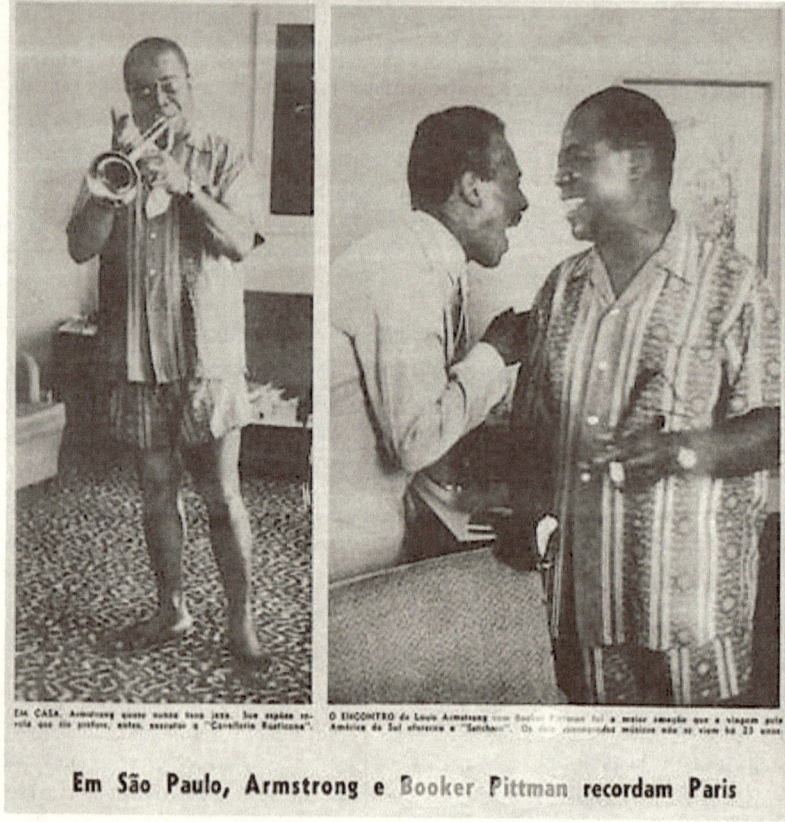

"In São Paulo, Armstrong and Booker Pittman remember Paris." *O Cruzeiro*. December 7, 1957. Public domain/fair use.

Yet unlike most of his contemporaries, Booker neither remained in Europe nor returned to the United States at the outset of World War II. Instead, he kept moving, traveling to South America in 1935 and remaining in Brazil, Argentina, and Uruguay for the better part of three decades in conditions that were often far from ideal. In his episodic comings and goings, his myriad pitstops and long-term residences in large cities and frontier towns from the Atlantic rainforest to the pampas, Booker encountered a different side of the Black musical diaspora, made up not just of other US expatriates such as Claude Austin, Louis Cole, and Paul Wyer but also non-Americans such as the Chilean Cuban bandleader Isidro Benítez and the French Brazilian Argentine guitarist Oscar Alemán. During the late 1930s and early 1940s, South America ostensibly promised a safe harbor from the ravages of World War II. But the struggles and exploits of the burgeoning South Atlantic jazz diaspora at once mirrored and exceeded those of Europe-bound musical expatriates.

Only in rare cases did the great port cities of South America sustain wayfaring musicians in any permanent way; these cities did not provide them the same publicity or exposure to musical trends and transcendent talent that they could find in Paris or London before or after the war. All the same, the streets of Buenos Aires and Rio de Janeiro offered the full array of the modern vices and temptations of the northern metropoles. North American musicians, and particularly Black Americans, injected shots of what many locals considered jazz authenticity and cosmopolitanism into what were still, in the middle decades of the twentieth century, mostly provincial, if uniquely vibrant, musical scenes. Thanks to their talents and also their relative novelty and outsized notoriety in local media, Black *jazzistas* made ideal teachers and promoters. They also served as racial weather vanes, especially in cities like Buenos Aires, where local identities had long been fashioned in tacit or explicit opposition to conceptions of *negritud*, or Blackness. Even in Brazil, the official embrace of racial democracy as national destiny belied the segregation and white privilege that reigned in the casinos and nightclubs of the period. Foreign Black performers like Booker Pittman, therefore, had crucial work to do there in the sense that their presence provoked long-suppressed discussions about race, nationality, and modernity. And so, celebrated yet often fetishized, a relatively small but influential transnational community of primarily Black musicians plied their trade, sometimes for decades, in economic semi-precarity and big-fish glory.

In many ways, Booker Pittman and other musicians on the South American circuit embodied what Brent Hayes Edwards has called "vagabond internationalism." For Edwards, Jamaican American Claude McKay's landmark Black expatriate novel *Banjo* (1928), set in the rough streets and bohemian dives of Jazz Age Marseilles, at once exemplified and radically defied the dominant strains of Black internationalism. McKay's characters, Edwards notes, "[C]hallenge the very logic of civilization itself and, moreover, expose its underbelly, its elusive escape hatch—precisely by proving with 'happy irresponsibility' that civilization can be defied."[8] Booker was not a full-time vagabond in the style of *Banjo*. Yet beginning in the 1930s, he and a steady stream of his compatriots participated in a distinct brand of marginal Black internationalism thousands of miles from the hallowed terrain of Harlem and Montmartre. The roles and challenges of these far-flung musicians were fundamentally different from those of white American expats or Europe-based troubadours. As transatlantic migrants and sometimes racial exiles, they are perhaps best described—to combine concepts developed by Ana María Ochoa and Éduoard Glissant—as agents of *aural errancy*.⁹

In a period of Nazi menace and the US Good Neighbor campaign in Latin America, and later, of Cold War propaganda, scores of mostly African American musicians playing in casinos and nightclubs up and down the coast between Rio de Janeiro and Mar del Plata at once fled the toxicity of mainstream US nationalism and at the same time served unwittingly as alternative cultural attachés, doing the essential shadow work of Pan-Americanism in places that the US State Department either could not reach or did not wish to. Among these globetrotting artists, Booker Pittman was an anchor and lodestone, an "errant" pioneer of the South American musical diaspora (in Glissant's sense of difficult yet productive wandering) who emerged as a seminal figure of several jazz scenes. Booker would hardly have considered himself an ambassador in the same sense that Louis Armstrong was. A floating fixture of myriad musical communities in Brazil, Argentina, and Uruguay, Booker always carried home with him, for better and for worse.¹⁰ Yet his lifelong odyssey was marked by a centrifugal arc of travels and uprootedness with countless variations of exile, return, and revival. For nearly three decades, Booker bounced around, erratically and often ingloriously, at times triumphantly and other times off-the-grid entirely. When Buenos Aires grew too big for him to take, he caught a ferry to Montevideo. When smaller cities became too stifling for him to bear, he fled them by train or bus for tiny backwaters. More than exile, Booker embodied a rare kind of escapism and oblivion—what might be called *infra-exile*. During long stretches, he seemed to enjoy roughing it in out-of-the-way places. Perhaps for this very reason, during his comeback years in the late 1950s and early 1960s, Booker rarely spoke about his lost periods in tragic terms: he had long been trying hard to forget about himself, and he had many reasons to. His travels to ever more remote corners of South America gave outward form to a willful forgetting of who and what he had once been, a means to outrun the long shadow of his family name and the deep hauntings of his youth.

At the same time, Booker's drift across the ocean and back again on southward currents paralleled his slow death in North American and European cultural spheres as new musical styles and idioms came and went during his long periods of isolation and obscurity. This abiding oblivion ate at the musician for decades, and it showed: Booker's stubborn addiction to alcohol and harder drugs dogged him for much of his adult life, the persistent weight of melancholy and anger masked by his drug-fueled affability and exuberant virtuosity. After his resurfacing and subsequent revival in the late 1950s and early 1960s, the final chapter of Booker T. Pittman's life coincided with the culmination of his circuitous route to fame in South America as well as his triumphant 1964 return to the United States, where he and his stepdaughter and jazz apprentice, the singer Eliana Pittman, performed on television talk shows and in Manhattan nightclubs for nearly two years; they were aided by Eliana's mother and Booker's wife, Ofélia, who served as an agent and manager for both. Back in Brazil in the late sixties, Booker lived the chaos of celebrity together with the delirium of sickness and palliative drug cocktails, writing and painting in fits and starts while he fought laryngeal cancer.

What Booker Pittman put down on paper in his final months reflects the fever and the fugacity of the life he led. His memoirs—stored among the rest of his scant belongings at his stepdaughter Eliana Pittman's apartment in Copacabana—are not what could properly be called "memoirs." They are rather a pastiche of scraps and scribbles, remembered oblivion and oblivious memory. They abound with lucid descriptions of joy and devastation, with damp, broken-off pages full of half-legible names and smeared telephone numbers of hotels and nightclubs, promotors and physicians, friends and cabaret dancers. Scores of pages are blank or nearly blank, mottled with an outline of Booker's best intentions: the address of a temporary residence in Buenos Aires, the first name of a fry cook in Paraná, a drugstore in Montevideo. A week or a month or a year of life reduced to a banal haiku: "I hunted frogs and drank." Errata, repetitions, and annotations are common, as though Booker were trying in vain to remember despite the fog of morphine and fear, of a body being eaten alive from the inside. Booker T. Pittman's memoirs are also his *immemoirs*.

More than a decade after his death, these shards of memory were translated and included in his widow Ofélia's book *Por você, por mim, por nós* (*For You, for Me, for Us*) (Rio de Janeiro: Editora Record, 1984), which featured Booker's writings almost in their entirety alongside her own, more complete memoirs in alternating chapters. Booker's *immemoirs* also became the logical starting point for *Jazz Odyssey*. In my previous research on jazz in Latin America (for my last book *Tropical Riffs: Latin America and the Politics of Jazz*), I had often bumped into Booker's name in newspapers and magazines, books, liner notes, and occasionally scholarly articles. The wandering Texan was nothing if not elusive. When it came to the cultural history of jazz in Latin America, Booker was at once central and slippery. For decades, he came and went, disappearing and appearing again somewhere else, shaping musical and cultural scenes at key moments—at times emphatically, at other times spectrally—but never remaining in places long enough to be completely synonymous with them. Many of the secondary sources on Booker's descent into obscurity and subsequent triumph in the 1960s were unreliable and often contradictory. The dates of his various arrivals and departures varied wildly, episodes and even entire countries were sometimes left out of Booker's timeline, and yawning gaps abounded.

Still, the more I ran into Booker Pittman's name in print, the more I became convinced that his story deserved to be brought to a wider audience. One Brazilian contemporary of Booker's wrote in the 1960s that the American's musical adventures could only be compared, in sheer color, drama, and variety, to those of musician Mezz Mezzrow, as recounted in the classic jazz memoir *Really the Blues* (1946).[11] The question remained, though, about how Booker's tale should be told. I quickly ruled out conventional fiction. As a non-Black scholar of Latin American cultural studies writing in the third decade of the twenty-first century, I felt it would have been presumptuous of me to attempt to paint Booker's inner landscape based purely or primarily on imagined empathy and creative guesswork. If collecting evidence of Booker's odyssey proved as circuitous as the musician's meanders, however, it was precisely the saxophonist's shapeshifting, elliptical qualities that piqued my curiosity, especially as they spoke to the interplay of memory, ambition, and escapism that teased and tormented Booker throughout much of his adult life. The backbone of *Jazz Odyssey* is the musician's fragmentary writings and interviews along with Ofélia's more reliable memoirs, the oral testimony of his living stepdaughter Eliana Pittman (whose access and assistance were essential to this project), and selected periodicals from the 1930s through the early 1970s, though with conspicuous gaps until Booker's definitive return to the spotlight in the mid-1950s. The very precariousness of the archive has compelled me at times to adopt a method akin to what Saidiya Hartman has called "critical fabulation." In the interstices of private and public records, I have occasionally sought to fashion a narrative consisting of "a critical reading of the archive that mimes the figurative dimensions of history" by imagining "what cannot be verified." Conversely, the majority of the book is indeed based on written evidence, which becomes overwhelmingly the case in the last chapters, in which I chronicle Booker's much more widely covered life and career since his reemergence and marriage to Ofélia. As such, *Jazz Odyssey* is a story at once "written with and against the archive."[12]

By definition, as Hartman warns, such a hybrid approach renders any historiographical or biographical project "unfinished and provisional."[13] In the chapters that follow, I have attempted to recover the memory of a man whose life, in many ways, defied memory. The only common witness to all the permutations and episodic shifts of Booker Pittman's world—Booker himself—is long since gone. Even while he lived, the musician's own capacity to remember was frequently befogged by drugs and trauma and, when he finally tried to put down his recollections in words, terminal illness. In trying to bring to life a patchwork quilt of personal testimony and archival evidence, nonetheless, I hope to do justice to an extraordinary man who lived his life in danger of extinguishing himself at every turn.

*Chapter One*

# THE ESCAPE ARTIST

Did I believe escape was possible? I suspect not. But I had no option but to proceed as if it were.

—STUART HALL, *FAMILIAR STRANGER*

## PARANÁ, 1953

THE MEMORIES HURT, PULLED HIM IN AND REALLY HURT HIM. EVER SINCE Booker Pittman had moved to this remote inland region of Brazil, one that vaguely reminded him of northeast Texas, all too often he found himself hunkered over a chisel plow, gathering coffee cherries in the sun, sweating out the sins of the previous day or hour. When the buzz of hard labor wore off, he slept, or he blew a saxophone or a clarinet if he happened to have either in his possession, and when his hands were not trembling from alcohol abuse. More frequently, when he had work at all, he drank again before he played and during shows as well, and then, if he was not rationing his supplies, once again before sundown. The wayward musician's body was now fully and ingloriously middle-aged, his bones achy, his mind murky, and his daily ritual of drunken self-flagellation left its imprint on him like never before. He could feel it crushing him down, a double dose of gravity, a triple dose. Sometimes, he would crawl out into a remnant of the Atlantic rainforest during a morning shift just to feel the jungle wrapped around him in a cool embrace. A part of him wished that this was how it would end. A big branch heavy with bromeliads would land on his head just so. A jaguar would ambush him. Something.[1]

One day, they found him on the edge of a plantation, holding a saxophone with one hand, with the other directing a make-believe orchestra of coffee trees.[2] Booker knew things had gotten bad, very bad, to the point that he was half-surprised when he woke up alive, his body still intact; the surprise itself surprised him. The worst part was that even knowing he had to pull himself out of it, he could not pull himself out of it. The weight was just too great. In this way especially, he felt that he had failed himself and others. Friends who knew something of his past often told Booker he was stronger than strong for making his own way through life, braving the elements so far from home and what they imagined were the creature comforts of his family name and upbringing. But in his present state, his struggle did not feel like strength. It felt like weakness—weakness and avoidance.

The recriminations rushed in with each swing of the sickle and then again with each footfall as he stumbled home from a brothel to wedge himself inside his latest closet-sized abode: a cabin, a toolshed, a stable. The memories swarmed him anew with every small-time *empresário* whom he failed to confront, every contract he broke, every whispered promise he did not keep. And especially with every swig of the bottle of *cachaça* that he kept with him as though it were a medical necessity. Drinking was a paradox: a source of his shame and also a coping mechanism; it numbed his physical pain and, at the same time, made his memories more vivid.

Except the memories did not behave. They could not be tamed into a sweet narrative for very long. Images of his more recent conquests, of his standing-room-only performances in São Paulo and Rio de Janeiro since the war, led him backward in time to casinos in Montevideo and nightclubs in Buenos Aires, and before that, to jam sessions and romantic trysts in Montmartre and Harlem, of ocean liners and beaches and comely smiles in Philadelphia or Chicago or Kansas City. He tried to hold fast to these visions of youthful promise and inchoate glory, but then came the other ones, the snapshots of abject failures and savage insults, needles in dead-end alleys, of handcuffs and hospital rooms. As he lay on his back at the edge of the jungle canopy, his memory went dark, and the kaleidoscope of recollections gave way to indelible images deeper in the recesses of his mind. To the Dallas of his youth, the smell of gasoline and cologne and shoe polish, the sound of cicadas and train whistles and the blues. But mostly he saw the faces that populated his childhood: teachers, bosses, relatives, parents. Sometimes, they smiled faintly, but mostly, they did not. Mostly, their faces glowered down at him between the branches, daring him to make another mistake.

One of the faces that haunted Booker was that of his maternal grandfather, Booker Taliaferro Washington. He only vaguely remembered meeting Washington when he was very young, perhaps three years old. But it was the framed portrait glaring at him unflinchingly in the parlor of his childhood home that stuck with him the most. In his delirium, Booker Pittman

Booker T. Washington, circa 1910. Photograph by Harris & Ewing. Library of Congress. Public domain via Wikipedia Commons.

could now see it clearer than ever: his grandfather sitting upright in a dark jacket and bowtie, his light-colored eyes aiming their gaze just to the right of the camera in ready stillness like a hunter not wanting to startle his prey. In his right hand, he holds a folded newspaper tightly as though it were a ready-made weapon; with his left hand, he touches, almost fondles, what looks like a pocket watch. The portrait outwardly evokes calm and steely reserve, the embodiment of hard-earned success in spite of the odds. But below the surface, there is tension in Washington's pose, a mixture of calculation and pride, judgment, and pain.

## BOOKER THE FIRST

From an early age, Booker Pittman must have known his grandfather's story by heart. Born into slavery, by the end of the nineteenth century, Washington had become one of the most visible and renowned Black intellectuals of his generation. He was an outstanding orator, the founder and first president of the Tuskegee Normal and Industrial Institute in Alabama, and the author of *Up from Slavery*, one of the most cited and moving slave narratives ever published. Booker T. Washington was such a seductive public figure in part because of the way he pitched himself to his audience: the former enslaved person as forgiving self-made man, a Black embodiment of the Protestant work ethic. "Cast down your bucket where you are," he said famously in an 1895 speech delivered in Atlanta at the Cotton States and International Exposition. The message was aimed at Washington's fellow Black Americans at a time of grinding hardship, abiding racial injustice, and dizzying social and demographic change, a time when Black southerners increasingly felt the pull of the city, the North, and increasingly the allure of other countries and continents.

Landbound grunt labor as racial pride and provisional destiny: Booker T. Washington's message was too seductive for white America to ignore.[3] Washington's power, Michael Rudolph West has argued, lay in his "special persuasiveness, as historian as well as pundit, and his extraordinary ability to enchant, enthrall, and seduce an eager audience motivated by an odd mix of idealism and bad faith, racism and wishful thinking."[4] This knack for winning over more than one public at once was always the plan, or at least that is what Washington's great rival W. E. B. Du Bois claimed. Du Bois wrote that Washington had risen to power "as essentially the leader not of one race but of two," an embodiment of "the old attitude of adjustment and submission."[5] The subtext of what came to be known as Washington's Atlanta Compromise speech, Du Bois suggested, came through loud and clear: Do not blame the guilty, do not take revenge on them, do not compete with them, but also do not flee from them. To abandon Mississippi for Chicago or New York or Africa was treason, was weakness. What was needed was forbearance, sweat, savings, sobriety. What was needed was not just depoliticization and conciliation. It was deliberate avoidance and forgetfulness. It was oblivion.

The Atlanta Compromise was such a smash hit with Black and white audiences alike that Washington repeated it as an encore many times over the coming years. In 1908, a recording was made that eventually became a staple of early Black American aural history right alongside blues, jazz, and spirituals. Booker T. Washington's activities and accomplishments did not stop there. Particularly in the later years of his life, faced with abiding segregation and Black disenfranchisement, especially but not solely in the US South, he often spoke out vociferously against racial injustice.[6] He remained extremely, almost uncannily, adept at currying favor with the white establishment, from mayors, college deans, and common businessmen, from Andrew Carnegie to Theodore Roosevelt. But as would be the case a half-century later with his wayfaring grandson, Booker T. Washington's late-life fame masked crippling pressure and premature physical decline. An in-demand public speaker practically until the day he died, Washington also oversaw the day-to-day management and expenses of the Tuskegee Institute, traveled constantly, wrote long letters and sent long telegrams, and juggled various appointments with local civic leaders and charitable organizations.[7] In another way, too, Washington would leave his imprint on his namesake. One of the keys to Tuskegee's acceptance by the power elite of the nation's capital was the way in which the institution embraced and pursued the United States' "civilizing mission" elsewhere in the world. A telling example of Washington's capitulation to imperial designs was a 1901 to 1904 expedition that Tuskegee mounted to German Togo on the West African coast. Invited by the German government and ostensibly designed to export cotton cultivation methods and technologies to local farmers, the expedition also hoped to showcase Tuskegee's "emancipatory, even revolutionary" potential, even if the Institute ultimately served the interests of the United States' global profile and German elites' business interests.[8]

The toll that Washington's constant endeavors and contradictory politics took on his body was increasingly apparent to those who surrounded him, even if he tried to hide the damage. While still only in his late fifties, he suffered from crippling digestive ailments, extremely high blood pressure, nervous exhaustion, arteriosclerosis, increasingly severe headaches, and kidney disease.[9] The myriad pressures of celebrity, the perpetual demands on his time, and the heavy expectations that came with being a leading spokesman for Black America were more than his middle-aged body could take. To make things worse, Washington's celebrity was never great enough to protect him from standard racist abuse. On one occasion, he and his young daughter Portia, Booker Pittman's mother, were forbidden by a white security guard from signing the ledger at the Washington Monument.[10] And in 1911, at the height of his fame, Washington was savagely beaten by a random bystander and arrested for reputedly harassing a white woman on the streets of the Upper West Side of Manhattan. In both instances, Booker T. Washington refrained from lashing out publicly at his accusers. Even as he lay dying four years later, he was forced to endure one last insult: a white Canadian-born doctor, after examining him at New York City's St. Luke's Hospital, not only leaked Booker T. Washington's illness to the press but baselessly speculated that the stateman's "nervous breakdown" was due in part to "racial characteristics." It was code language for syphilis.[11]

## PORTIA

To be faithful to his own convictions of persistence and accommodation, Booker T. Washington—during his relatively short but eventful existence—felt he had no choice but to absorb the blows of racism stoically. This was his way of confronting hate and vitriol as well as their polar opposites, love and affection. Impeccably polite in social settings, upright in financial matters, and outwardly devoted to family, Washington was almost as sparing emotionally with kith and kin as he was with thugs and foes. Despite his formal demeanor, he developed a close bond with the eldest of his three children, Portia, whose biological mother (Washington's first wife) died when she was one year old. Her father soon remarried; twice, in fact. But Portia's aloof second stepmother Maggie, an English teacher at Tuskegee, had little interest and even less experience in raising children. She preferred to travel with Booker on his nearly constant fundraising and lecture trips.

To cope with her beloved father's absence and her stepmother's coldness, young Portia turned to the refuge of music. Her father bought her a piano on which she learned to play Negro spirituals, and later, European classical music. Though her father enjoyed hearing her tickle the ivories in the parlor of the Washingtons' stately brownstone house, Portia's devotion to music was rebellion in disguise. What could be further from the feminine practical skills championed by the institution whose air she had lived and breathed as long as she could remember? Booker and Maggie had little use for music, though they fooled themselves into believing that the piano was an extension of women's etiquette—advanced training wheels for a girl born into Black American society.[12] Portia never saw music this way. Her father's stature rubbed off on her. Having seen the global success of the Fisk Jubilee Singers firsthand, she knew that her ambitions were not mere flights of fancy. Perhaps it was the very impracticality of music that wooed her as much as abstract beauty or celebrity. Music as a vocation and vehicle of free expression and collective lament was the antithesis of what Tuskegee prescribed for young women with its toothbrushing and hygiene lessons, with its rigorous classes in dressmaking and housekeeping.

Portia became restless, her energy centrifugal. She yearned for higher rungs of learning and wider social circles. As she grew out of adolescence, her father tried to support her desire to seek opportunities beyond Alabama. Using his expanding web of connections among New England philanthropists, Booker T. Washington enrolled his daughter in a series of schools in the Northeast: first Framingham State College, and then, after a failed stint at Wellesley College, Bradford Academy. As the sole Black student virtually wherever she went, Portia experienced alternating waves of isolation and acceptance, curiosity and scrutiny.

## THE APPRENTICE

Once she graduated from Bradford Academy, Portia Washington continued her studies of music and German once again from the comfortable confines of Tuskegee. She was beginning to show flashes of virtuosity on the piano. What was missing, her father felt, was a trip to the Old Continent. With the encouragement of her former piano teacher at Bradford Academy, Samuel Morse Downes, the blessing of her family, and the funding of Andrew Carnegie, Portia set sail for Europe in 1905.[13] And so it was that Booker T. Washington's favorite came to study in Berlin under the tutelage of Martin Krause, Franz Liszt's star pupil and a former teacher of Downes. It was this period, a year of freedom sandwiched between the pleasant captivity of The Oaks and the imminent turmoil of her married life, which gave her the greatest happiness. During one marvelous year, Portia Washington lived beyond the reach of her father's own well-intentioned and puritanical demands and her stepmother's spartan sense of domestic order and, far from white America's envious whispers and recriminations, immersed only in the ardent tonal universe of Beethoven and Wagner.

By all accounts, Europe turned out to be a transformative experience for Portia. But it was not all about the music. An attractive young woman in her early twenties, daughter to a man who had become a household name in many parts of the world, she had her share of suitors. Before and after her time in Germany, Portia had a few chaste flirtations, one with Samuel Coleridge-Taylor, a well-known Black composer who had transcribed some of the very spirituals that she had mastered on the piano, and sometime later with a Venetian named Leo Ziffer, who courted Portia so insistently that her stepmother (who had joined her for some sightseeing in France and Italy) was called on to intervene.[14]

In the meantime, Portia's correspondence with a handsome, ambitious man in the United States began to intensify. She had met William Sidney Pittman in Tuskegee years prior to her period abroad, and since then, he had courted her persistently, albeit mostly from a distance. One day, she relented. Though her father was ambivalent about Pittman, her stepmother was unusually, even suspiciously, encouraging of the match. Giving into the pressure of Victorian domesticity and wooed by the sheer ardor of Pittman's letters, Portia abandoned her burgeoning career, returned to the United

William Sidney Pittman, 1916; Portia Washington Pittman, circa 1925. Both images public domain/fair use, William Sydney Pittman's via Wikipedia Commons.

States, and married her father's protégé. Her German teacher would never pardon her for giving up on her ambition to be a concert pianist. Portia had her own doubts as well.[15]

Born in Montgomery, Alabama, in 1875, the child of a white father and a Black formerly enslaved woman, William Sidney Pittman was driven by a special brand of ambitiousness that seemed at once well suited and excessive for the mostly staid educational ethos of Tuskegee. In addition to architecture and design, he studied wheelwrighting, a nod to the institution's trades-oriented philosophy. Once he graduated, he was asked back to serve at the institution that had schooled him. It was a practice reserved for Tuskegee's brightest stars, though the savvy Booker T. Washington also used it as a mechanism for graduates to pay off loans they had accrued while attending Tuskegee.[16] Even before his marriage to Portia, Sidney Pittman had begun to establish himself as an up-and-coming architect in and around Washington, DC, catering to the emergent Black middle class. His breakthrough came in 1906 when he became the first Black architect in US history to design and supervise the construction of a federal building, the Negro Building of the Jamestown Tercentennial Exposition. The event drew national attention, with the *New York Times* writing that Pittman was "believed to be the only Negro in the country supporting himself in this difficult and exacting field."[17] More contracts soon followed in Washington,

DC, and beyond, from schools and hotels to cultural centers such as the African American branch of the YMCA on 12th Street. He was elected president of the local Negro Business League and kept frequent company with his father-in-law. With the money that was coming in, Sidney Pittman built the house where Booker T. Pittman was born, in Fairmont Heights, Maryland, just outside the District of Columbia, on October 3, 1909.[18]

Soon thereafter, Sidney Pittman received an offer that would change the course of the Pittman family forever. Already, using his family ties to Booker T. Washington and his personal acquaintance with President Theodore Roosevelt, Pittman had been asked to submit plans for a building in Brownsville, Texas, in the wake of the infamous 1906 Brownsville Affair.[19] Around this same time, the members of a Black Masonic society, The Colored Knights of Pythias, hired the young architect to design their new Grand Lodge in Dallas, Texas. The family moved there in 1913. A dusty provincial city on the edge of the southern plains, Dallas in the second decade of the twentieth century was a far cry from cosmopolitan Washington, DC. For one, it was a focal point of deep racial conflict throughout the US South, a region that had only recently emerged from two decades of atrocious racial violence and hostility against Black people. Lynching had reached historic heights, claiming around 1,700 victims between 1889 and 1909 alone, a figure that does not take into account the much more frequent, if less public, instances of murder and rape, not to mention routine harassment, intimidation, and segregation. Moreover, racial violence tended to be more intense in cities like Dallas where whites frequently encountered traveling and itinerant Black populations, including touring shows of commercial "coon song" performers—music, scholar Karl Hagstrom Miller has written, that in and of itself, served "as both a fantasy enactment and a rhetorical justification of white attacks on black southerners."[20]

Still, the Colored Knights of Pythias made Sidney Pittman an offer he could not easily refuse: a big contract and a signature building in what was—despite its many flaws—a dynamic young city, with more offers in the pipeline from all over Texas. Notwithstanding the racial tensions of Dallas, this was a chance for the up-and-coming architect to make his mark far beyond the judgmental gaze of his father-in-law. Pittman moved his family from Fairmont Heights to a Dallas neighborhood east of downtown near where the Grand Lodge would be built. Deep Ellum, as the area would later come to be known, was a fulcrum between the rural past and urban future of the city, a unique Jim Crow contact zone between races and classes, worlds and underworlds. Even more so than other areas of Dallas, life in Deep Ellum was rife with contradictions. The city's codification of segregation in 1916 (three years after the Pittmans arrived) did not keep the Black and white (particularly Jewish) populations from interacting in and around the business district of Elm Street. Known for its danger, vice, and entertainment, Deep Ellum in the early twentieth century was also home to many successful businesses and stately homes.[21] In short, the neighborhood presented the DC transplants a uniquely diverse and vital setting in which to live and work—a seemingly ideal place to build a new life.

Sidney Pittman worked on his signature creation day and night. And when he did not work on the building, he thought about it obsessively, imagined its contours, its soaring grandeur, its importance as a hub of the Black community, locally and nationally. When the Grand Lodge, a striking five-story tower in the Beaux Arts style, was completed, it became *almost* everything Sidney envisioned. The building immediately stood out as the tallest and most distinguished structure in Deep Ellum. It proved to be a cultural and economic lodestone as well. On the first floor, there was an enormous and enormously popular barbershop. On the second and third floors, attorneys and physicians rented offices alongside meeting spaces for the most eminent African American organizations of the region. The dance floor on the fourth floor hosted high school glee clubs and community theater productions and also well-traveled luminaries like the Fisk Jubilee Singers, the controversial intellectual Marcus Garvey, and the scientist George Washington Carver, a colleague of Booker T. Washington's at Tuskegee. Carver's 1923 lecture on the virtues of sweet potatoes drew a crowd of eight hundred people to the Grand Lodge of the Colored Knights of Pythias.[22]

## TORN ASUNDER

Sidney Pittman was no Booker T. Washington. Though brimming with talent and ambition, Sidney lacked the personality to realize the stolid and pacific dreams of his towering mentor. When he was younger, Sidney was as ethically upright as he was confrontational. As he grew older, he became vengeful and belligerent, the bright apprentice turned bad disciple: brilliant but mean and acutely attuned to the toxicity of his environment. Deeply resentful of the pressure, injustice, and hypocrisy of the Jim Crow era, all the contradictory and infuriating forces that Washington also felt in his bones, he and his father-in-law were tormented by the same "double consciousness" that Du Bois wrote about so trenchantly, the self-perception of Black Americans through the gaze of a white majority who loved and despised them, who wanted to forget about them and yet could not leave them alone.[23] But whereas Booker T. Washington disavowed his own contradictions in a vain attempt to rise above them, an almost heroically sustained effort of self-denial that likely led him to an early grave, Sidney Pittman fought, suffered, and survived.

Like his mentor, Sidney cherished the *idea* of work almost as much as he did work itself. He was determined to be the most venerated architect in all of Dallas, of any race. In this narrow sense, he was faithful to the principles of his father-in-law. And for a time, at least, the building contracts kept coming: a college dormitory in Waco, the Colored Carnegie Branch library in Houston, churches in Dallas, Ft. Worth, and Waxahachie; more Masonic lodges in San Antonio and Houston.[24] Sidney Pittman's fortunes turned even before the Great Depression seized Dallas and building contracts dried up at the end of the 1920s. The same men who built and later frequented the buildings that Booker T. Washington's protégé had designed quickly grew tired of the architect's rudely proud temperament, his moodiness, and especially his sharp tongue. The light-skinned Sidney Pittman, for his part, felt a mixture of disdain, distrust, and condescension toward Black Texans. One day, during the Grand Lodge's construction, Sidney berated one of his workers so mercilessly that the man tried and nearly managed to hurl the architect off the roof of his own building. The moneyed African American elite, on the other hand, tried to finish off Pittman through more insidious means: ostracization and economic attrition.[25] They iced him out of the same associations and social networks that had embraced him in Washington, DC, shunned him at picnics and barbecues, nodded coldly or averted their gaze entirely when they ran into him at the market or at church. The message came through loud and clear. When Pittman did not confront his growing ranks of adversaries directly, he bridled and seethed, waiting for the moment to exact his revenge.

At home, Sidney Pittman turned into an even more extreme version of the taskmaster who had always thrived on rules, regulations, and punishment—on "primitive discipline," as Booker Pittman called it.[26] The term did not do his father full justice. Especially as his children got older, Sidney Pittman beat them with such fervor that he would only stop when he was too tired to go on, his offspring left in a wet heap on the floor, whimpering and semi-conscious. Booker's brief, almost blithe mention of his father's abusiveness in his memoirs seems incongruous alongside his other descriptions of his childhood. In his tender final years, Booker downplayed his father's severity by reviving his amusing nickname, Big Pitt, as if William Sidney Pittman were a beloved guard dog instead of a tyrant-savant.[27]

Once, when he was twelve, at a Sunday dinner of fried chicken, sweet corn, and peach cobbler, Booker and his brother Sidney Jr. were celebrating the beginning of summer vacation when Big Pitt suddenly grew dead serious. He said that the next day, the two of them should leave the house and return home only if and when they had found steady jobs. Their mother protested, but to no avail. It was not just the sheer physical force and emotional intensity of her husband that intimidated her but also his moods, his threats, large and small. It was also the strength of his arguments. The elder Pittman's intelligence was formidable, and it rarely rested. He saw in his boys' entitled expectation of leisure a teachable moment, one impossible to pass up. It went beyond cruelty. In his grandiosity, Sidney Pittman improvised not one but two Washingtonian lessons at the same time: how to work and how to save money. When the two brothers landed jobs, Big Pitt opened a bank account for each, their salaries under their father's name and strict control.[28] He could not stand to think that Booker T. Washington's grandsons might end up as soft, feeble, spoiled young men. He simply would not allow it.

## THE SHOESHINE BOY OF ELM STREET

In Sidney Pittman's dictatorial regime, spending one's own money was prohibited. Booker's mild-mannered, studious, and pragmatic brother obeyed his father's edicts. But Booker was quietly rebellious. He found jobs paid in tips rather than salary, so he could squirrel away coins and cash for small pleasures and peccadillos without Big Pitt finding out. He ended up working as a shoeshine boy on a stretch of Elm Street full of dance halls, movie theaters, and tailor shops.[29] For Booker, as he tells it, this experience was fundamental, like being born again. Only he soon learned there was a pecking order to the shoeshine stand. The lower-numbered chairs were fancier, and as such, occupied by wealthier customers. At first, Booker worked from Chair #10, the least coveted of them all, but with the distinct advantage that it lent him easy access to a big stack of blues and early jazz records on the Okeh label. This way, he controlled the music on the record player, a privilege he used to set the rhythm and mood with which to polish work shoes and cowboy boots for hours at a time. As he wrote in his memoirs, "[Y]ou had to keep rhythm with your brushes and pop out sounds with the shining flannel rag with the music that came from the gramophone."[30]

It was, Booker wrote later, "the beginning of my spiritual contact with music."[31] He felt the deep echo of the blues in his bones, the thrill of improvisation. But he was not satisfied just listening to records. There was also music to be heard in the streets. And what music! Strolling along Central Track, the name of the railroad and the neighborhood that connected Deep Ellum to North Dallas, he could sometimes hear several different blues interpreters at the same time: a guitarist from Memphis, a harmonica player from Arkansas, a banjo virtuoso from Mississippi. It was no coincidence that blues musicians could be found congregating near the railroad tracks: many of them played on trains in exchange for travel throughout the region, Lead Belly (Huddie Ledbetter) later recalled.[32] Occasionally, players like the guitarist Lonnie Johnson came up from New Orleans. And then there was Blind Lemon Jefferson, a Texas musician and composer who sang on a street corner close to the shoeshine stand where Booker worked, belting out original tunes that would soon become blues standards with names that evoked backwoods entanglements and numinous marshes, traps, and escapes: "Mosquito Moan," "Black Snake Moan," or another of Booker's favorites, "Rabbit Foot Blues":

> Baby tell me something 'bout the meatless and wheatless days
> I wanna know about the meatless and wheatless days
> This not being my home, I don't think I could stay

The song alludes to President Herbert Hoover's campaign for food conservation during World War I when American families were encouraged to eat "meatless" and "wheatless" meals on certain days of the week.[33] Yet Jefferson's words must have resonated with Booker Pittman not just because of their emphasis on self-deprivation but also their evocation of an itinerant world of pleasure, independence, and escape.

## PORTIA

The sinful and spendthrift world of Elm Street was the opposite of Big Pitt's cult of hard labor and forbearance at The Oaks, located just a few blocks away. But the Pittman household was far from being an anti-musical abode. On the contrary, musicians, including famous ones like Bessie Smith, constantly stopped by the house on Liberty Street.[34] For all his other faults, Sidney Pittman had a good ear and listened to the sitting room concerts with a fervent delight that he took pains to disguise. Until a certain age, he even plucked out blues melodies on his guitar.

But the sonic force of the Pittmans was Booker's mother. Once settled in Dallas, her internationally famous father had bought her a grand piano, and Portia became an eminent, sought-after teacher, if somewhat out of the public eye, at least initially. From the parlor of the Pittmans' comfortable middle-class home, she offered classes for children and adults, including young musicians who would later become well-known jazz players like the pianist Sammy Price and the saxophonist Budd Johnson. Booker also studied briefly with his mother, but he found the staid and stuffy world of classical music antithetical to his aesthetic sensibilities as well as to his very being. The piano scales imposed on him by Portia, he would write later, ravaged "every nerve in my dreamy body."[35]

*Dreamy, dreamer*, and *adventure* are words Booker Pittman often repeats in his memoirs. Another is *geography*, a term he generally writes in Portuguese, *geografia*, as if the concept did not stick to his native tongue. By his own admission, the young Booker was such an incurable dreamer that he frequently complained that his body ached with a perpetual desire not so much to improve as to improvise his life, to test its boundaries unshackled.[36] Where did this fugitive impulse come from, this restlessness and disquiet that years later would drive him abroad, much as it drove his mother abroad, only to lead to more restlessness and augment his itch to flee over and over? Booker T. Washington coined his most celebrated phrase at a speech he gave in Atlanta at the end of the nineteenth century, more than a decade before his musical grandson was born. "Cast down your bucket where you are," he said. This is how the elder Booker implored emancipated Black Americans and their descendants to remain where they were and as they were in the South, to resist the temptation to uproot their families and move to other states, or nations, or continents. It was a call to stay put and to stand pat—as the younger Booker knew too well—to work and live the way they always had. Which meant, for the great majority of former enslaved people and their offspring, to remain cast off, separate and unequal, to gaze downward with their mouths shut and their hands in the dirt. To live and toil without the imprudent dreams of mobility, of foreign adventures, of hope of elevation. To live without *geografia*.

## TIP-TOP

The dance hall did not have an official name. People called it the Tip-Top Club after a tailor shop on the ground floor called the Tip-Top. But the two-story building was slightly higher than the others on Elm Street, so the nickname stuck. It was there that the young Booker discovered live jazz, gawking at musicians and bands from Louisiana that, until then, he had only heard about by word-of-mouth or on the Victrola at the shoeshine stand. Name-brand performers like Kid Ory, Sidney Bechet, and the Eureka Brass Band would play teaser sets on the street on Saturday afternoons before the main event upstairs later that night.

One day when he was fourteen or fifteen, Booker was sent out on an errand when he stumbled on a performance in front of the Tip-Top that left him in such a long and deep trance that he almost lost his job. "I stood there hypnotized by that music," he wrote in his memoirs, "which caught me in such a spell that I forgot the time." Although he fails to mention the name of the band, it was the clarinetist who bewitched him.[37] Given the year (likely 1923 or 1924), it could have been Sidney Bechet, who played clarinet and soprano saxophone in large and small venues throughout the country before his departure for Europe in 1925. But even a bedridden, dying Booker would surely have remembered Bechet's name. (In a radio interview four decades later, Booker says he first saw Bechet perform at a traveling circus).[38] A better possibility is that he had seen Dink Johnson, the clarinetist for Kid Ory's Creole Jazz Band, which had cut a record in 1922, widely considered the first jazz recording by an African American band.

Either way, Booker Pittman was clearly witnessing something historic, something seminal. Yet for the teenage Texan, the most important thing was his personal experience, the intimate backstory of what was not yet history. Dink Johnson's sinewy improvisations seemed to want to tell Booker a tale in the abstract. In this tale, the clarinet was a wily king, moving in nimble circles around the brassy cornet and the clumsy trombone, all without getting in anybody else's way. The physical appearance of Johnson's instrument said something else, though. The clarinet's keys were so banged up, Booker recalled, that Johnson was left with little choice than to bind them together with rubber bands so that they would not come loose while on stage.[39]

Dink Johnson's clarinet told a history of hardship that contradicted the elegance of Kid Ory's sound. This contrast also seduced young Booker Pittman so completely that he knew he had to learn how to learn to play Dink's instrument. One week after the decisive encounter with Ory and Johnson, Booker spotted a clarinet in the shop window of a pawnbroker on Elm Street. The owner had a long beard, a black hat, and a benevolent twinkle in his eye; he offered the boy the instrument for three dollars. Booker only had fifty cents in his pocket, but the owner did not have the heart to deny him the instrument. When, a few days later, Booker returned to pay off the remainder with tips he had saved from shining more shoes than usual, the bearded man was pleasantly surprised. Booker left the pawnshop in ecstasy, his instrument swaddled in newspaper like a gleaming baby.[40] He immediately began to learn how to play. Or rather, he immediately began *to try* to learn how to play. Booker tried to think of a place where he could practice in silence for hours, a chapel of sound. He went to the garage on Liberty Street, where Big Pitt kept his Ford Model T. For the first ten minutes, he could not coax any sound whatsoever out of the clarinet. He kept at it, though, and for his efforts, he was "rewarded with a piercing shriek."[41]

The next day, Booker decided somewhat reluctantly to ask his mother for some guidance. She looked doubtfully at the shabby instrument, then recommended a teacher who would give him the basics of technique: embouchure, correct fingering, and basic scales. In person, the man exuded authority and seriousness and wisdom; he looked the part. Except Booker could not help but notice how his highly touted teacher snoozed furtively throughout their lessons. Without a word to his parents, the young pupil decided to take things into his own hands, pocketing the money meant for the lessons and becoming his own teacher. He culled what knowledge he could from the Victrola at work, from the live bands he heard at the Tip-Top Club, and even from his own mother. Unbeknownst to her, Booker, ears pressed against the wall, would listen attentively to the scales her students practiced endlessly in the parlor.[42]

Soon, he could reproduce some of these same scales on the clarinet, and what he did not know, he made up. The thing was to make notes and more notes, sequences of notes, simple and complicated sequences; blues scales at first, then arpeggios and glissandos, almost without any desire to learn popular melodies. Songcraft could wait and so could busking on the street corner. Above all, Booker searched for a big fat sound, a round and unique tone: *his* sound, *his* tone. Only when he stopped playing by himself, when he shed the cocoon of the Model T garage, did he begin to play tunes and not just music. With the help of his younger sister, Fannie, already an able pianist, Booker Pittman felt his way through his first melody, W. C. Handy's "St. Louis Blues."[43]

## BLUE MOON CHASER

Any musical odyssey contains an episode of instructive humiliation, and Booker Pittman's story is no different in this regard. Booker attended a high school located a few blocks north of his house that happened to be called Booker T. Washington High School. It was not the only school in the nation to be named after young Booker's illustrious grandfather after his death in 1915, though it was one of the first. To say that the school's name cast a shadow over Booker and his siblings would be an understatement. Big Pitt would tell his children, "You are a Pittman. You must always remember that, so whatever you do in life, make your own name. Don't lean on your grandfather's name." But Booker T. Pittman still received his share of teasing and gawking. It was not that he felt ashamed to be the scion of the school's namesake. But his father had instilled in him and his siblings the conviction that they did not deserve the attention, good or bad. Booker's reflex was to be as inconspicuous as possible. But the strategy did not always work. "[O]n the street or in school or in public places, people would say, 'That's Booker T.'s grandson.' Boy was I mixed up."[44]

One day, most likely in 1926, the school's principal decided to invite a professional jazz band to perform in the auditorium. The band had two stars. The first, Willie Owens, was a loud-mouthed dandy who played the clarinet and saxophone with clean technique, admirable tone, and little imagination. The second star, Buster Smith, had less formal training than Owens. When he performed, he whispered the notes rather than belting them out. But Buster more than made up for it with an ineffable quality that Booker chased while he practiced scales and tore through tunes in his father's garage: he could improvise like mad.[45] Booker was not the only musician impressed by Buster "The Professor" Smith in the 1920s. In fact, Smith was so eccentrically brilliant on the alto sax, so unique in his approach, that years later, in Kansas City, a young Charlie Parker gladly became one of his acolytes.[46]

The problem was that during the intermission, Booker declared his admiration for the wrong musician. Perhaps it was because Willie and not Buster possessed the type of round and rich tone that Booker coveted, a tone that some musicians, by the end of the decade, would call the "Texas sound." Or maybe it was Willie Owens's flashy confidence and beautiful girlfriend, two things that Booker sorely wanted, almost as much as he coveted Willie's round, rich tone. All that Booker could think of saying to Willie was that he would love to be able to play the clarinet like him someday. Accompanied by the most arresting woman at the party, his ego further inflated by the boy's praise, Willie could not resist the temptation to make small of young, earnest Booker. He told him that while *he* was a born musician, "you couldn't make it sound like me never. Forget it, son. Try something else besides music. You're not cut out for it." Then, just like in the silent pictures, the bully and his date laughed uproariously in young Booker's face. The woman led Willie by the hand to the middle of the salon, the other boys admiring her figure as she walked.[47] It was the type of insult that came in the guise of jocularity, an insouciant trifle that only stung badly if you happened to be the butt of the joke. And it was absurd on the face of it. Willie had never even seen Booker play. His bullying was likely the preemptive bravado of a musician who knew deep down that he was just an average player, that if anyone should hang it up, he should. Even so, the insult cut Booker to the quick.

Intent on proving Willie wrong, for the next year, Booker practiced his clarinet every opportunity he had, memorizing scales and developing, as he put it, "a solid tone and a moderate technique." One afternoon, months after the humiliation, it was his turn to shine in front of his entire high school. He had been invited by his friend and schoolmate Budd Johnson and his brother Keg to join their band, called the Blue Moon Chasers, as a clarinetist to replace Willie, who had left the city. Budd was a precocious multi-instrumentalist and arranger bursting with talent and ambition. Two days before the dance, he decided that the band needed *two* saxophones so that the Chasers could soar like the modern ensembles in Chicago: Louis Armstrong, Bix Beiderbecke, Red Nichols. Booker had forty-eight hours to learn how to play the alto saxophone.[48]

It was an event that should have been a disaster, but somehow it was not. On the morning of the show, Booker lay fast asleep, dreaming that he was already on stage. He was awoken by the sharp sound of pebbles thrown at his bedroom window by Trezevant Sims, the Chasers' tuba and trombone player. At first, Booker heard the sound in his dream as a snare drum beat that seemed to come out of nowhere, throwing off the rhythm of the band. The third or fourth pebble was more like a rock, though, and it shattered the window. Booker leaped out of bed, his first instinct to run for his life. How would he explain the broken window later to his father, or even his mother? They would blame *him*, of course, not his brother or sister, and certainly not Trezevant Sims. The solution that presented itself to him was to get as far from the house as possible, and fast. And then it dawned on him when he saw Trezevant hustling his tuba down Liberty Street: the concert started at 9 a.m., and he was late; *they* were late.

When it came time to play his first solo, Booker was still so groggy that his body barely registered the nerves expected from an alto sax ingenue blowing for the first time in public. Not only that, it was a large and demanding audience, made up not just of students but also teachers and school administrators, boosters and alumni, mothers and fathers. Booker took in a deep breath; he did not know how this would go. The crowd gasped audibly when Booker began playing. Did he really sound that bad? He kept blowing nonetheless, trusting his breath, trusting his fingers, because what else could he do? By the time he finished, most of the crowd was standing and applauding loudly. Before the show, Booker was a nobody with a somebody's name. Now, suddenly, people he did not even know were shouting praise at him. Girls who had never noticed him before smiled and rolled their eyes at him flirtatiously. Cool boys slapped him on the back. The school principal congratulated him personally. Booker was still half awake and fully incredulous, dazed as much by his ability to improvise under pressure as by the audience's reaction. His mother might have been the most astonished of them all. The same woman who just two years earlier had said that her son lacked musical qualities now practically demanded to know where his sense of invention and creativity came from.

The only explanation he could give her was that it all came from the blues, Booker recalled.[49]

## THE MUSE

It was during a school dance at Booker T. Washington High School when Booker properly met Paula Moore. Though, really, it was the second time they met. If Paula did not remember the first time, Booker surely did. She was Willie Owens's ex-girlfriend and, as such, the bully's sidekick in the first school dance one year prior. But this time, Paula came to the show without Willie and with no desire to humiliate Booker. Just the opposite: she could not take her eyes off the graceful young man. The Blue Moon Chasers now wore a mostly convincing facsimile of tailored suits; they had more style than before, more panache, and plenty more technique. What was more, thanks mostly to Budd Johnson, they now sported an up-to-date set list and a modern, hot sound. They were, in short, a precociously slick outfit that oozed inchoate professionalism, and they knew how to get people dancing.

During the intermission, Paula smuggled a note into the dressing room, asking Booker to take a minute to talk to her after the second set. Though still a teenager, Booker now considered himself a real musician, and perhaps because he did, Paula now saw him the same way. It helped that the sultry ambience of the dance belied its physical setting. With the spotlights and the fancy attire of the guests, the auditorium bore little resemblance to a high school. It could have almost passed for the ballroom at the Grand

Lodge of the Colored Knights of Pythias or even a downtown theater. The girls and the women were dressed in formal gowns. The tuxedo-clad young men wore their hair slicked back, their shoes "glistening like light bulbs," as Booker remembered it.[50]

Amid the elegance and intoxication, Booker felt an odd mixture of resentment, lust, and fascination for Paula. A well-traveled showgirl bursting with innate charisma and vicarious ambition, she knew how to seduce with seemingly effortless precision. She told him that she had met many saxophonists in places like Chicago, Kansas City, and New York, and that Booker not only showed original talent on his instrument but also something rarer and more intangible: *stage personality*. The praise penetrated him as deeply as her derisive laughter had two years earlier. When he got home that night, Booker looked for his stage personality in the bathroom mirror. But all he saw was the same sleepy, vaguely sad young man whom Trezevant Sims had rousted out of bed that very morning. In truth, Paula possessed everything that Booker did not: experience, most of all, but also an ability to tell stories, to spin a good yarn. If Booker did not say much, Paula knew how to talk with her whole body, or as he put it later, "with her eyes, her mouth, her fingers, her hands."

Booker the memoirist hints at a sexual relationship lasting three or four months, although he never spells it out explicitly. Despite various gaps in his story, it was obvious that Paula Moore assumed giant proportions in the mind of the young musician. More than just his lover, Paula became his teacher, someone who perceived that Booker thirsted for some of the same kinds of adventure and knowledge she already possessed. Her words, her way of speaking, walking, dressing, even the scent of her body; they all evoked places and possibilities far beyond the limited, and racially segregated, social and cultural circles of Dallas. In Booker's memoirs, it is impossible not to infer a deep admiration for Paula but also a deathly fear of absolute possession, of invasion. "She was taking over, teaching me things about life," he writes.[51] If Paula was his teacher, then the act of *being taught* was synonymous with the annulment of his budding and precarious sense of liberty. Paula provoked in Booker at once a vision of a wide and marvelous world and the fear of losing this very world because of her.

## THE LAST STRAW

Meanwhile, seemingly all at once, the Pittman family fell apart. First, Booker's older brother Sidney Jr. left the house to pursue his studies at Howard

University in Washington, DC. This move was hardly unexpected: Sidney was a model student, and studying at Howard was beyond respectable; he left Texas with everyone's blessing and praise.[52] But Booker's sister Maggie had problems in school and worse ones at home. Like Booker, she was a rebel, but unlike her brother, she was unable or unwilling to disguise her true feelings and inclinations. On the contrary, when crossed, she reflexively confronted people; she yelled, sometimes she screamed. The big problem at home was her father, increasingly unstable, explosive, and drunk. One night, during an especially violent argument with Maggie, he struck his daughter in the face with such blunt force and fury that, for the rest of her life, she suffered sporadic convulsions.[53]

It was the last straw. Portia was loyal to the core and she deeply loved her husband, but she just could not take his abuse any longer. Dating back to her days in Fairmont Heights, she had carved out a career and identity of her own. At that time, she frequently gave piano recitals. A few years after coming to Dallas, Booker T. Washington's prodigal daughter, when she was not raising three children, earned considerable money and a sterling reputation as a teacher and a rising profile as a piano accompanist and choral leader. Beginning in the mid-1920s, she frequently appeared on local radio programs in a number of different formats.[54] In 1927, she directed a chorus of six hundred Booker T. Washington High School students in an impeccably prepared and moving spectacle that received considerable regional press coverage.[55]

After the epic family fight, Portia abruptly packed up, left the house, and accepted a position as a music instructor and choir director at the Tuskegee Institute, taking Maggie with her. Never again would they live in Dallas. This left Booker, to his utter horror, alone in the house with his father for the first time. It might as well have been a prison sentence. But the situation would not last long; it could not. Big Pitt never fully exhausted his will to inflict harm on others, but after his wife and daughter left, he changed his methods. Already effectively ruined as an architect and now without the income that Portia had brought into the household, he obsessively hatched a plan to found a Black newspaper, mostly to be able to publicly and freely criticize anyone and everyone who had ever spoken ill of him, who had denied him a contract or cast him an ambiguous look at a social function. He mainly aimed his wrath at the city's other Black intellectuals and power brokers, whom he considered, at best, shameless hypocrites.[56]

Meanwhile, Big Pitt waited impatiently for Booker to realize the futility of pursuing a musical career in Dallas. This would happen through his son's own failure, he reasoned. Once properly crestfallen and disillusioned, the prediction went, Booker would have no choice but to help his father pursue his no-less quixotic dream, one that soon would lead to the publication of a brilliantly irate tabloid newspaper called *Brotherhood Eyes*.[57] Booker had no interest in political journalism and felt an aversion to exacting revenge on enemies who were not his enemies. But in at least one way, he was not unlike his father: he was so totally fixated on his passion that he would do almost anything to help himself reach his goal. That included lying, which he did well and often.

Booker plotted his escape in silence. He waited, he practiced; he stumbled his way through high school. Meanwhile, the Blue Moon Chasers were expanding outward, both musically and geographically. The late 1920s were the golden age of what were known as *territory bands*: small-format orchestras that roamed the western States, particularly the Great Plains and the Southwest, and served as fertile training grounds for the swing craze of the 1930s. There were dozens of territory bands strewn about the hinterlands, playing in dance halls and roadhouses, where crowds could be rough and tastes differed widely, with some audiences asking politely for waltzes, polkas, and sweet jazz while others demanded gut-bucket blues, Western hoedown music, or torrid jazz.[58]

The Blue Moon Chasers, though still nominally high school students, wanted badly to break into the territory circuit. And to break in, you had to hit the road. At the tail end of summer vacation, the band traveled north to Oklahoma City for a brief engagement. Though Booker does not mention it in his memoirs, Buster Smith may well have been the facilitator, having already met Booker and the Johnson brothers in Dallas. The best part of the gig was meeting the other members of the established territory band that Buster played for: Walter Page's Blue Devils. Key figures in the transition to Kansas City swing, the Blue Devils was a band of all-stars, even if they did not know it at the time. At different moments in its history, the Oklahoma-based band featured the likes of pianist Bill "Count" Basie, the singer Jimmy Rushing, and eventually, the saxophonist Lester Young, though Buster Smith preceded him in this regard.[59]

The Blue Moon Chasers were still an unpolished lot by comparison, but the older, seasoned Blue Devils must have seen promise in the young Texans. The show went fine, but the Chasers needed to get home to Dallas right away since high school would be back in session soon. Booker and his mates had quickly burned through their lunch money and bus fare. Money problems among the territory bands, though, always seemed to have solutions. Despite the competitive atmosphere that generally reigned, there was great comradery among the musicians. Sometimes, competition and comradery were indistinguishable. Jimmy Rushing's family owned a restaurant in Oklahoma City, so they made sure the earnest musicians of the amusingly young band were fed properly. As for the tickets back to Dallas, the Blue Devils came up with the idea to stage a battle of the bands at Slaughter's Hall in the Deep Deuce neighborhood, with the proceeds going to the Moon Chasers, win or lose. Booker does not say whether his band came close to matching the verve and virtuosity of their benefactors—even more experienced bands could not touch the Blue Devils at that point. But the Blue Moon Chasers still made it back to Dallas, whether they wanted to or not.[60]

A few months later, another territory band swung through Dallas that would have an even more momentous impact on Booker. The band called itself Jesse Stone's Blue Serenaders, and they rivaled the Blue Devils as a magnet for talent in the region. By the time he arrived in the Texas city, pianist, composer, arranger, and bandleader Jesse Stone had already heard about the exploits of Booker and the other Blue Moon Chasers, most likely from someone in Oklahoma City. Then, in Dallas, he saw the Blue Serenaders for himself after the youngsters had added months of practice under their belts. He was impressed, and the attraction was mutual. For Booker and the Johnson brothers, Jesse Stone was one sharp cat, quick-witted and suave with an agile, refined style on the piano and a keen ear for melody.[61] Decades later, Jesse would compose what would become one of the first hits of rock and roll, the classic "Shake, Rattle, and Roll." But for now, he was just one of a number of young, talented, ambitious bandleaders who led the transition between hot jazz and early swing.

With Jesse Stone at the helm, the Blues Serenaders could do no wrong. Jesse projected commercial know-how and convinced the young Texan gunslingers that Kansas City was the place to be. As soon as he heard these words, Booker knew it was the opportunity he had been waiting for. It was *his time*, not just professionally but also personally. Once he created physical distance between himself and his father and began to earn some real money, he sensed, there would be no looking back. Without his mother and sister, and now out of school himself, Booker felt thoroughly orphaned. Dallas was next to meaningless, a place he wanted to forget about as soon as possible.

Booker knew his father would resist the move, maybe violently. Perhaps Booker needed a push from an older man as powerful and compelling as his own father to dislodge him from his unhappy childhood abode. A fast-talking seducer, but one who would not leave him broke or brokenhearted. Booker summoned up his courage and packed his things. "When the day of parting was near," he recalled, "I told my father my last lie. I told him that the band was hired to play for a week in Oklahoma, and when I returned, I would begin to work for him."[62]

Booker Pittman would not return to Texas for more than thirty years. He would never see or hear from his father again.

## KANSAS CITY

Booker's stint with Jesse Stone, though, did not last long. The Blue Serenaders had an extended contract to play in a roadhouse a day's travel from the city in the middle of the Kansas countryside. After a few weeks, Booker and Budd Johnson grew impatient. They did not want to be stuck in the corn and wheatfields forever.[63] Kansas City was no teeming metropolis, but by the end of the 1920s, it was an island unto itself, an unlikely center of musical vitality insulated from Prohibition and, later, the Great Depression by virtue of its city-sponsored cultural monopoly on general vice. This sanctuary of decadent fun was the creation of one corrupt politician and savvy investor by the name of Tom Pendergast, widely known as Boss Tom. In his pleasure dome of gambling and prostitution, the two main lubricants were moonshine and jazz. Alcohol, other illicit drugs like marijuana, and sex in various forms and configurations were readily available and tolerated virtually around the clock, as was entertainment of almost every kind imaginable. As a result, Kansas City flourished at a time when few other cities did, becoming at once a morally libertine space and one tightly controlled economically by a vast system of patronage. "[T]he Pendergast world and the powers it contained were direct challenges to the dictatorial and prevailing ideologies about morality, acceptability, and oppression," writes scholar Amber R. Clifford-Napoleone, while also noting that "the Pendergast machine controlled practically every club, cabaret, brothel, and infrastructural business in the city through its network of marginalized subcultures in the city."[64]

Kansas City's unique combination of economic opportunity, moral lassitude, and African American musical vitality was a siren song that young Black musicians could not ignore for long. One day, in the middle of the week, Booker and Budd fled the countryside and headed east. It did not take them long to find their way to the musical heart of the city—which extended a mile east from downtown and included upward of fifty cabarets on 12th and 18th Streets alone, recalled pianist Mary Lou Williams.[65] At the corner of 18th Street and Vine, Booker and Johnson heard propulsive music

> SUCH AS, JIMMY
> PAUL BARBARIN, EARL HINES, LOUIS ARMSTRONG
> JOHNNY DODDS — ETC —
> K.CITY WAS TO ME THE WAY TO N/YORK
> 4 BEATS TO A BAR — NOT 2 BEATS THE
> N.ORLEANS WAY TO CHICAGO
> THE SATURDAY NITE OR SUNDAY MORNING
> TO JAIL — BLACK MARIA — DAYLIFE
> VERY LITTLE. BL.& RECORD PLAYER
> FOR FIRST TIME — DUKE ELINGTON
> RADIO — COTTEN CLUB NEW YORK (WITH BAR.
> ST JOSEPH MO. 2 WEEKS HOME JESSIE JAMES
> UP TILL NOW MY ADVENTURE COLEMAN HAWKIN
> JAZZ? WHAT WAS I LOOKING
> FOR? DAYLIFE — NOTHING — FRIENDS
> MUSICIANS — ARTISTS OR PEOPLE CONNECTED
> WITH THEM — HOTELS — ROOMINGHOUSES —
> CABERET OWNERS — GAMBLERS
> UNDERWORLDS CATS. . SUPRISES
> COME WHAT MAY. LET JAZZ BE
> MY CONSIENCE, MY GUIDE, RELIGION
> FRIEND BEING LED ON BY THE
> BLUES. COUNT BASIE KNEELING DOWN
> TO PRAYER EACH NIGHT BEFORE
> SLEEPING —. LISTING TO ENDLESS
> TALES OF JAZZ BY MUSICIANS BY
> JAZZ MUSICIANS FROM ALL OVER.
> THE OLD AND THE NEW.

A page from Booker Pittman's memoirs. Courtesy of Eliana Pittman.

bursting from a basement venue, raw yet complex sounds of intertwining stride piano and drums. The place was a little, low-ceilinged cabaret called the Subway Club, and the musicians were Count Basie and Baby Lovett. Booker and Budd stood motionless in the stairway, bearing witness to blues as they had never heard the music played before. Without missing a beat, Basie and Baby invited them to take out their instruments and blow with them. At the end of the night, Basie told Booker that his playing had an unusual quality that needed to be developed. The Count asked him if he planned to stay long in Kansas City. Yes, that was the idea, he responded.[66] Booker always found it hard to think about the future in any structured or practical way. But the immediate promise of a tutorial of this level, added to the sheer vibrancy of a scene that teamed with talent, changed all that.

Booker stayed in the city for a year, jamming with Basie at the Subway Club at times until dawn. In his memoirs, Booker speaks of his Kansas City period with a style typical of him: ambiguous and elliptical, as though he were reluctant to conform to the truth-telling conventions of autobiographical writing. When he wrote that "each night was like a dream," it is unclear whether he was talking about musical bliss, the fog of drugs and alcohol that enveloped the Kansas City nightlife, or both.[67] At any rate, this was the first time Booker had been free from the watchful eyes of his parents for an extended period of time. With the newfound freedom came elation and also excess. Booker limits the acknowledgment of his nascent alcohol abuse in Kansas City to a single word: *vices*. Yet one page later, a revealing memory bubbles up about being picked up off the street and carried away in a Black Maria, shorthand for a police wagon. The episode foreshadowed a problem that would loom ever larger later in his life. For now, his binge drinking was apparently not so different from that of other musicians and merrymakers of Prohibition-era Kansas City, a place where club management and illicit distribution of drugs (including alcohol) were closely intertwined.[68] In any event, released from what amounted to house arrest in Dallas—an Old Testament world of sobriety and moral rectitude overseen, paradoxically, by a violent drunk of a father—Booker went wild. In his memoirs, his handwriting, clear and consistent when he writes about his childhood, suddenly becomes erratic, the narrative more fragmented and repetitive. It was as if the mind of the memoirist mirrored the period he wished to evoke, recollections of delirious, gin-soaked Kansas City filtered through the equally thick cloud of pain and morphine.[69]

## CREATIVITY

Count Basie was a precocious kind of sage, a jazz midwife who, as he had done with countless others, induced the birth of musical ideas that Booker scarcely knew he had in him. The fact that no recordings exist of the subterranean trio of Basie, Lovett, and Booker Pittman is regrettable but hardly surprising. As foundational jazz scenes go, late 1920s Kansas City was poorly documented musically. Count Basie still was not the famous Basie of the 1930s and 1940s, and even if he had been, musicians and record producers saw the jam sessions in places like the Subway Club as little more than tool-sharpening rehearsal spaces for the big bands that were beginning to grow more popular by the end of the twenties. The problem, if it could be called a problem, was that Booker never really took to big bands. He preferred duos, trios, and quartets, small and generally badly paid formats that gave ample space for improvisation and intimate musical interactions without the bothersome distraction of musical scores, noisy arrangements,

Jap Allen's Cotton Club Orchestra, 1930. From left: Joe Keyes, Ben Webster, Jim "Big Daddy" Walker, Clyde Hart, Slim Moore, Raymond Howell, Allen, Eddie "Orange" White, Al Denny, O.C. Wynne, Booker Pittman, Durwood "Dee" Stewart. Courtesy of the Kansas City Museum.

or overbearing bandleaders. In other words, the formal world of notation and discipline reminded Booker too much of the Pittman household, the world he left behind in Dallas. The small venues of Kansas City had other perks as well. The Subway Club, for instance, held the added attraction of supplying free food and unlimited booze to musicians.[70] And then there was the social life, wanton and abundant. As tenor saxophonist Buddy Tate later said, Booker "was a daring, pretty boy, who could outplay everyone" and drew plenty of attention from club-going women.[71]

Although he never felt the need for a life of luxury, Booker, like every other jazz musician, required money for clothing, daily expenses, and basic accommodations. He landed a steady job with the small orchestra of Jap Allen, a respectable mailman by day who played tuba by night. The orchestra proved to be a highly successful twist on the conventional territory band and was duly hired to play in different cities in the region. For Booker, the best part about performing in places like Omaha, Des Moines, and Fargo, besides not having to worry about covering room and board out of pocket, was that it gave him the chance to improvise in his spare time with the other members of the band, just the way he liked.

Two of the musicians were pioneers: the tenor sax player Ben Webster and the pianist Clyde Hart, who doubled as the band's arranger. In just a few years, Webster would be one of the hallowed names of the national swing scene. Hart never won the same level of recognition, but he was, if anything, even more intrepid than Webster, a proto-bebop sideman who, years later, would play with the likes of Don Byas, Dizzy Gillespie, and Charlie Parker. In the jam sessions with Hart and Webster, Booker encountered risky harmonies, nimble phrases, strange new riffs.[72] His self-portrait from the period was far from the image of the showman that would emerge years later in South America. The Booker Pittman of the Kansas City years was a paradox: a hard-drinking playboy and a devout jazz purist looking restlessly for an original voice, a means of expression at once personal and collaborative. He showed an almost excessive zeal for narrating his experience without bells or whistles—no gimmicks or easy money, no clowning around.

## TEACHERS

Count Basie, Ben Webster, Bennie Moten, Coleman Hawkins, Lester Young. Clearly, a dying Booker Pittman wished to underscore his link to the canonical names of a mythical moment in music history, to reenter the orbit of jazz history and reclaim ground zero for his own. He was certainly justified in doing so. Although Webster's name is far more renowned today in jazz historiography, it was Webster who apparently played in Booker's own short-lived orchestra in February 1931, not the other way around, an indication of just how highly respected a player Booker was.[73] Curiously, Booker never mentioned this episode in his memoirs. The topic Booker dwells on the most in his writings about the period is not celebrity but rather tutelage. Count Basie played this role in Kansas City for Booker and others. Basie's genius was not that of a self-centered virtuoso who wished simply to be adored. For this reason, he became a bandleader and arranger instead of a soloist. He knew he could never be the best jazz pianist in a world that included Fats Waller and Art Tatum. He also realized that a good bandleader was a teacher and that truly first-class teachers were less common than second-class performers. The way Booker saw it, his mentor "taught you and you didn't know at the time you were being taught."[74] He knew that teaching effectively meant teaching with judicious generosity and strategic aplomb, with *purpose* and with selflessness. And this sometimes required loaning out one's pupil to another teacher.

This is what happened one night at the Subway Club. Booker saw Count Basie out of the corner of his eye, speaking with rare deference to a trumpet player, a gaunt, middle-aged man with a disarmingly sad and tired face. Later, Booker learned that the man's name was Peter Davis, Louis Armstrong's first cornet teacher from his New Orleans days. Basie asked Davis if he would mind playing a blues tune, and the man played the song with such delicacy and touch and such indescribable pain that it was as though he were playing his instrument for the last time or that he was not a musician at all, but a country preacher putting a poor soul to rest. Booker heard in the impromptu performance a melancholy so profound, so genuine, that he knew it had to be the product of suffering, neglect, and oblivion. At that moment, Booker identified so completely with the feeling of the music that he could almost glimpse his own suffering, not just that of his Texas past but also, somehow, that of his future as well. He asked Mr. Davis for advice, any advice.

Jazz was a way of life that should reflect the good as well as the bad, Davis said. "Tell what you feel [and] be truthful about it."[75] Davis had just stopped working on a traveling minstrel show, he told Booker, and he was sick and tired of working endlessly for the pittance that he received for his toil and trouble. The man's words conveyed to Booker the sense not that pain and suffering were odious and avoidable but rather the inevitable markers of an authentically lived life of risk and adventure: the enablers of soulful creativity. If there were a Hollywood version of the fateful encounter, the battle-worn Peter Davis would die from tuberculosis soon after imparting his last words of wisdom to the young and cocky upstart. But the episode's real-life denouement was much longer and more pedestrian than that. Louis Armstrong's first teacher was not as far gone as he seemed in 1930. In fact, Davis kept playing sadly and authentically for decades. In 1965, he even resurfaced on the American game show *I've Got a Secret* alongside his most celebrated student.[76]

## MANHATTAN IN KANSAS CITY

The young Booker Pittman was not greedy or materialistic. But he was as ambitious as anyone else, and his star was rising fast in Kansas City and beyond. Booker was more than just good: his talent intimidated people. Ben Webster himself later recalled that Booker was clearly the saxophonist to beat at the time. Buster Smith had made his way to Kansas City by this time, and he was another player in the same category, according to Webster. But where Buster practically whispered his notes, Booker was the opposite—potent, loud, and audacious.[77] Booker felt that the time was coming to leave Kansas City and, in fact, to leave the Midwest entirely. At the beginning of the 1930s, few people thought Kansas City was the center of the musical universe, even if it was. Chicago came closer to fitting the bill, and Booker's Kansas City–based circuit took him there more than once. Later, he recalled bullets flying while he played in a cabaret owned by Al Capone's brother.[78] In another instance, he met and briefly played with Louis Armstrong in a small combo format in Rock City, Illinois.[79] But the world's jazz capital in everyone's mind was Harlem. Established bands had already put down roots there: Duke Ellington, Fletcher Henderson, Chick Webb. And then there were the musicians from the Northeast who had never had much use for Kansas City or the territory circuit, top-tier saxophonists like Benny Carter and Johnny Hodges. Even the band Booker played for, Jap Allen's Cotton Club Orchestra, evoked Harlem even if few, if any, of the band's members knew the storied neighborhood firsthand.

Booker Pittman prepared for his imminent exodus to New York in the only way he knew how: by keeping his ears open and eyes peeled to every new sound and style and quickly absorbing them. Above all, he listened to records, taking in the exciting runs and exquisite timbre of Hodges and Carter. For Booker, it was not only a matter of imitating their styles but of copying their solos. For all that has been written about the innovations of hot jazz and early swing, musical poaching and copycatting were all too common at the time.[80] And it was not just Booker. His brilliant bandmate Clyde Hart used to sit down next to the jukebox at a diner and transcribe the records of a rival up-and-coming band, McKinney's Cotton Pickers, note for note. One day, the Cotton Pickers happened to come through Kansas City and challenged Jap Allen's orchestra to a battle of the bands. The Cotton Pickers somehow had lost their playbook on the road, so they were forced to muddle through their performances by ear and memory. When they heard the Cotton Club Orchestra's repertoire and arrangements, so uncannily like their own, they became so convinced that Clyde Hart was the culprit that they tried to have him arrested by the Kansas City police, accusing him of stealing their charts.[81] The notion of absolute originality or pure improvisation was a farse that belied the fact that stealing riffs from others was the very bedrock of innovation. Booker, Clyde Hart, and the other top musicians in Kansas City could only know with complete certainty when they had chanced on something new if they had already fully plagiarized the great inventors of jazz. But in order to have full access to the fluctuating archive of the mandarins of the sax, trumpet, and piano, they needed to live closer to the source.

## JOY BOYS

Booker Pittman's first clear signal to head to the East Coast was Count Basie's graduation from the intimate world of the Subway Club and promotion to the bigger stage of Bennie Moten's band, where he would play a more and more prominent role until, finally, he left Kansas City entirely some years later.

The second catalyst was Blanche Calloway. Like her more famous younger brother, Cab, Blanche was a charismatic, extravagant, and clever bandleader. And just as Booker and others stole riffs from Hodges and Hawkins and Tatum, Blanche absconded with Booker and his bandmates, hiring away several members of Jap Allen's orchestra while touring the Midwest when she caught wind of some financial problems and tensions within the band.[82] The slick maneuver effectively ended the musical career of the former postal worker Allen and launched Blanche Calloway into a brief period of semi-stardom. One of the first female bandleaders in history, Blanche had apparently coined the call-and-response "hi-dee-ho" routine that made her brother famous. In that same year, 1931, with a band of crack musicians like Booker, Clyde Hart, and Ben Webster, the newly formed orchestra, Blanche Calloway and her Joy Boys, almost immediately recorded several sides with RCA Victor.

The Joy Boys' records are a mixture of blues, hot jazz, and commercial foxtrots that showcase the unique talent of Blanche as a bandleader and vocalist. As a singer, she sounds like a more polished and extravagant version of Bessie Smith and every bit as lurid. As a leader, perhaps to mask her modest abilities as an arranger, she relies heavily on humor and gimmickry. Webster is the band's main soloist, though Blanche leaves little room for improvisation. In the last few bars of "Sugar Blues," however, Booker has his shot, and he does not miss, attacking the clarinet with a skittish brilliance that seems to want badly to leave a good impression. He makes the most of the little space he is allotted, leading with an audacious blue note followed by several ethereal, almost timid phrases, like eloquent mumbling. Like all the musicians in the band, Booker knew this was not just any performance. It was an audition, personally as well as collectively.[83]

Since the stock market collapse of 1929, the sale of records and record players in the United States had fallen precipitously, so much so that the recording industry almost died, dipping in the early 1930s to as low as five percent the size of what it had been just a few years earlier.[84] Blanche wanted club access to the small world of commercially successful recording artists and so did her young, ambitious bandmembers. But it was not to be so. Practically the only sustained success stories of the period belonged to Duke Ellington, who assumed the throne of the King of Jazz that he had long deserved, and Cab Calloway, who recorded his massive hit "Minnie the Moocher" just weeks after the Joy Boys' RCA Victor sessions. In little time, Cab Calloway not only eclipsed his older sister; he made her nearly disappear from public memory.

While they were still in fashion, Blanche Calloway and her Joy Boys toured for several weeks in the other big cities of the Northeast: Philadelphia; Washington, DC; Boston; and Baltimore. There was a part of the experience that appealed to Booker. Blanche was nothing if not a showwoman, entertaining audiences with musical gags that bore thick traces of vaudeville and minstrelsy, and she must have seen how seamlessly Booker stitched visual theatricality into his performances. The money was better than it had been in Kansas City. Still, Booker soon tired of life on the road.[85] Blanche could be a demanding boss, for starters. But that was not the only issue. Booker's flagging interest points to one of the great paradoxes of his personality: he was an impulsively itinerant musician who, deep down, could not stomach life on the road for long; an incurable troubadour who suffered from motion sickness. He needed a place he could call home, if only for a while.

Booker Pittman got his first taste of Harlem playing with Blanche Calloway's band at the Lafayette Theatre on 132nd Street.[86] With the help of Leroy Hardy, the Joy Boys' other saxophonist, Booker quit the band and remained in New York City. His next big opportunity in New York was with the Congo Knights, the ensemble of the young bandleader Ralph Cooper. Here, Booker met a different set of excellent musicians: Bill Coleman, Bill Dillard, Henry Goodwin, and a tenor saxophonist and clarinetist named Alfred Pratt, whom Booker would quickly befriend. Cooper saw not just talent but charisma and budding showmanship in Booker and encouraged him to assume the spotlight as much as possible. The band did so swimmingly in venues like the Apollo Theater and the Harlem Opera House that, in 1932, they were invited to tour the states on the RKO circuit—not just the Eastern Seaboard but as far west as Denver.[87]

As long as there were new, faraway places to see, Booker was fine with the touring. But he especially savored his time in Harlem. With all the traveling, he felt as if there was still so much of the city and the city's music to explore, the minutiae of each block, the pint-sized meat markets and hat repair shops, the seafood lunch places and barber shops. And then there were the small music venues and speakeasies. Soon, Booker was blowing, watching, and dancing in the best clubs in the neighborhood—The Cotton Club, Savoy Ballroom, Small's Paradise, Connie's Room. It was through the club scene that he met most of the biggest names in jazz whom he did not already know personally: Fats Waller, Chick Webb, and of course his idols, Benny Carter and Johnny Hodges. Booker knew how to ease himself into the in-crowd. He was quietly charming, a well-dressed and understated hit with women, and too polite and good-natured to be a threat to the men. He had musical talent that he never seemed too eager to peddle. And he was also not *just* interested in music, and this also played well with the big shots.

Harlem's cultural scene in the early 1930s went far beyond music alone. For some subsequent historians, the Harlem Renaissance referred first and foremost to a literary and artistic movement.[88] But Harlem was already a musical mecca well before writers channeled the sights and sounds of the neighborhood, as captured in Alain Locke's seminal anthology *The New Negro* (1925). As one scholar has written, Black music "already existed in the night and day of Harlem life, naming it as a vernacular precedent for the acts of independence that the Renaissance would achieve in print."[89] And it was not just the music. By the time Booker Pittman arrived, the neighborhood was a widely diverse center of Black popular entertainment that appealed to a multiracial, international public. Beyond the jazz and blues musicians, beyond the poets and the painters, swirled a nocturnal world of boxers, baseball players, street hawkers, entrepreneurs, magicians, actors and actresses, reefer dealers, tap dancers, and chorus girls. For Booker, the tap dancers were as memorable as the musicians and just as ubiquitous. Figures with resonant names like Bill Bojangles Robinson, Buck and Bubbles, and Clayton "Peg Leg" Bates graced the same large theaters as Ellington and Webb and the same cabarets and speakeasies as late-night jam bands. Even on the sidewalks, dancers engaged in spontaneous artistic duels, all while competing for space and pocket change with peanut vendors and banjo savants.[90] In this atmosphere, at once segregated and democratic, collaborative and competitive, serious and capricious, holding people's rapt attention was essential.

## WILLIE THE LION

The best introductions, the ones that opened doors, naturally came from the famous and the well-connected. An old friend of Count Basie's, the pianist Willie "The Lion" Smith, was a case in point. The Lion was an enigma: a relic of ragtime and a fixture in the 1930s Harlem scene, an extravagant clown and a decorated veteran of World War I, a showman and a seminal figure of stride piano, one of the original "big three" along with James Johnson and Fats Waller. If The Lion was a clown, he was one with pedigree and complexity—a snappy dresser but also "an iconoclast and fiercely independent," as Waller put it years later.[91] One night, Willie was playing in a speakeasy called Big John's where, according to an English writer of the period, the gin was of incredibly poor quality.[92] Booker, dressed elegantly as always, his alligator skin wallet tucked into his pocket and a brand-new King alto saxophone under his arm, strode into the bar and ordered his horrible gin on the rocks as though he were not new at this.

Booker quickly discerned that a rival of his was in the house. Without asking ("just like a mother takes a baby," Booker wrote), Charlie Holmes, one of the pretenders to the throne of best alto sax player in the city, borrowed Booker's gleaming instrument and began jamming with the Lion. Holmes played in a style that was tonally impressive and audacious, Booker observed, but also repetitive and derivative: a well-rehearsed but badly disguised replica of Johnny Hodges's best moves. Booker saw his opportunity. He grabbed his saxophone back more assertively than was his style. Willie, maybe out of loyalty to his friend Basie, orchestrated a musical mini-revenge, payback for Charlie Holmes's insolence. "Get ready," he whispered to Booker. "This is going to be fast."[93]

And fast it was. Booker closed his eyes, took a swig of bad gin, and blew the frenetic melody of "Chinatown, My Chinatown" as cleanly as he could, his tongue vibrating with such force that he feared he might injure himself. At first, it was hard for him to catch the tempo. He felt clumsy, cold, struggling to keep up with the pace set by the fleet-fingered Lion. He felt a surge of low-level panic course through his veins, then hot on its heels came the dark gift of adrenaline. He tasted the salt of blood in his mouth, his lips, his tongue. Every so often, Willie would shout "Keep blowing, boy!" or simply "There you go." It was like an incantation. Simple as it was, the words of encouragement worked their magic. First, Booker noticed that he was treading water in a sea of piano chords. Then he realized that he was swimming, and then that he was swimming well. So this was the *pocket* that Count Basie had always talked about. It was a strange sensation. Without doing so willingly, Booker was summoning all the unspoken lessons he had learned in his years playing with Basie and Clyde and Ben. He had no other choice.

"Keep blowing," Willie said. "There you go."

And away he went, flying blind, so far in the pocket that he lost any conventional sense of time and direction. Finally, when Booker felt that he had said what needed to be said, he finished with a quick cadenza: eloquent, potent, devastating. When he opened his eyes, he saw that the empty speakeasy was now nearly full, the applause filling the void left by his suddenly mute saxophone. And no Charlie Holmes for miles.[94]

## JOYCE

Though no doubt there were others, Booker only spoke of one long-term lover from his New York period. Her name was Joyce, an Irish American redhead who, according to Booker, felt unusually at home in the world of Black jazz bands and vaudeville acts. Booker met Joyce in Nebraska while he was touring with Jap Allen, and she followed him on the circuit. Though Booker speaks relatively little of her in his memoirs, Joyce (surname unknown) seems to have been a combination of talented dancer and fanatical groupie. She embraced the world of African American cabaret with such zeal that her performances, in a realm of popular entertainment where racial impersonation, shock, and novelty were highly valued, likely flirted with the toxic desire for blackface. Irish and Jewish immigrants often occupied this niche during the long period of transition between theatrical revues and early film when the common tropes of minstrelsy lingered.[95] Although the practice ultimately benefited European-born performers at the expense of African Americans, Joyce's apparently earnest admiration for jazz culture may also have masked a desire to escape from her own family of disenfranchised white immigrants at the nadir of the Great Depression.

What made Booker most uncomfortable about Joyce, though, was her ardent wish to be married. And to *him*, no less, to Booker Pittman. At the time, flush with promise and ambition, he regarded any attempt at commitment and domestic life with Joyce as sticky and burdensome, if not downright impossible. His misgivings were not unfounded and went beyond his fear of commitment. As late as the 1950s, about one percent of white Southerners approved of Black-white marriages; in the northern states, the figure was five percent.[96] Attitudes were even more extreme when it came to romantic or sexual relationships between white women and Black men. Whereas a white man would inevitably encounter fierce resistance from his family if he chose to marry a Black woman, purely sexual encounters did not carry the same degree of risk. Conversely, any relationship between Black men and white women "not only challenged the racial order but also rejected the authority of [white women's] fathers and brothers," a perceived offense that could quickly spiral into physical violence.[97]

Booker Pittman clearly faced a difficult decision. Despite her earnest affections, Joyce was phenotypically white. But she apparently came from a lower social class than Booker, and her lack of elegance and good manners seemed to eat at him in ways he scarcely wished to admit to himself. Working as a cabaret dancer carried with it a connotation of licentiousness, if not prostitution. Therefore, not only might their marriage have challenged the racial mores of Joyce's family, but Booker's own relatives would have likely viewed Joyce as beneath them. Since it was not Booker's style to summarily kick a woman out of his life, he tried gentle persuasion. The prognosis for the long-term success of their unconventional relationship was not good, he told her. They would have to win over too many people, people who could not be won over. Joyce was undeterred; she pressed on. Finally, out of sheer desperation, Booker T. Pittman invoked the ghost of Booker T. Washington. Booker admired his grandfather for his courage in combating racial prejudice, he told Joyce. But as for himself, he just "wasn't called on to do that sort of work."[98]

Despite his gut instinct to do the opposite, Booker agreed to marry Joyce in what he called a "surprise wedding." There is no evidence of their legal matrimony, formal or otherwise. This is hardly a shock, given the political climate of the times. Succumbing to deeply entrenched racism and xenophobia, anti-miscegenation laws in the United States had grown considerably more widespread and prohibitive between the 1860s and the 1940s. Even though in the early 1930s, Black-white intermarriage was technically legal in the state of New York (whereas it was not in Texas or Missouri, nor in the large majority of states), it was neither common nor socially acceptable.[99] Yet surely there were other factors that compelled Booker to agree to a union with Joyce, with or without a ceremony. Perhaps he reasoned that the mere promise of commitment might put an end to the visceral terror that overcame him whenever he gave the issue any thought—the dread of settling down with a woman and of settling down generally, let alone at this stage in his life. Maybe he simply capitulated to the pressure of Joyce's own passionate arguments. After all, how could he oppose someone who agreed to move where he moved, drink what he drank, sleep when he slept? Joyce was a rare find, a live wire, a desirable fellow traveler. And besides: *No women*, he wrote, *no adventure*.[100]

In the end, though, travel itself would prove Booker Pittman's greatest muse.

*Chapter Two*

# ⁕LE ⁕JAZZISTE

*May I?*
*Mais oui.*
*Mein Gott!*
*Parece una rumba*
*Play it, jazz band!*
—LANGSTON HUGHES, "JAZZ BAND IN A PARISIAN CABARET"

BOOKER PITTMAN'S EUROPEAN ADVENTURES BEGAN WITH A HARLEM-based bandleader named Lucky Millinder. Encouraged by promoter, publisher, and lyricist extraordinaire Irving Mills, Millinder convinced most of Ralph Cooper's Congo Knights to join up with his globetrotting outfit.[1] Like Blanche and Cab Calloway, Millinder was equal parts showman and businessman, a savvy dynamo who knew how to attract first-rate talent and land lucrative contracts. After doing a series of shows with the newly minted ensemble at the Harlem Opera House and the Apollo Theater, Lucky Millinder's orchestra headed for Europe, embarking on the transatlantic liner Il Conte Grande in late June 1933.[2]

It was a voyage to remember. The weather was fair, the food excellent, the rooms luxurious, and the drinks unlimited. Most of the orchestra members, joined by two chorus girls and a tap dancer, were not used to a high life this high. The rest is not hard to imagine: Booker and his bandmates likely spent ample time at the swimming pool and playing cards, finishing off crab and scallops and untold bottles of wine while they beheld the flying fish of the Atlantic with the intense lyricism of the inebriated. After eleven days on the open sea followed by brief stops in Gibraltar, Naples, and Ventimiglia, Il Conte Grande finally dropped anchor in Monte Carlo in early July.[3] Lucky and his band were to open a casino in the Sporting Club d'Été, a commitment that kept them in the Riviera for several weeks. Right away, Booker would have been exposed to a level of scale and cosmopolitanism that he was not accustomed to. He must have felt as though he and the other performers were happy impostors in a gaudy palatial playground, crashing the party en masse. Lucky Millinder and His Orchestra were part of an enormous revue that encompassed dozens of cabaret dancers, comedians, acrobats, and two other orchestras besides their own: the Catalan Enric Madriguera's Latin American orchestra and the Hungarian Bela de Racz's "gypsy" ensemble.[4]

Booker later remembered how the spectacle of seminude female dancers somewhat upstaged the music. Nonetheless, audiences took to the sounds of Harlem, with Lucky's band serving as a conduit to the New York jazz and swing scenes, introducing European vacationers to dazzling new songs such as Cole Porter's "Night and Day."[5] In their time off, meanwhile, Booker and his chums toured Nice and the Palace of the Prince of Monaco; they lounged and flirted in the all-night cafés that dotted the beach. Many of the musicians found the atmosphere of the Riviera irresistible. The band's tenor saxophonist, Alfred Pratt, was so smitten by a woman he met there that they were married before they departed Monte Carlo.[6]

Leaving Monaco might have proven more difficult if it were not Paris that awaited them; Booker was especially eager to get there.[7] 1933 was an intoxicating time to behold the City of Light. As the Great Depression began to make itself felt throughout France, many white American expatriates returned to the United States. However, much of the Black American migrant community who had arrived in the previous decade, from writers and artists to students and musicians, remained in the city. Jazz had taken hold in Paris to a degree that it rarely had during the Jazz Age proper and now included a growing number of French musicians as well. As the phalanx of African American talent showed few signs of abandoning the city, their music found audiences in a network of cafés, nightclubs, and larger auditoriums that only seemed to expand with each passing year of the decade. Most, though not all, these venues could be found in Montmartre, places like Frisco's, the Melody Bar, and Bricktop's—the latter an elegant nightclub frequented by royals and aristocrats and owned by Bricktop (née Ada Beatrice Queen Victoria Louise Virginia Smith), along with Josephine Baker, one of the most powerful and influential Black American expats in the city.[8]

The first stop in Paris for Lucky Millinder and His Orchestra was Le Grand Rex, the large and sumptuous art deco movie theater and performance space built the year before on Boulevard Poissonnière. One of the musicians who traveled with the orchestra was the trumpeter Bill Coleman, like Booker Pittman, a carryover from the Congo Knights who, with time, would become one of the most notable jazz musicians of the transnational musical scene centered in the French capital. For Coleman, Paris was a completely different scene from New York. Even so, there were already a considerable number of Black Americans in the City of Light, many of them, like the pianist Freddy Johnson, lodged at the Hôtel Lisieux in Montmartre.[9] Paris in 1933 was not just about touring Harlemites and sundry American expats. There were musicians and artists from other corners of the globe as well. The Bal Nègre, for instance, drew performers and audiences from the French West Indies, especially from islands such as Martinique and Guadeloupe. Located in Montparnasse on the Left Bank, the club featured orchestras playing beguine, a French Caribbean musical style and dance, made widely fashionable in jazz and swing circles by Cole Porter's 1935 composition "Begin the Beguine." As historian Tyler Stovall has noted, the Bal Nègre attracted considerable numbers of Black American writers and intellectuals as well, drawn to the kindred novelty of the beguine and its unique rhythms and instrumentation, not to mention spectators and dancers who brought to the venue sounds and experiences distinct from their own yet also familiar. The club's success revealed the many ways in which Black performers and audiences of the period coalesced around Parisian cultural venues and specifically how they exposed American musicians, artists, and expats to Black cultural practices of different climes.[10]

Back in Montmartre, meanwhile, a brood of Cuban musicians and artists clustered around La Cabane Cubaine on Rue Pierre Fontaine. Lucky's orchestra quickly caught wind of the Cubaine, and several of the musicians showed up with their instruments and jammed there with rumba and *son* players. Coleman was astonished by the Cubans' ability to adapt so quickly to the harmonic modalities of jazz.[11] The admiration and knowledge-sharing were mutual. Cubans brought to the stage a rhythmic complexity unknown to the recently arrived *jazzistes*. The cross-pollination continued outside the confines of La Cabane Cubaine and spread throughout Montmartre. This intensely transnational, integrated subscene lent Paris a distinct flavor beyond anything that African American jazz musicians had experienced in the United States. Coleman and his colleagues regularly jammed and jousted with other musicians from France, the Caribbean, Africa, and Eastern Europe. Afterward, they would share stories and reefers in Freddy Johnson's room, where nonmusician guests like the Cuban boxer Kid Chocolate would sometimes show up as well, bringing ample marijuana with him. The tea party did not end until it was time to play again.[12]

Booker and the recently married Alfred Pratt enjoyed Paris so much that when their ship was set to embark for the United States, they did not show up.[13] Bill Coleman did. Upon his return to Manhattan, Lucky Millinder's band broke up and Coleman joined up with Benny Carter's new orchestra, along with colleagues of Booker's like Cozy Cole and his hometown friend Keg Johnson.[14] In short order, Lucky replaced Cab Calloway as house bandleader of the Cotton Club. Later, he would lead other famous artists: Dizzy Gillespie, Buster Bailey, Sister Rosetta Tharpe.[15] The birth of the Swing Era signaled the gradual resurrection of the music industry, unceremoniously buried alive during the early depths of the Great Depression. The rebirth of popular music also meant the return of records, the ascension of radio, and the professionalization of hordes of musicians toiling in Bohemian obscurity for years: by missing the boat, Booker had also likely missed out on the gravy train.

It was not hard for Booker Pittman to imagine what would have happened had he gone back to Harlem with Millinder and most of the rest of the band. No doubt he would have landed more gigs than ever and perhaps earned more money than he knew what to do with. He would have played more solos and made more records, perhaps—who was to say?—becoming one of the most visible and venerated instrumentalists in the city and, therefore, the world. Given his intrepid disposition, his formidable chops, and his distaste for the regimentation of commercial big band, it is not outlandish to picture Booker eventually eschewing the bandstand and jamming with like-minded stateside musicians: Lester Young, Clyde Hart, Coleman Hawkins, Ben Webster, even Parker and Gillespie themselves.

But as always, Booker was the faithful heir to his own complex temperament. Equal parts laid back and stubbornly principled, he prized above all else conviviality, variety, and intimate creativity. For this reason, he never took to playing in large commercial orchestras, which required extra preparation, repetition, and generally little magic—work that really seemed like work, complete with headaches and deadlines and imperious boss men. Beginning in 1933, the year Booker Pittman stayed behind in France, the Big Band Era would intensify, only slowing down at the end of World War II. Although the commercial swing scene did not appeal to the Texan, there may well have been other considerations. The rise of big band signaled a new reign of clinical musicianship and crisp arrangements. Since his days in Kansas City, respected peers and elders like Bennie Moten and Count Basie had begged Booker to further his studies in music theory and notation, but he resisted these calls to become another "paper musician." He felt that the hours spent on perfecting his scales and charts would take away from something more essential to him: the "sweet adventure" of improvisation.[16] But the Montmartre scene, he was finding, was closer to his platonic ideal of jazz than Harlem was; music and booze flowed just as fast, and friendship came easier. Musically and personally, Booker felt more at home in Paris than he had in New York City.

## LE JAZZ HOT

Booker Pittman experienced a blend of comfort and stimulation in the streets and restaurants and cabarets of Paris that he had never felt elsewhere.[17] Perhaps it had more to do with absence than presence. It was as though the City of Lights existed only to expose the rest of the Western world as intrusive and petty, weighed down with self-imposed and unnecessary rules, barriers, and biases. Of course, the insulation that Paris offered was not absolute. To Parisians, being a Black American, for instance, meant something quite different than being Congolese: a different kind of Blackness, one freer of Francophone colonial stigma and less subject to hostility and surveillance. This was especially true when it came to jazz musicians. As one historian noted, "The contrast between the treatment of Black American performers (and Black Americans more generally) and Black French was obvious, and it added to the anti-colonial political sentiment among Black French who witnessed it."[18] In either case, interwar Paris was as attractive a place as any for an interracial American couple like Booker and Joyce. Unlike New York, moreover, France supplied ample opportunities to play in smaller formats. And not only that. While in the United States, orchestras were growing bigger by the day, Paris embraced the intimate, complex world of hot jazz as a phenomenon that went beyond the *tumulte noir* spectacle of the 1920s.

Nonetheless, in one sense, the timing of Booker's arrival was less than ideal. More than a decade earlier, when the jazz rage was still in its infancy, the French government had passed legislation decreeing that music and entertainment venues must limit the number of foreign musicians to 10 percent of the total number. The so-called "10% Law" initially did little to stymie the growth of Black American bands in Paris. Yet by the early 1930s, the Great Depression and dwindling opportunities for French musicians pressured more and more cabaret and club owners to enforce the law. By the summer of 1933, just as Booker made his entrance, the situation had driven many foreign resident musicians and entertainers to resorts in the South of France, where business was also relatively slow. Others fled the country entirely, traveling as far as Shanghai, where the jazz expat scene quickly eclipsed that of Paris.[19] Only in the following spring were the owners of some Parisian establishments, such as Chez Florence, able to effectively exploit loopholes in the 10% Law to ensure the survival of Black American orchestras.[20] In an interview later in his life, Booker mentioned hunger as a defining feature of his time in Paris. Although he managed to piece together a living by playing in cabarets, jam sessions, and concerts, as a whole, he earned less than he had in New York.[21]

On the other hand, if it were not the perfect moment for someone like Booker Pittman to break into the Montmartre scene, it was not an entirely bad one, either. It helped that the Texan had never played better. All he had to do was to look the part, partake gamely in the madness, forge networks out of friendships, not get too drunk, and play his heart out. Or at least not get too drunk *before* he played his heart out. For Booker, social intercourse led to all others. Working a room came naturally to him. In new terrain like France, he might not be able to rely on his old contacts or tried-and-true strategies, but Booker was nothing if not adaptable. As always, he was perpetually interested in getting to know new people and places. And he was not afraid to ask questions in whichever language moved him or to listen. Through his friendship with Freddy Johnson, Booker met other musicians like the trumpeter Arthur Briggs, the tenor saxophonist Frank "Big Boy" Goudie, and the singer and tap dancer Louis Cole. He began to frequent and then play in an assortment of cafés, cabarets, theaters, and other cultural spaces, principally in Montmartre. Meanwhile, the Hot Club de France, brainchild of the writer Hugues Panassié, was inaugurated that same year in a small record store in Montparnasse, later moving to a larger space in L'École Normale de Musique, and finally multiplying and migrating to other cities in France and elsewhere in Europe.[22]

If the hot jazz scene in Paris was exactly what Booker was looking for, it was looking for him as well. Hugues Panassié encouraged Freddy Johnson to create a band that would exhibit the most authentic side of *le jazz hot*. Freddy obliged by forming the Harlemites, a band that brought together the best African American talent Paris had to offer, beginning with musicians like Briggs, Goudie, and Cole. Initially playing to nearly empty audiences at the Hot Club, the Harlemites quickly gained a following and, by summer, had managed to sell out a show at the Salle Pleyel. In June and July 1933, Freddy's ensemble recorded several sides with the Brunswick label and even one curious record with Marlene Deitrich called "Wo Ist der Mann?"[23] A few months later, Booker joined the Harlemites along with his close friend Al Pratt. It was the second time Booker had performed in

Lithograph poster of Freddy Johnson and His Orchestra by Charles Delaunay, 1934. © Cooper Hewitt, Smithsonian Design Museum/Art Resource, NY.

a band whose name referred to Harlem. It was also the second time his bandleader was an ex-postman. Maybe this is why Freddy Johnson was so well-connected. The man who had convinced Freddy to leave among the steadiest of African American jobs for the insecurity of jazz was Benny Carter. The person who had convinced Freddy to leave the United States and go overseas was Sam Wooding, who had first arrived in the 1920s and was by now the spiritual leader of Black American expatriates in Europe.[24]

Despite the sense of displacement that plagued Sam, Arthur, Freddy, and other American musicians, the symbolic ground zero for the Harlemites was still New York City, a fact made evident in the song titles that the band recorded with Decca: "Sweet Madness," "Tiger Rag," "Harlem Bound," and "I Got Rhythm." In the two versions of the latter Gershwin tune, Booker Pittman shows off even more refined and confident technique on the clarinet than what he had exhibited on the Blanche Calloway sessions two years earlier. He had clearly stepped up his game. Especially on the first version of "I Got Rhythm," recorded in October, he bobs with quicksilver agility atop the galloping rhythm laid down by Freddy, emitting sharp cries and coos, followed by sinuous, syncopated runs, at once playful and powerful. On "Tiger Rag," without exhibiting the tonal audacity he had shown on the clarinet, Booker's alto sax, anchored by quieter, eloquent arpeggios, is more structured and expressive. For the first time on record, Booker was telling a *story*, as he had always wanted to do.[25]

## HOT BABEL

Everything pointed to a long stay in Europe for the young Texan. The arrival of Duke Ellington in 1933, followed the next year by Louis Armstrong and Coleman Hawkins, signaled the definitive consecration of Black American jazz in France. Satchmo was probably the most legendary of the three at this early stage. By the time he took the city by storm, Armstrong was already the patron saint of Panassié's Hot Club. But many French people were not satisfied with simply adoring and imitating the great American performers; they also wanted to forge a new national expression from the raw material of *le musique negre americain*. French interest in jazz grew stronger thanks to the emergence of two first-rate homegrown talents, the Romani French Django Reinhardt and the Italian French Stéphane Grappelli. The style they invented had its roots in hot jazz, to which they added rich, novel tonalities gathered from Romani music and European string instrumentation techniques more generally. Along with the Afro Caribbean hybrids centered in New York City and Havana around this same time, the new sounds forged by Reinhardt, Grappelli, and others (now sometimes referred to generically as *jazz manouche*) were arguably the beginning of jazz's internationalization beyond mere copies and tributes.[26]

As had been the case in Kansas City and Harlem, whether by intuition or blind luck, Booker Pittman found himself in the middle of a profoundly vibrant scene still in its infancy, riding the wave of yet another musical avant-garde. By now, Booker already knew nearly everyone and had blown his alto in a variety of settings for vastly different audiences. He had appeared in prestige venues such as Salle Pleyel, where he played with Ellington's formidable orchestra.[27] With another band, Harry Cooper and His Rhythm Aces, Booker played at the École Normale, an event where the soon-to-be-famous Quintette du Hot Club de France had its debut.[28] The following year, Booker and Arthur Briggs performed at a dance in Zurich, Switzerland, with Django and Grappelli.[29] This did not include the countless gigs in cafés, *boîtes*, cabarets, and other intimate venues in Paris and beyond.

But Booker Pittman's culminating moment was being recruited by Louis Armstrong to play with him and his orchestra at the Grand Rex and other shows, including a run at the Salle Pleyel.[30] During his time in the territory circuit, Booker had played briefly with Armstrong in Rock City, Illinois.[31] However, he owed his fruitful reacquaintance with Satchmo largely to Alfred Pratt, who recorded with Armstrong's orchestra on several sides that same year at Studio Polydor.[32] In an interview three decades later,

Armstrong singled out Booker as one of the most memorable musicians he played with in his maiden voyage to Paris. Booker was one "lively cat," he remarked.[33]

A testament to Booker's ubiquity as well as his talent was the publication of Hugues Panassié's landmark book *Jazz-Hot* in 1934. Word must have spread quickly among the city's expat musicians when the book hit the shelves. It was likely that Booker still could not read French all that well, but Freddy almost certainly could. Perhaps he was the one who explained to Booker the importance of *Jazz-Hot* and how it gave many Black musicians their due, many of whom had never seen their names in print before. The book was as informative as it was long, with ample descriptions of the leading figures and even a preface written by Satchmo himself. And Booker was in it. In his summary of leading alto sax players, Panassié declared Booker one of the best in the world, placing him just behind Benny Carter and Johnny Hodges.[34] Flipping through pages of prose he mostly did not understand, feeling the weight of the book, Booker must have sensed that he *existed* for the first time, really existed. Though only scant sonic evidence of Booker's 1930s prowess remains on record, Panassié's assessment does not appear to have been an exaggeration. Over two decades later, the ever-discriminating Arthur Briggs remarked that the Booker Pittman he knew in Paris was "an exceptional alto man, the Charlie Parker of his day."[35]

Despite French nativism and the city's best attempt to domesticate Black American jazz and blues, Paris was becoming a global music scene, not just a French or American one. The singer, dancer, and entertainer Josephine Baker had a big part to play in the accenting of jazz, just as she had, as one scholar has argued, in the "theatricalization" of racialized bodies in the 1920s and 1930s.[36] Not only that, she "Latinized" the music of Paris, perhaps more than anyone else at the time. Born in the United States, she came to France in the 1920s riding the wave of *le noir*. But unlike most musical acts, she stayed. Using Paris as her base camp, in little time, Baker became a truly global star, bringing her quirky hodgepodge of music and dance to the rest of the world, a US import turned lucrative French export who was not easily reducible to either country. In 1929, she took her *primitif-moderne* spectacle to Latin America for the first time. With her unapologetic *negritude* and racy Charlestons, assaulting audiences with her strange brew of baubles and bananas and cardboard skyscrapers, "la Baker" scandalized priests, racists, and prudes alike. But she seduced many more: first in Argentina, Chile, and Uruguay, then Brazil, making waves and new friendships in Rio de Janeiro and São Paulo, jump-starting discussions of race, sex, and morality wherever she went.[37]

Far from being a frivolous woman, the Empress of Jazz (as she was commonly referred to by South Americans, though her touring show was hardly just a jazz spectacle) had a nose for business opportunities and stellar musicians. In Buenos Aires, she had discovered the guitarist Oscar Alemán. A unique talent who spent part of his childhood in Brazil, Alemán was tailor-made to be Josephine's go-to sideman: a quiet showman with a vast encyclopedia of popular music in his songbook, a musical polyglot equally adept at playing and singing sambas, tangos, rumbas, and even Hawaiian music. While in Brazil, Baker also made the acquaintance of the well-traveled bandleader Romeu Silva and a number of the musicians from Silva's Jazz-Band Sul Americano, including the bass saxophonist Luis Lopes da Silva, the trumpeter Mário Silva, and the drummer and percussionist Bibi Miranda, all of them future collaborators of Booker Pittman.[38]

## THE BAKER BOYS

Never satisfied limiting herself to one language or musical tradition on stage, Josephine Baker needed adaptable musicians with a wide-ranging skillset and repertoire. With this in mind, she recruited Oscar and several members of the Jazz-Band Sul Americano to form the basis of a new orchestra called the 16 Baker Boys. The fact that Oscar and Bibi Miranda were Afro Latin American solidified the interracial and international credibility of the band. What was more, they were fabulous musicians capable of playing the diverse new idioms that Josephine had learned to love during her long stay in South America. Oscar, Bibi, and the Silva brothers took up residency at the Casino de Paris with the orchestra Le Melodic Jazz and set down several sides with Baker on Columbia Records in 1930 and 1931, including the hit "La Petite Tonkinoise."[39]

After embarking on a weeks-long European tour, Baker and her boys returned to Paris, where Baker dedicated herself to theater and film for a spell. In the meantime, Oscar Alemán was fast becoming one of the most important guitarists in the city's competitive music scene. His subsequent fame may have been overshadowed by Django Reinhardt, whose Francophone profile meant he could be more easily assimilated as a musical hero, albeit with a certain ambivalence.[40] But Oscar ended up working with some of the best musicians in Europe until his hurried departure in 1939, under the threat of war and finally Nazi occupation. Of the many maestros who sought out his talents, the most prestigious, and the most insistent, was

Duke Ellington himself. Josephine Baker prized Oscar so jealously that she refused to let him go, not even for the new King of Jazz.[41]

Despite her taste for the foreign and the exotic, Josephine Baker was now fully settled in France and, outside of Oscar Alemán, had no more urgent need for the Baker Boys. The ousted Brazilians of the band looked for other engagements. Enter Romeu Silva. The great dandy of the Brazilian bandleaders of the 1920s, Silva, like other globe-trotting compatriots such as the great flautist, saxophonist, and composer Pixinguinha (Alfredo da Rocha Viana Filho) and the composer Donga (Ernesto Joaquim Maria dos Santos), had learned years before that jazz, the modern popular idiom par excellence, generally paid better than still-limited national exports such as samba and *maxixe*. Playing up his light skin and elegant demeanor for all they were worth, Silva leveraged the entrenched racist tendencies of the era, absorbing the music of Black Americans and Afro Brazilians while providing a visual contrast to Black musical contemporaries like Pixinguinha and Donga.

The latter two performers first traveled to Paris in 1922 as part of the Oito Batutas, a nimble Afro Brazilian orchestra specializing in samba, maxixe, and *choro* (like maxixe, a Brazilian idiom that predated samba) that quickly assimilated the trappings of the modern jazz band as well, playing to rapt audiences of the cabaret Scheherazade for six months. The Batutas' long and successful stint created something of a scandal in Brazil as a number of white journalists and overseas travelers were aghast that their country would be represented abroad by a "savage and rabble-rousing gang of blacks."[42] For Parisians, though, already somewhat prepared by the composer Darius Milhaud and the poet Blaise Cendrars, both of whom had traveled extensively in Brazil and spoken widely of the nation's musical richness, the Batutas would prove the christening of samba in Europe, inciting a wave of interest in the music that would not soon wane. They would also prove pivotal in bringing elements of jazz instrumentation and arrangement back to Brazil and Argentina upon their return to South America.[43] Donga, meanwhile, would return to Europe in 1926, first to Lisbon and two months later to Paris, where, with the Brazilian orchestra Carlito's Jazz-Band, he performed at the Cabaret Palermo and the Café Anglais before returning to Rio de Janeiro.[44]

Romeu Silva's orchestra came hot on the heels of Carlito's Jazz-Band. Like his American role model, Paul Whiteman, Silva was musically skilled and commercially savvy. He was so clever at self-marketing, in fact, that he frequently changed the name of his orchestra to suit his ever-changing purposes, even when the music and the musicians remained much the

Lithograph portrait of Booker Pittman by Charles Delaunay. Included in a collection of works under the title *Hot Lithography*, 1939. Division of Culture and the Arts, National Museum of American History, Smithsonian Institution.

same. When the Jazz-Band Sul Americano began to find work in venues outside the country, Silva changed its name to the Orchestre Brésilienne. When the band caught a cruise ship to the United States in 1932 to represent Brazil in the Olympic Games in Los Angeles, the Orchestre Brésilienne became the Brazilian Olympic Band.[45] There was an important motivation for the bandleader to keep moving and changing. Romeu Silva complained in Brazilian newspapers that work conditions in Paris were becoming more protectionist by the day. If foreign-born musicians were fortunate enough to obtain work permits, they were less inclined to leave the country, yet many needed to travel outside of France from time to time to take advantage of opportunities in neighboring countries—Spain, Switzerland, Portugal, England—often in lucrative contracts to play at casinos. Brazilian entertainers in Paris likely began to speak more openly about the possibility of returning to their homeland. It is not clear who among the former Baker Boys met Booker first. What is certain is that by February 1934, Booker and Oscar Alemán had played together at the Hot Club de Paris, a memorable night later remembered affectionately by the critic and artist Charles Delaunay, who was so impressed by Booker that he later included his portrait in a collection of lithographs of jazz musicians called *Hot Iconography*.[46] Alfred Pratt had previously performed with Romeu and his musicians, so it is likely that Booker was introduced to Brazilian musical society through his American friend. In a short time, Pratt had become a central figure in Booker's life. And it was not just the wives. Like Booker, Pratt already had a track record with American orchestras from Louisiana to Harlem. Born in New Orleans—or Barbados, according to one source—by 1931, Pratt had played with Willie Wilkins's band, Ray Parker's Orchestra, and King Oliver's New Orleans Creole Jazz Band.[47] But Pratt had a calm cosmopolitanism about him that seemed one step ahead of Booker's. He knew some of the same people Booker knew, but he knew them better, and he could grasp the political intricacies of Europe and the Parisian music scene with clearer eyes.

Booker also gleaned knowledge from Bibi Miranda, who had been in Paris since 1931, well before Booker's arrival. Like Pratt, Miranda also seemed to know a little more about the world than Booker did. From a working-class family in the semi-rural neighborhood of Engenho de Dentro on the northern outskirts of Rio de Janeiro, Bibi began working as a courier for Western Union while still a teen, yearning even then to travel overseas. His two main options, as he saw it, were to enlist in the Brazilian marines or to become an entertainer. He chose the latter and made his debut dancing maxixes and telling folktales at the Cassino Beira-Mar in 1925 in the coastal city of Santos, not far from São Paulo. At the casino, exposed to unseen varieties of music and spectacle, he quickly learned that he had the talents as a musician and showman to go far. From the port hub of Santos, the intrepid Bibi caught an ocean liner as soon as he could to Lisbon, later moving to Paris, where he became known as *le chansonnier brésilien*. Brazilian music had become popular in the city, he found, in part thanks to trails blazed by Pixinguinha and Donga. One night at a bistro where Romeu Silva and his orchestra were playing, Bibi Miranda found himself listening from the sidewalk, singing a samba and laying down the *batucada* rhythm on a matchbox. Silva was so impressed that he hired Bibi as an all-purpose percussionist on the spot, confident that the Engenho de Dentro native could learn what he must on the fly.[48]

Before coming to Europe, Bibi Miranda was familiar with samba, maxixe, and choro—the holy triumvirate of Brazilian popular urban genres in the 1920s—as well as the rural styles he had heard as a boy in Engenho de Dentro. Perhaps even more so than Booker, Bibi was highly adaptable to new musical idioms and new techniques. In very little time, playing alongside musicians like Alemán, Al Pratt, and Booker, absorbing the lessons of Millinder, Armstrong, and Ellington, the Brazilian percussionist fell head over heels in love with jazz and tweaked his game plan accordingly. To say that Bibi was unique would be an understatement. He played the drums in such an intuitive way, Booker wrote later, that he seemed to have been born with swing inside him; this even though he still frequently played the drums in a way that went against the international norms of jazz: without drumsticks.[49] It was a vestigial technique from a country where most percussion instruments were still played with one's bare hands and where the modern North American drumkit was still rare.

But Bibi Miranda was no staid folk musician. He was a clever, industrious man, and like Booker, he harbored a deep thirst for novelty and *aventura*. To feed his friend's curiosity about the urban landscapes of the United States, Booker told him stories about the bohemian life in Kansas City, Chicago, and Manhattan. The American inadvertently fed his own nostalgia for New York whenever he shared details about his old stomping grounds, spaces increasingly distant from his everyday life in Paris, like dreams he forgot the longer he lay awake. For as much jazz as Montmartre had to offer, Harlem had more. Perhaps Bibi sensed the risk in Booker's sharing the highlights of his homeland since he might, at any moment, begin to miss things so badly that he would catch the next ocean liner back to Manhattan. (In truth, if it had not been for Joyce, Booker likely would not have given it much thought.) At any rate, the Brazilian began to tell his own tales of origin: Rio de Janeiro, the sugar plantations, samba, the Atlantic Rain Forest, the women, and the food of his native land.[50] The strategy, if it was a strategy at all, seemed to work. Since his days as a schoolboy in Dallas, Booker had proven susceptible to well-told tales of exotic climes and easily seduced by the idea of escape, of liberation, even when he was not precisely sure from what or whom. Being surrounded by Latin Americans in Paris, especially Brazilians, and given the strange affinity he felt with people like Bibi Miranda gave some specificity to his yearning. Once again, he thought of his inevitable and immediate destiny as tied to *geography*; only now, he had a slightly better idea of where he was on the map.

## GANGA FINA

Booker Pittman did not stay that long in Europe mostly because he did not stay that long anywhere. But there were other strong incentives to leave as well. The 10% Law, though it had lost its teeth somewhat, still favored French musicians over Americans and Brazilians. Meanwhile, Romeu Silva had secured a one-year contract by telegram to play with his orchestra at the Cassino Atlântico in Rio de Janeiro. The band would have the honor of inaugurating the elegant new casino located in the same beachside neighborhood as the swanky Copacabana Palace.[51] Dom Romeu needed to fill out his band somewhat, so he invited Booker, Al Pratt, Louis Cole, and a few other Americans to join the fold. Booker was a logical choice: a crackerjack musician and a multi-instrumentalist to boot, he had a reputation for getting along with others and not causing much trouble, if you set aside his occasionally wild jags in Pigalle.

Intoxicated by Bibi Miranda's descriptions of Brazil, Booker did not hesitate long to give his reply, but he did hesitate. In Booker's mind, one year was a long time to commit to anything. He came from the churning musical worlds of Kansas City and New York, where contracts were counted in days, weeks, and only occasionally in months. However, there was a darker calculus to consider: if he brought Joyce with him, Booker would, in effect, be committing to a job *and* his wife for twelve months. His friend Al Pratt, married and now with a child, likely did not think twice about bringing his family with him for what would be a long and scenic voyage and an even longer stay in the famously beautiful Rio de Janeiro. But Pratt was a steadier character than Booker, who had begun to view the breakup of his marriage as inevitable, even desirable. He already had his reservations in Harlem about their relationship, but in Paris, it had only become clearer to him that they did not see eye to eye on a whole host of issues. The problem was the more time he spent with Joyce, the harder he feared it would be for him to extract himself from the marriage when the time came. And the time was coming.[52]

The work part of the decision to leave Paris was simpler for Booker to sell himself on. He could always leave the band; he had done it before, and he probably assumed that Brazil would be no different from the United States and France in this regard. Anyway, club work in France was getting somewhat harder to come by. Despite French-first legislation, musicians from all over the world were flooding Paris. Good musicians, too. Benny Carter himself had just begun performing in the city and would be a fixture in Europe until the beginning of the war.[53] In 1935, Nazi aggression was still a somewhat distant possibility. But spending an entire year on another, cheaper continent and not having to worry about how to pay the rent must have sounded better to Booker Pittman the more he thought about it. And it was Brazil they were talking about, after all. The mere mention of the country had become synonymous in the Texan's mind with unfathomable remoteness and exoticism.

*Chapter Three*

# ℬECOMING CARIOCA

BOOKER TALIAFERRO PITTMAN'S TICKET TO PARADISE WAS THE SS *SIQUEIRA Campos*, a modest-sized transatlantic ocean liner that changed names, flags, and purposes almost as often as Romeu Silva's orchestra did. Before being rechristened the *Siqueira Campos*, the liner went by the *Gertrud Woemann*, the *Curvello*, and the *Cantuária Guimarães*. Built by a German company in 1907, the ship was captured and claimed by Brazil during World War I, leased by the French in the 1920s, and would be used in World War II to transport Jews and other wartime refugees to the Americas.[1] The *Siqueira Campos*, in other words, sailed under the sign of war and persecution but also liberation.

From the beginning of his voyage to South America in April 1935, he associated the SS *Siqueira Campos* with something called *cachaça*, rum that was not exactly rum. He did not know it yet, but for Booker, the liquor's aroma of moist, limpid earth would forever be the scent of Brazil. No matter how many hundreds of pungent plates of *feijoada* (bean and meat stew) and *bobó de camarão* (shrimp bobó) he feasted on in the future, cachaça always lingered on his breath and in his mind. He had his first taste with the friends and bandmates who made the trip with him: Al Pratt, Louis Cole, and Bibi Miranda. Later, he absconded with a bottle and sipped at the liquor furtively while he wandered around the first-class cabin, trying to feel majestic and debonair even if all along he felt like a giddy impostor.[2] On the *Siqueira Campos*, especially as the ship churned through the choppy waters of the Bay of Biscay, almost everyone succumbed to seasickness. But not Booker. His mates were amazed but suspicious; they wanted to know what his secret was. The Texan hesitated to tell them until later that he had been pilfering all the good cachaça he could get his hands on; he was sure this was his antidote.[3]

Before reaching Rio de Janeiro, the SS *Siqueira Campos* made two stops in the Brazilian Northeast in the states of Pernambuco and Bahia. At the ocean liner's first port of call in Recife, Booker caught his first glimpse of

Brazil's modern side. At a cabaret close to the beach, Romeu Silva and company listened to a large ensemble playing harmonically sophisticated pieces that resembled tunes Bibi Miranda had whistled to him in Paris. To the American ear, the cabaret orchestra must have sounded like jazz with an accent—at times marked, other times subtle. Like the cachaça, the music flowed so freely and easily that Booker and his bandmates could be forgiven for putting Paris out of their minds so soon. In fact, Romeu's boys were so astonished by the quality and feeling of swing displayed by one musician they encountered—a trumpeter and pianist named Fats Elpídio—that Romeo Silva invited him to join the orchestra in the final leg of their trip to Rio de Janeiro.[4]

Though Pernambuco was captivating, Booker formed his first deep impression of the country strolling along the docks of Salvador's Cidade Baixa neighborhood at the ship's second stop in Bahia.[5] With its fishing boats and seafood markets, Salvador felt rawer than Recife, and the taste of the sea in the air was even stronger than in the middle of the ocean. The smoke-filled corner bars served cheap beer, cachaça, and big plates of a spicy seafood dish called *moceca*. Outside on the sidewalks, dressed in resplendent white, Bahian women peddled a strangely pungent substance called *acarajé*. People on the street remarked that Booker looked like one of them.[6] It was here, perhaps, that he first perceived Brazil as a kind of echo chamber playing back to him his own voice and his own identity in altered form, a theme repeated in his memoirs and in later interviews. Maybe it started with the music he heard on street corners, rhythms hammered out on gourds and small drums, with melodies sung and sometimes strummed with seemingly endless variations. The sound would have vaguely reminded Booker of the blues, not the blues of Bessie Smith records but rather the plaintive strains he had heard by the railroad tracks in Deep Ellum: improvisation disguised as repetition; freedom dressed up as constraint, as incantation.

On May 3, 1935, the daily newspaper *O Jornal do Comércio* announced that the Orquesta Sul-Americana Brasileira, led by Romeu Silva, "the aristocratic *maestro* who for the last ten years has been spreading the gospel of our music in the most noteworthy fashion to the best cities of the Old World," would be dropping anchor in Rio de Janeiro the next day. The article mentioned a few of the Brazilian musicians on board, including Fernando de Albuquerque, Luis da Silva Lopes, Mário Silva, and Bibi Miranda. The American musicians slipped into the country virtually unannounced and largely unnoticed.[7] As the ship approached the harbor, Booker Pittman would have found the capital city itself rather small, dwarfed by the green fairy tale mountains and the enormous Guanabara Bay that seemed designed for either a larger metropolis or none at all. Once the passengers exited the ship and spilled into the colonial center's maze of small streets and big commotion, some surely could not resist passing judgment: all these days at sea for *this*? It was true that Rio de Janeiro was no Manhattan, with its shiny stand of soaring skyscrapers, or Paris, with its wide stately avenues and *Tour Eiffel*. But Booker did not want another New York or Paris. He wanted a *new* experience in every sense of the word.

Booker and Joyce, along with Al Pratt and his family, were initially lodged in one of the old, dignified-looking hotels on the Avenida Rio Branco, a wide thoroughfare that cut through the commercial heart of a city in transition, precariously suspended between the colonial and the modern. The hotel was more elegant than anywhere they had stayed since Monte Carlo. But Booker was not content just lingering in the room or the lobby. Once on the street, what first caught his attention were the blindingly white, shiny suits of the men seated in cafés, their tables full of beer—*chope*, they called it—a diaphanous pilsner served in thick frozen mugs that well-dressed waiters filled over and over again, whether Booker asked for it or not.[8] In one direction, in Cinelândia Square, a parade of beggars and snappily clad moviegoers shared the same ceramic sidewalk. In another, the modern veneer of Avenida Rio Branco yielded to the tumult of Rua Uruguaiana and the teeming side streets of old Rio. With its pamphleteers and donkeys, soothsayers and macaw vendors, the area, though a short walk from the hotel, would have left the American with the distinct and marvelous impression that he had stepped back in time.[9] Booker was already partially inured to novelties, having encountered his share in Paris and elsewhere in Europe. But what he saw in Rio de Janeiro was on a different scale. Bibi Miranda's descriptions had not quite prepared him for the sheer exuberance of the Brazilian vegetation. "Rio was too much of a natural paradise, too beautiful to believe," he marveled.[10] But it was not just that. It was also the disarming sociability of the *cariocas* (residents of Rio de Janeiro) and the city's bracing variety and vitality, its heady combination of grit and grandeur, the handsome brown faces, the salty street slang that one heard everywhere. Booker felt both at home and strangely outside of himself.[11] Wandering without clear direction in this new world, he unsteadily but ecstatically took in his new surroundings, unsure of how to process the bewitching mishmash of colors, smells, and sounds. "I thought I was as close to heaven as anyone could get," he would later write.[12]

## RIO NOCTURNE

Al Pratt and the other Americans were eager to see Copacabana, the suburban beach neighborhood that had recently become the center of the city's casinos and upscale nightlife and where Romeu Silva and his orchestra were slated to spend the next year of their lives. But Booker first wanted to tour what he had been told was the city's Harlem. He and, presumably, Joyce ambled their way to Lapa, on the southern fringes of the colonial downtown, where they met up with Bibi and a few other Brazilians. Lapa in the 1930s was ground zero for Rio's bohemian excess: a vortex of prostitution, booze, and samba that drew from all walks of carioca life, from musicians, pimps, and hustlers scraping together a living to rich playboys looking for a respite from the stifling front of bourgeois respectability. In Lapa, Booker would have found all the spectacular energy and variety of Black Manhattan except that the Brazilian neighborhood was smaller, the cabarets and common bars poorer and seedier, and the music mostly alien in terms of rhythm, instrumentation, and dance accompaniment. As one of Brazil's chroniclers of the neighborhood, Luís Martins, would later put it, the *cabarés* of Lapa were vibrant and melodious but also "humble, run-down, [and] quite tacky."[13]

Because the musicians whom Booker saw and heard in Lapa looked and sounded so unlike anything he had experienced before, he figured they had different stories to tell, other messages to share with the world, which was why he was astonished when he turned a corner and ran smack into an eerily familiar scene. In one of the neighborhood's small dives, three musicians were playing the blues together with such honest, down-home simplicity that something told Booker they had to be his countrymen, fellow exiles from the American South. This was indeed the case with two of the musicians, the banjo player David Washington, who hailed from Alabama, and the trumpeter Jack Braggs, originally from Georgia. The third member of the trio, Lovett Price, was a drummer and tap dancer from Philadelphia. Together, they had made their own long journey to Brazil as part of the traveling musical called *Bimbo*, which Booker may well have read about or even seen in Kansas City years before. When the show had ended a few weeks prior, the three musicians decided to stay on in Rio, seduced by the sweetly chaotic rhythm of the city and tempted by the prospects of making easy money in a less competitive environment for talented jazz novices. The three still could not play their instruments very well, Booker observed. But they made up for their technical flaws by dancing and singing with real exuberance and soul, selling their songs any way

Copacabana Palace Hotel, anonymous, 1935. Public domain/fair use. Wikipedia Commons.

they could.[14] It was at the same time a raw spectacle and a charming one, and it seemed to make Booker mildly homesick, giving him a first glimpse of something he would go on to witness in countless venues across South America over the next few decades: a multinational circuit of drunk tourists, low-grade fugitives, cultural castaways, and lost and hungry musicians feeling their way blindly through the outskirts of the modern world. This South Atlantic society of the musical anonymous tried to make names for themselves by re-creating raw, immaculate sounds imported from another time and place, reconfigured for the imperfect present of a faraway land.

## DAWN IN THE TROPICS

Once he began his work at the Cassino Atlântico, Booker moved from his downtown hotel to a *pensão* in Copacabana on Rua Siqueira Campos. It is unclear whether or not he made the short trip alone.[15] In his memoirs, his marriage to Joyce is mentioned only in passing. Booker simply writes that he was too young to be tied down in a serious relationship.[16] Ofélia Pittman, in her own memoirs, does not mention Joyce, and Booker spoke little about his pre-Ofélia romantic life to his stepdaughter Eliana. The cabaret dancer probably lingered in Brazil before returning to the United States, remaining with Booker for a few weeks or even months. What is certain is that sometime after their arrival in Brazil, Joyce completely disappeared from the picture. What is also certain is that something had fundamentally shifted inside Booker.

It hit him as he walked back to his room at dawn after one of his first nights at the *cassino*. Pleasantly buzzed on excitement and applause, beer, and cachaça, he jogged across the Avenida Atlântica to the beach promenade and took in the multicolor spectacle of the aurora, the sweetness of the breeze, and the soft rhythm of the waves. "Then," he later wrote, "I began to notice something was happening to me, but I didn't know just what it was."[17] It was a conventional scene of rapture: Copacabana at the break of day. Booker would have seen it in magazines many times before he witnessed it in person. But there was something almost painful about the moment nonetheless, a distillation of all that he had felt since his arrival in the city. He was making 100,000 *réis* per day to play in a coolly elegant and stylish hotel where he was the secret star of the show. Romeu Silva would not let him play that role openly; he paid the American the salary of someone who could shine but only so much and for so long. For Booker to walk the fine line each night between virtuoso and orchestra grunt, he needed this moment of seaside rapture as a bonus.[18] To take this early morning stroll, to witness this dawn, this daily rebirth, the windswept oracle of an empty beach, was everything to him. The beach and the jungle were integral parts of the Brazilian city, ones that Paris and New York could never touch. In its glorious, dirty, chaotic, contradictory way, Rio de Janeiro was *the place*, a realization of all the vaguely imagined adventures that had dazzled Booker's mind since childhood. He was so moved by the photogenic beauty of the beach and the impossibly vertical mountains that, for the first time in years, he began to pray out loud, pray and weep, with such intensity that he reminded himself of a maudlin, heroic pastor: a Texas preacher.[19] "Yes sir, if you've never felt the spirit," he wrote in his memoirs, "then you should try and see Rio."[20]

## JAZZ CARIOCA

Housed in a brand-new art deco building on the far end of Copacabana, the Cassino Atlântico was indeed "the marvel of *Posto 6*," as the newspaper ads at the time put it. The idea was to compete with the city's two recently established, highly lucrative casinos, Copacabana Palace and Cassino da Urca. Like its rivals, the Atlântico was aimed at a clientele of local elites mixing freely with tourists from all corners of the world. The casino built its international profile on the quality and diversity of popular music and performance, hiring musicians and acts from all over the globe who delivered the goods in an exotic array of languages and accents. Romeu Silva's orchestra fit in swimmingly. His musicians played to entertain, and for Atlântico's customers, that meant dancing to foxtrots, sambas, rumbas, beguines, tangos, and maxixes. After two months of banging out American standards—the obligatory sweet renditions of Ellington, Gershwin, and Cole Porter, over and over—he could also swing to the melodies of Noel Rosa, Pixinguinha, Moisés Simons, Carlos Gardel, and Alfredo Le Pera. Pretty soon, he could, in good conscience, call himself a South American musician and not just a Southern one.

Booker took a special liking to Pixinguinha. Already a seasoned veteran and local legend by this time, the peerless flautist and composer had a smooth regality about him that reminded Booker of Duke Ellington. After his stint in Paris in the early 1920s, Pixinguinha had taught himself how to play the saxophone as well, to the horror of puritanical Brazilian music critics and the amazement of carioca musicians, several of whom took up the instrument themselves. Pixinguinha avoided pigeonholing himself as either a samba or a jazz musician, and he was not the only Brazilian musician who dabbled in jazz.[21] In the wake of the Batutas' sustained success in Paris, the group splintered into other combos. By 1923, other ensembles emerged who openly identified themselves as jazz bands, beginning with the Oito Cotubas, led by the former Batuta, Donga. Unlike the Pixinguinha-led Batutas, the Cotubas were openly jazz-oriented, playing predominantly foxtrots, while the Batutas still featured a healthy number of choros, sambas, and maxixes.[22]

The jazz band craze reached such a fervor in Rio de Janeiro in the mid-1920s that even string ensembles—ones bearing little resemblance to the hot orchestras in Chicago, Harlem, and Paris and that could be heard in fashionable cafés and *confeitarias* in the nation's capital—were calling themselves jazz bands.[23] Even so, most of the music was not jazz in name only. The extended presence of foreign combos lent knowledge and authenticity to local scenes and was also, as one music scholar has noted, "a testament to the fluid nature of musical genres" in the 1920s.[24] The Black Liverpool-born drummer Gordon Stretton, for instance, led a combo touring Brazil and Argentina in 1923 that introduced the jazz drums, banjo, and the sleek moves of the shimmy to southern climes, all while backing European vedettes and cabarets.[25] Sam Wooding passed through Rio briefly on his way back from Argentina in 1927 with a hot orchestra that included Freddy Johnson on piano, providing what one Brazilian writer later described as the "aural shock of modernity" to carioca audiences.[26] And then there was Josephine Baker, whose barnstorming tour of the southern cone of South America culminated in Brazil in the latter part of 1929. Despite the hysterical press corps' focus on her body and scant attire, the Jazz Empress also brought with her a crack team of musicians and introduced the Charleston to Brazilians much as Stretton had popularized the shimmy. Baker epitomized the frenzied enchantment of the modern, wrote one journalist of the time, even if she was the "noisiest sister" of the Jazz Age.[27]

By the early 1930s, a new generation of Brazilian musicians had cut their teeth in jazz bands such as Romeu Silva's and Carlito's, musicians like Bibi Miranda but also Ary Barroso, Benedito Lacerda, and the pianist, composer, and arranger Radamés Gnattali. Originally from the southern Brazilian state of Rio Grande do Sul, Gnattali formed his Ideal Jazz Band there before moving to Rio de Janeiro at the beginning of the decade, founding the Trío Carioca with Luiz Americano on clarinet and Luciano Perrone on drums.[28] By this time, though, it had become, at best, awkward and, at worst, risky for most Brazilian musicians to identify themselves primarily as jazzistas. Getúlio Vargas seized power, and his cultural policy championed the medium of radio and favored musical nationalism, which facilitated the consecration of samba as the de facto soundtrack of the nation. This was not to say that Vargas's Estado Novo orchestrated the samba's institutionalization in heavy-handed ways, at least most of the time. Indeed, the consecration of samba likely would have happened with or without Vargas thanks to radio's reign and the eager participation of popular musicians in the urban cultural sphere.[29] However, Vargas's ascent to the presidency and his belief in the essential vitality of Brazilian cultural forms and mass media certainly did contribute toward the institutionalization of carnival and samba schools, a move that gradually, if only partially, squeezed jazz from setlists and radio programs.[30]

Booker Pittman fit in well in Rio's quickly evolving jazz scene, thirsty for "authentic" Black Americans who knew how to play. But since he would not only be playing jazz numbers, Booker knew that he needed a bit of tutoring. Initially, he hung out a great deal with his friends Pratt, Cole, and Bibi. But in his free hours, Booker took to jamming with the orchestra of Fon-Fon (Otaviano Romero Monteiro). Until his premature death in 1951, Fon-Fon was one of the essential musicians and bandleaders of the Brazilian swing scene.[31] From the moment he heard him solo, Fon-Fon knew Booker was a rarity: a true-blue jazz virtuoso living in Brazil, of all places. Whenever possible, the Brazilian monopolized Booker in the hopes that his Harlem-honed chops and up-to-date Parisian stylings would rub off on him and his orchestra. In exchange, Fon-Fon taught the American the rudiments of Brazilian popular music.[32]

And so it was that Booker Pittman, who just a year earlier haunted the dives and alleys of Montmartre whistling "J'ai Deux Amours," now found himself working out the lithe melodies of fashionable sambas that he heard everywhere at once: in nightclubs, on radios and record players, at corner bars, on the lips of maids in streetcars. The tunes lodged themselves into his mind and refused to leave. It is not hard to imagine Booker tapping out the rhythms as he walked the streets and sat at bus stops and as he lay in bed at night, saxophone still in hand. The sounds were so hypnotic and so ubiquitous that he likely did not quite know what to do with them. He turned to Fon-Fon, a patient teacher who helped Booker transcribe the melodies he heard into lines on the saxophone, infusing the American's somewhat limited repertoire with Brazilian songcraft and rhythm: serenatas and carnival marches but also sambas, naturally, songs like "Eva querida," "Arrependimento quando chega," "É bom parar," and "Cidade maravilhosa."[33] Booker did not only devote the melodies to memory but the lyrics as well. "Cidade maravilhosa" was one of his favorites, a siren song that became more and more intoxicating as his Portuguese improved:

> Cidade maravilhosa
> Cheia de encantos mil
> Cidade maravilhosa
> Coração do meu Brasil
> Oh marvelous city
> Full of a thousand delights
> Marvelous city
> Heart of my Brazil

## SIMPLY BUCA

Booker took to Rio de Janeiro in other ways as well. Weeks into his stay, he left his *pensão* and found a place to rent on Rua Aires de Saldanha, one block from the beach in Posto 5.[34] It was an easy walk from the Cassino Atlântico and a scenic one; the air and light of the *orla* never ceased to dazzle him, day or night. But Booker no doubt liked to walk the inner streets of the neighborhood as well, with their shaded sidewalks and intense commercial life: fruit markets, corner drugstores, tailors, shoeshine businesses that reminded him of his first job in Dallas. And then there were the tiny, ubiquitous *botecos*—popular bars—where the barmen quickly learned his name, though they pronounced it differently: "Bookah" instead of Booker. Buca. *Tudo bem, Buca? E aí, seu Buca?*

There was a slight playful irony in these voices, but there was warmth and acceptance, too. The other advantage of the commercial streets and boulevards of Copa—Avenida Nossa Senhora de Copacabana, Rua Sá Ferreira, Rua Sousa Lima—was their easy access to beer and booze. In his memoirs, there are hints that Booker was, at this time, succumbing more and more to the siren song of alcohol, a tendency that would only intensify with the years.[35] But it was not just free-flowing chope and cachaça that tempted him. In fact, everything lay within reach: restaurants, shops, peerless beaches, dense tropical forests. Despite its size and stature in Brazil and abroad, Rio de Janeiro still felt small in the 1930s and, after the frontal cosmopolitan assault of New York and Paris, somewhat provincial as well. The consolation was that Booker very quickly met many of the top musicians in the city. Sometimes, work or curiosity took him back to downtown Rio, and when they did, he frequented Café Nice on Avenida Rio Branco. The place fascinated him, not just because of its Parisian ambience but also because he found he could rub shoulders with *sambistas* like Noel Rosa and Wilson Batista. At first, he did not know who these musicians and composers were any more than they knew who he was. But soon enough, he was hobnobbing with the likes of Rosa, Wilson, and Benedito Lacerda, who introduced him to other musicians, journalists, politicians, even soccer players—anyone whom they happened to run into at the Nice.[36]

Samba may have been king, especially in its native Rio de Janeiro, but casinos were another story. Casinos were upscale international spaces where foreign tourists and well-heeled Brazilians expected a variety of musical styles to dine and dance to. Despite the emergence of new talent and swing combos in the mid-1930s, Romeu Silva's orchestra was still more synonymous with jazz than other Brazilian ensembles. Of the three

Newspaper advertisement of Rádio Ipanema and the Cassino Atlântico, featuring Romeo Silva's orchestra. Rio de Janeiro, 1935.

principal casinos of Rio de Janeiro, the Atlântico was the only one linked to a radio station that transmitted from the same building, Rádio Ipanema.[37] As a result, Romeu Silva e sua Orquestra Sul-Americana, including the occasional solos of Booker Pittman on sax and clarinet, could frequently be heard on Rio's airwaves in 1935 and 1936. But the performances of the orchestra and Booker were not limited to the casino or Rádio Ipanema. The local newspapers of the period painted a picture of the orchestra's diverse activities, which usually revolved around the city's elite. In May 1935, the orchestra played at the Teatro Recreio along with the celebrated singer Francisco Alves and other local stars.[38] In June, Silva's band performed at a charitable event at the Clube dos Marimbás, with an entrance fee of 13,000 réis per person.[39] One of the sponsors, Jorge Guinle, a young scion of the wealthy Brazilian family that built Copacabana Palace, was an astute cultural critic and devout jazz enthusiast who befriended Booker almost as soon as he saw him play. Still a teen during the musician's first stay in Brazil, Guinle's impeccable taste, bon vivant spirit, and playboy charm—he would reputedly go on to have affairs with scores of Hollywood stars over the next few decades—would have appealed to Booker's lust for life. Moreover, Guinle's economic and political autonomy and unorthodox sensibility lent him "relative immunity to the constraints that befell other Brazilian critics" of the time, according to one scholar.[40] For Guinle, as for Fon-Fon, Booker was a living embodiment of jazz aristocracy who had, incredibly, chosen to live in Brazil, of all places. They would remain lifelong friends.

Meanwhile, Romeu Silva and Company were in high demand. In August, the band participated in a fashion show at the Cassino Atlântico as part of a benefit for impoverished newspaper delivery boys, an event sponsored by the First Lady of the Brazilian government, Darci Vargas. The party was supposed to showcase "an entire garden of beautiful girls" dressed in the fabulous inventions of Etienne Drian, a Parisian fashion designer, who was to make a special trip to Rio for the occasion. The famous Drian, however, never showed up.[41] That same month, the orchestra played at a private party alongside Francisco Alves, the composer Noel Rosa, and a young samba singer named Carmen Miranda.[42] Later in the year, Romeu's band dazzled at a dinner for wealthy debutantes at the Copacabana Palace. But the musicians were more background sound than the main event. The party's culminating musical moment was reserved for the "senhorinha" Alzira Camargo who, accompanied by two young men, sang "waltzes and ballads from a small boat floating in the swimming pool."[43]

## AN EXIT PLAN

The new year began with more glamour and also more shows. In January 1936, the Orquestra Sul-Americana Romeu Silva furnished the soundtrack for a dance-and-ice-cream social at the Fluminense Football Club. The following month, the band was hired to participate in a prestigious Carnival Ball at the Cassino Atlântico. The ad for the party promised elegance, sophistication, and extravagant decorations, "surpassing the grand spectacles in American films." The creator of the Carnaval extravaganza was, in fact, a Brazilian film director named Luiz de Barros. Either during or after the costume ball, Barros invited the orchestras of Silva, Gaó, and Martí—all of them under contract with the Atlântico at the time—to take part in a film that he planned to shoot at Cinédia studios.[44] Called *O jovem tataravô* ("The Young Great-Great-Grandfather"), the picture turned out

Video captures from *O jovem tataravô* (dir. Luiz de Barros, 1936). Romeu Silva, top; Bibi Miranda, middle; Louis Cole, bottom; the orchestra's saxophone section sans Booker Pittman. Public domain/fair use.

to be a unique yet ultimately forgettable science fiction comedy about a man from the nineteenth century who awakens in the 1930s, where he must contend with modern "dangers" such as jazz.

In a story dated May 1, 1936, the Rio-based film magazine *Cinearte* reported that Romeu Silva's orchestra had been increased to fifty musicians.[45] It is quite possible that Booker Pittman took part in these early rehearsals. In the version of the film that survives, though, a much smaller ensemble appears on screen, one in which Louis Cole and Bibi Miranda made their movie debuts. In the scene in question, Romeu Silva introduces "Night Falls," a foxtrot dominated by trombones and trumpets and a long solo by Bibi. Louis Cole does his best to sing the song in the suave style of Bing Crosby, then tap dances somewhat less gracefully to end the number. The scene captures the precariously charming style of early 1930 Brazilian film musicals. In the closeups and midrange shots, the musicians and even Romeu himself project a certain misplaced modesty—as if camera-shy, half-embarrassed by the medium itself. The director, meanwhile, brings an overly theatrical approach to the silver screen, still unaccustomed to the technical demands and aesthetic strengths of the talkies. Like the characters in the film, the performers and the director appear stuck in a state of limbo between the past and the present.

Booker is absent from the film's musical cast, and the explanation is simple on the surface: he had left for Buenos Aires, not to return to Brazil for a decade. Yet it is puzzling why he would bypass such a chance to appear in the pictures, which would also have allowed him to remain in Brazil for longer. In a matter of twelve months, he had fallen hard for the country, likely attained a serviceable knowledge of Portuguese, and forged an ever-widening network of musicians, promoters, fans, and friends. Booker had no legal obligation to remain in Rio; his contract with Romeu Silva and the Cassino Atlântico expired in May, not long before filming was to start on *O jovem tataravô*. But there were no doubt other factors at play: racism, for example, and not just the routine and deplorable treatment from certain customers and employees of the casino. Booker says little about Romeu Silva in his memoirs, and when he does, he remarks only that he was an "exceptional gentleman."[46] But other Black performers clearly had issues with the white bandleader. According to film and theater actor Grande Otelo, one of the few Black Brazilians who managed to penetrate the wall of segregation in the mid-century Brazilian entertainment industry, Silva swindled him out of 300,000 réis that he owed him.[47]

In any case, Booker could have left the orchestra without leaving Brazil. It is more likely, therefore, that artistic and existential restlessness was a stronger motivation. Doing contract work at a first-class casino certainly paid the bills, but as work went, the socialite circuit was as mercenary as it was elegant. The brand of music demanded by the well-heeled audiences of the Atlântico, not to mention those of society parties and benefits, was exactly what Booker least liked about being a professional musician: yielding to the regime of a large commercial orchestra where everything was prearranged, sweetened, and endlessly repeated. The Brazilian highlife of the 1930s, in other words, was too often a fragrant and lucrative exercise in creative inertia. A part of Booker no doubt began to long for the Parisian scene, with its nightly jam sessions and its taste for hot quartets and quintets. There was one fundamental problem. Besides the fact that a return voyage to Europe would be long, costly, and possibly embarrassing, Booker simply did not *return* to places. Going back meant going backward, and staying put was just another way of going back, of condemning himself to recycle the same shows for the same audiences, to blow the same melodies in the same ways, over and over again. If he dared break from the program, Romeu Silva was there to set him straight; all it took was one look askance, a cutting word in the dressing room. The problem was that Booker needed constant variation or else he felt he was selling himself short by failing to wring all the novelty he could out of life. He needed to feel like he was not just moving but moving *forward*, even if it meant running the risk of getting himself good and lost.

The chance for a clean break from his routine came in the form of another bandleader, the Afro Cuban maestro Isidro Benítez. Central to the early history of jazz and Caribbean music in South America, Benítez is nonetheless a mostly forgotten figure and something of an enigma. According to one Cuban source, Benítez left for Chile in 1926 with his orchestra Los Negros Cubanos (The Black Cubans) to inaugurate a recreation center in Santiago. He and at least some members of the orchestra decided to remain in Chile, in part to avoid the racist cultural milieu of Havana. By the early 1930s, Benítez seems to have temporarily resettled from Santiago to Argentina before moving back to Santiago later in the decade.[48] He would remain there for the rest of his life, frequently playing in venues like the Casino de Viña del Mar, the studio auditorium of Rádio Carrera, and the Santiago nightclub La Quintrala.[49] Benítez arrived in Rio de Janeiro from Buenos Aires in April 1935, one month before Booker. With his band now named the Orquestra de Pretos Cubanos (Orchestra of Black Cubans), the maestro worked at the Cassino da Urca, sharing the stage with Chinese acrobats, French chanteuses, American tap dancers, Argentine tango orchestras, and a Viennese vocal ensemble calling itself, of all things, As Baianas da Urca (The Bahian women of Urca).[50] This was in addition to dependable Brazilian acts like the Bando da Lua, who would strike gold a few years later by backing an ascendant Carmen Miranda.[51]

At the time, there was fierce competition between the top casinos of South America. Still, among the musicians themselves, a culture of comradery and cross-pollination generally prevailed. Even if they worked for rival orchestras, Rio de Janeiro's diverse cast of international characters often played together at parties, weddings, and special events, drinking and gossiping after hours in the same *boates* (nightclubs) and botecos. When Booker first met Isidro, he was so impressed by the Cuban's musicality and panache that he likely realized this was his chance to break with Romeu Silva and travel to other parts of South America.[52] It was just a matter of riding out the one-year contract. Bibi Miranda and Al Pratt, meanwhile, had had more history with Romeu than Booker and apparently felt loyalty toward him beyond the Cassino Atlântico. When the bandleader approached them with a chance to make a film, they both jumped at it and stayed with Romeu for some time afterward.

Romeu Silva and Booker Pittman were clearly headed in different directions. All the recent time spent in his native country had managed to Brazilianize Romeu's songbook. Nativist politics had a part to play in his shift. By the time the bandleader finally left again for France in early 1937, his orchestra was playing more sambas and *marchinhas* than foxtrots.[53] Booker, on the other hand, despite his love of Brazilian music, was increasingly inclined to play in smaller, hotter, jazz-only (or at least jazz-mostly) orchestras. Isidro Benítez promised him just that. It pained Booker to split with his friends Bibi Miranda and Al Pratt, but they were all still young and he knew he would run into them again sooner or later. In their place, several Cuban and Brazilian musicians embarked southward with Booker and Benítez on the SS *Highland Monarch* on May 14, 1936, along with three familiar faces: the much-improved David Washington, Jack Braggs, and Lovett Price.[54]

*Chapter Four*

# SOUTHERN STAR

Pobre gringo solo y triste
que a la América viniste
con tu carga de ilusión.
—JUAN ANDRÉS CARUSO AND ALBERTO VACCAREZZA, "POBRE GRINGO" (1928)

ONE OF THE FEW ITEMS THAT BOOKER PITTMAN BROUGHT WITH HIM ON his maiden voyage down the Atlantic coast of South America was a dark camel hair coat that he wore almost nonstop until the first hot spells of November. The coat was a rare item in Rio de la Plata, an exotic curiosity from a distant land, which seemed fitting: Booker arrived as a dark-skinned foreigner speaking a strange hybrid of English, Portuguese, and French. In his Parisian attire, he resembled an elegant black bear as he shivered his way down the Avenida 9 de Julio in Buenos Aires. Few people stopped, but many stared.[1] If the American were not especially put off by the quiet scrutiny of the *Rioplatenses* (inhabitants of the River Plate region), it was only because he was a shy brand of extrovert. Being conspicuous was a simple way to remedy the common symptoms of solitude and timidity—better to leave invisibility to a spy. In a place like Argentina in the 1930s, it behooved errant jazz musicians like Booker Pittman to draw attention to themselves one way or another. It was good for business.

What Booker discovered during his first meanders in Buenos Aires was a paradisiacal forest of popular culture: street artists, *bandoneón* players, classically trained violinists, clowns, jugglers and magicians, small theatrical troupes. And that was only on the city's sidewalks, small plazas, and parks. The central neighborhoods were packed with *confiterías*, corner bars, restaurants, nightclubs, dance halls, cabarets, cinemas, and larger theaters and auditoriums, and everywhere jazz was almost as common as tango. The busy streets and avenues of the Bajo Porteño—Corrientes, Lavalle, Suipacha, Esmeralda, Maipu, and especially Calle Florida—echoed eerily

A view of Calle Florida from Bartolomé Mitre in the center of the Bajo Porteño. Horacio Coppola, "Florida y Bartolomé Mitre," Buenos Aires, 1936. Municipalidad de la Ciudad de Buenos Aires. Public domain via Wikipedia Commons.

with the Great American Songbook of Duke Ellington, Cole Porter, and George Gershwin. Much more than Copacabana, more than even Harlem or Montmartre, Buenos Aires struck Booker immediately as his ideal of authentic bohemian life, an exuberant expression of culture in motion rooted in local traditions, yet roiling day and night with modern disquiet, with constant flirtations with faraway fashions. A culture with swing.[2]

## SYNCOPATION AND RHYTHM

Isidro Benítez y sus Black Stars' first gig in Buenos Aires was at the Confitería Esmeralda. For their debut, the line out the door was so long it stopped traffic on the corner of Calle Esmeralda and Avenida Corrientes. Despite only having rehearsed together one time, the orchestra showed remarkable chemistry from the get-go. It helped that Benítez was a seasoned, self-assured bandleader with an up-to-date playbook of first-rate composers. He also knew that River Plate audiences had different expectations from those elsewhere in South America. Booker, on the other hand, was not at all prepared for the effusive response that the band received nor did he quite expect to be the focus of their applause.[3] If, during his year in Rio de Janeiro, Booker had managed to elevate himself to being one of the featured soloists in Romeu Silva's orchestra, he had not been a headliner; his name had not appeared on the marquee or in newspaper ads.

Buenos Aires promised to be different. Here, although Booker did not arrive as the star of the show, before long, he would soon be one of the city's spotlight performers. In general, porteños (residents of Buenos Aires) proved more discerning than jazz audiences elsewhere in South America. When they heard a first-tier American musician like Booker Pittman blow his horn, they demanded that he take solo after solo. Booker was delighted. Here, he soon found, one did not just play to Rio-style dance crowds, the smartly dressed couples of the casinos who paid good money for a well-paced selection of foxtrots, sambas, rumbas, and boleros. In Buenos Aires, there were also specialized live-music venues where some customers moved silently in their seats and others sat seriously, sipping their coffee or whisky slowly so they would not miss a beat. Jazz enthusiasm was not limited to clubs and cafés. At the newsstands, besides the publications focused on popular music like *Sintonía* and *Radiolandia*, Booker also found a little magazine dedicated entirely to jazz, *Síncopa y Ritmo*—the first of its kind in Latin America and one of the first in the world.[4] And not just that: Booker soon discovered that there were more local record labels and more access to jazz records in Buenos Aires than in any other city in South America. If jazz was still carving out a niche on the airwaves of São Paulo and Rio de Janeiro, in the Argentine capital, American music had already taken radio by storm, sometimes at the expense of local styles, provoking ardent defenses of tango in the same newspapers that announced swing dances and jazz shows at places like the Confitería Esmeralda.[5]

Confiterías were an unusual staple of Rioplatense musical performance in the 1930s. Primarily seen as places to eat sweets, snacks, and cheap meals, they appealed to a wide-ranging clientele in part because they lacked the exclusionary ethos and stigma of many late-night venues, generally opening earlier and charging less than the competition.[6] Besides La Esmeralda, there was the La Richmond, with two locations, one on Calle Florida and another on Suipacha; and La Adlon, also on Florida. The confiterías were, however, often just the first stop of the night for jazz fans and musicians like Booker Pittman. Bars and nightclubs in Bajo Porteño included the Odeon Bar, La Chaumière, and the Charleston Club. A number of movie theaters, such as the Cine Teatro Baby and Cine Teatro París, also featured jazz bands on occasion, as did public spaces like the Parque Japonés and luxury venues like Le Cigale and the Grill Room at the Alvear Palace Hotel.[7] Finally, as in Rio de Janeiro but more so in Buenos Aires, there were radio stations that hosted live shows of the city's big bands: Radio Belgrano, Radio El Mundo, Radio Excelsior, Radio Splendid, and Radio Municipal, among others.

In this vibrant scene poised between the diurnal and the nocturnal, the vernacular and the modern, the sheer volume of newspapers, magazines, street performances, radio programs, records, and film musicals exalted jazz as a *local* expression and not just an exotic one. There were the sweet bands like the Santa Paulo Serenaders, led by Guy Montana; hotter ensembles like the Dixie Pals, with their crackerjack pianist Adolfo Ortiz; and lady crooners like Lois Blue (Lucía Bolognini Míguez) and Blackie (the Jewish Argentine Paloma Efron). Even so, jazz demand exceeded supply. To staff all the orchestras and slake the thirst of aspirants and aficionados alike, an educational infrastructure emerged. First, the best local instrumentalists, such as the Turkish-born guitarist Ahmed "Mike" Ratip and the saxophonist and clarinetist Ismael "Pibe" Paz, began to offer private lessons in their apartments. Then, toward the end of the decade, the American expatriate Gene Poole founded the Academia Americana. Soon realizing that the *porteño* public demanded more than just English classes, Poole opened a jazz school where some of the city's top musicians taught classes to new generations of Buenos Aires jazzistas. Poole even published an *Encyclopedia of Swing* in which he defined not just the basic concepts and instruments of big band jazz but also information about illicit drugs associated with the jazz scene and the undesirable (or "icky") markers of inauthentic playing and players, from corny sound effects to street slang deemed uncool.[8]

## THE SPECIAL EXPATS

Icky affectations aside, for devoted fans and music critics in mid-1930s Argentina, the only truly authentic jazz player was an American jazz player. This desire for authenticity was reflected in the ersatz nomenclature of Rioplatense performers. Local magazines and newspapers were full of suspicious-sounding artistic monikers: Aileen Lark, Buddy Day, Ken Hamilton, Guy Montana, and Bob Hylton—Argentines and Uruguayans all. To further muddy the waters, a brood of actual American musicians had settled in the city by the middle of the decade. Besides relatively minor figures like Russ Goudey and George Hines, two of the most prominent local bandleaders were Harold Mickey and Don Dean.

A native of North Carolina, Mickey arrived in Argentina in 1933 and stayed for the rest of his life, though he made frequent trips back to the United States in subsequent years. In the 1930s and 1940s, his Orquesta Pan-Americana emerged as a mainstay of the River Plate swing scene, a competent and professional ensemble with a reserved, almost somber sound. Known more for its consistency and stability than its innovation, Mickey's band specialized in melodic jazz in the style of Paul Whiteman or Ray Noble, found considerable success on Radio Excelsior and Radio Splendid (among other stations), and recorded several sides for the Argentine outposts of Victor and Odeon. It helped that Mickey maintained connections with the United States and Europe; he was hired not just by prestigious musical venues such as the Alvear but also by well-monied entities as diverse as the Jockey Club de Buenos Aires, the Club Atlético Belgrano, Pan American World Airways, and several foreign embassies.[9] Additionally, Mickey was a key sonic importer on more than one occasion. By the 1950s, sensing the waning interest in big band swing, he first dabbled in boogie-woogie and commercial rumba, then brought one of the first incarnations of rock and roll to Argentina.[10]

Born in Oklahoma as Arthur Dean McCluskey, Don Dean was precociously talented and joined up with first-rate big bands at a young age. Like many "paper" musicians (ones with formal training and technique), he aspired to be a bandleader and traveled to South America to recruit musicians. Arriving in Argentina in 1932 amid somewhat murky political circumstances, Dean initially stayed thanks to a stranded airplane and remained in the country after he met his future wife.[11] Though he benefited from some of the same privileges as his compatriot and played at many of the same venues, Dean was a more charismatic character than Mickey and also an edgier one: a talented and marketable dandy. With his orchestra Estudiantes de Hollywood, Dean presented his composition "Bailando en el Alvear" in the Argentine film musical *Ídolos de la Radio*. There is something unnerving about his 1934 screen debut. The dapper bandleader presents his signature number in Spanish with a heavy American drawl, the inverse of so many Argentine and Uruguayan crooners singing in English with River Plate accents.[12] In the upside-down jazz world of Argentina, it was as if the aura of translation were the ultimate trademark of authenticity.

Despite the presence of white Americans like Dean and Mickey, the terms "jazz" and "*música negra*" were nearly synonymous in the Argentine press of the 1930s. The pinnacle of authenticity to the Rioplatense was not the American jazz musician but the *Black* American jazz musician. Race and particularly racial Blackness have had notoriously slippery histories in Latin America, and perhaps nowhere is this truer than in Argentina. As late as the mid-nineteenth century, Afro Argentines comprised nearly a third of the nation's population. By the end of the century, however, the racial admixture and Black Argentines' disproportionate participation in wars and epidemics combined with a widespread "whitening" campaign buttressed by scientific racism and the official targeting of European immigrants greatly reduced the country's Afro-descendant population by the beginning of the twentieth century.[13] Nonetheless, Blackness as a concept did not merely disappear. Instead, the word "Negro" gradually began to acquire connotations of social class and national origin that have continued to the present day. Whereas in many other Latin American nations, including Brazil, governments began to promote mixed-race identities in the early decades of the twentieth century, Argentina never did, per se. Such was the efficacy of the state's whitening project that Afro-descendant and indigenous populations were largely disavowed as relics of the previous centuries and the still-substantial *mestizo* populations subsumed under the sign of compulsory whiteness.[14]

At the time of Booker Pittman's arrival in Buenos Aires, as a number of scholars have pointed out, it was common for Black, indigenous, mixed-race, and darker-skinned European Argentines to refer to themselves as *trigueño* (wheat-colored). A capacious form of racial classification and declassification, the term also provided cover for those who wished to avoid the subject of Blackness altogether. "As in other parts of Latin America," as historian Paulina Alberto has noted, "Argentine republican ideologies of racelessness and racial harmony displaced older practices of marking difference. But they provided clear pressures and incentives for Afroporteños to shed any marks of Africanness in order to fully claim their rights as citizens."[15] Nonetheless, when porteños encountered someone whom they were unable to categorize as white, they sometimes used the term *negro mota*, alluding not to the person's dark skin but rather to other putative traits of African descent. Yet *negro mota* also carried a strong whiff of foreignness precisely because a living, breathing Black Argentine was seen as anomalous to the prevalent notion of national identity.[16] Perhaps for this very reason, Black American jazz musicians served not just as idle curiosities but also as antipodes of normative Argentineness: emblems of racial otherness that local audiences otherwise denied as incompatible with themselves.

Booker Pittman was not the first foreign Black performer to leave his mark on Buenos Aires. Shortly after their long tour of France in 1922, Pixinguinha and the Oito Batutas dazzled music and theater audiences in the Argentine capital for several months, even recording sides on Victor between gigs.[17] In June 1923, Gordon Stretton left Brazil to tour Buenos Aires and Montevideo with his Orchestre Syncopated Six, accompanying the French revue Ba-ta-clan for the remainder of their three-month stint in the region; the sextet was praised by the *Buenos Aires Herald* as a "jazz band of the jazziest order."[18] In 1927, nine years before Booker's regional debut, Sam Wooding's distinguished orchestra, the Chocolate Kiddies, appeared in the Argentine capital. One of the pioneering bandleaders of the first half of the 1920s—surpassed in New York only by Fletcher Henderson and Paul Whiteman—Wooding, the so-called "Christopher Columbus of jazz," planted his flag in Europe before bewitching Argentine audiences on the way back from the Continent in an afterthought tour of South America, one that—similar to the Oito Batutas' and Stretton's residency—ended up lasting months. Much like the Brazilians, the strengths of the Chocolate Kiddies were their technical mastery, unfailing elegance, and versatility. They were equally adept at playing sweet or hot styles, depending on the atmosphere of the venue or the mood of the audience. In this way, the band created and shaped Argentine fans of different stripes and won over jazz-leaning bandleaders such as Adolfo Carabelli and René Cóspito.[19]

Hot on the heels of Sam Wooding came Josephine Baker in 1929. The orchestra of the "Ebony Venus" was too eclectic to be considered just a jazz band. But with its dazzling musicianship and unique spectacle of race, sexuality, and dance, Baker's multimedia combo represented the Jazz Age like no other on the transatlantic touring circuit. In her first long stay in South America, Baker transformed the cultural and moral landscape of Chile, Uruguay, and Brazil.[20] If anything, she had an even greater impact in Argentina, where her presence on the bandstand whipped up debates, triggered priests and politicians, and provoked scandals that made the headlines of the Buenos Aires dailies. Less conspicuous Black American performers were already embedded in Rio de la Plata, figures like Paul Wyer, violinist, clarinetist, and ex-collaborator of the famous blues composer W. C. Handy.[21] Despite not possessing either the virtuosity or pedigree of Booker Pittman, Wyer formed the respected orchestra Dixie Pals with Adolfo Ortiz and maintained a modest profile in the region for decades. But after Wooding and then Baker returned to their respective northern metropoles, there was no one of comparable stature to lend visible continuity to the fervor of *música negra* without falling into the trap of rote imitation or racial ventriloquism. It was as though porteños were waiting for the arrival of someone like Booker Pittman to kindle their very own Jazz Age.

## SWING STARS

To be a bandleader was the goal of countless jazzmen and a few jazzwomen in the 1930s. But leading a band and being a leader were two different things. At times, the will to lead sprang organically from a certain artistic or even educational vision, and to realize the vision logically meant assuming artistic control of the orchestra. Other times, the motivation was more venal than that, with profit and prestige being the driving forces. What united circumstantial and born bandleaders was their ambition. If not for glory, then for visibility: the bandleader was the person the orchestra looked *to* and the audience looked *at*. They had the power to decide who took solos (which sometimes meant the bandleader himself) and who receded into the background (almost never the bandleader). Once Isidro Benítez returned to his adopted home in Chile, the Black Stars disbanded, and Booker Pittman saw his best chance to form his own orchestra. He had already made a name for himself as an alto sax soloist extraordinaire. There was no one within five miles—or really, five thousand miles—who could touch him. Booker had never been all that interested in money, and in a later interview, he claimed to be too proud to ask family or friends to help him out financially.[22] But the spotlight and the baton were something else entirely. In Benítez's orchestra, he had had his chances to shine. But with an even smaller, more intimate band, one that gave its members space to improvise, he felt he could shine in exactly the ways he wanted.

Booker did not have the organization, the managerial aplomb, or the elite technical knowledge of a "paper" musician to be a bandleader like Silva or Benítez, and perhaps he knew it. When sober, Booker certainly had discipline as a musician and was not averse to long hours of practice. But having discipline was one thing, and instilling discipline, or worse, *imposing* discipline, on others seemed beyond his reach. Maybe it reminded him too much of his own upbringing: Big Pitt's *primitive discipline* and the terror it sowed in the entire family haunted him still, as it would throughout much of his life. Whatever the reason, Booker needed a local partner who could assume the more mundane and disciplinary responsibilities of the band—the scheduling, the transcription of scores, the publicity, the logistics of booking and budgeting shows. An overseer, in other words, who could complement Booker's creative leadership. He found this person in Adrián Russo, a capable pianist and arranger who had a head for details and a serene manner and sober disposition that Booker lacked. Bringing together the nucleus of the Black Stars—Dave Washington, Jack Braggs, and Lovey Price—and several others, notably the Australian accordionist

Bob Stewart and the West Indian bass player David Meneses, Russo and Booker founded a band that would make a big splash in the region: the Swing Stars.[23]

## URUGUAY

For some musicians, like Paul Wyer, the road to the Southern Hemisphere led to stable respectability and a permanent address. Booker Pittman, on the other hand, tended to move even when he seemed to be staying put. This had partly to do with the seasonal nature of the regional music scene. The center of jazz activities in Rio de la Plata in 1936 and 1937 was not just Buenos Aires, or at least, it was not *always* Buenos Aires. Once or twice a year, the scene shifted to resort hotels, casinos, and nightclubs of provincial capitals like Mar del Plata or Córdoba or floated across the delta to Uruguay, landing on the beaches of Montevideo or Punta del Este. In this sense, Uruguay's musical scene more closely resembled Rio de Janeiro's than it did Buenos Aires's. In the hot, humid months of December, January, and February, the biggest jazz public consisted of well-to-do summer vacationers in places like the Hotel Casino Carrasco, the Hotel Casino Míguez in Punta del Este, and the Rambla Hotel Casino in Montevideo, as reported in a number of newspapers and magazines of the period.

In December 1936, Booker Pittman, Adrián Russo, and the rest of the Swing Stars were playing at the Rambla Hotel on the exclusive Pocitos Beach. A few weeks later, they moved to the Restaurant Municipal "El Retiro" inside the Parque Rodó, a stone's throw from the swanky Parque Hotel. Booker felt like remaining in Uruguay beyond the summer holiday, in part because an old friend of his was also staying in Montevideo: at the beginning of the year, the new orchestra Al Pratt and His Entertainers was invited to headline at the Show Boat nightclub and perform a series of concerts at a local radio station.[24] Led by radio, modern mass media in Uruguay was growing at the same time as Argentina's, just to a lesser degree. As news spread about their incendiary live performances, the Swing Stars received other invitations. They played in the studios of Edison Broadcasting, their shows at the Rambla Hotel were transmitted live on Radio Carve, and they appeared on a Radio Águila jazz program hosted by the local aficionado, Ruben Picón Olaondo.[25] Booker later recalled having played alongside Carmen Miranda and her group Bando da Lua while they stopped in Montevideo after a trip to Argentina, though this may well have happened in Buenos Aires.[26]

The Swing Stars' several-month stint in Uruguay would prove a watershed in the country's musical history. Booker's performances electrified countless people but none more than the critic and musician Juan Rafael Grezzi, the founder of the Jazz Club Uruguayo. As was the case with seemingly every devoted jazz critic whom Booker encountered, the American quickly won over Grezzi with the combination of his explosive chops and personal charm. Before the Swing Stars set foot in Montevideo, Grezzi commented, local audiences had only really heard sweet jazz and inoffensive swing played by competent Uruguayan and Argentine musicians who, if they happened to be professionals, were still a far cry from *jazz* professionals. *Montevideanos* had never seen or heard the likes of anything like Booker Pittman. And it seems the Americans also took to the charming seaside capital, with its beaches, parks, trams, and *candombe* rhythms—the latter of which, with its infectious sound and Afro-diasporic provenance, reminded Booker vaguely of Brazil—and the surprising number of dark faces in the squares and on the sidewalks, which did as well. But the city was sleepy compared to Buenos Aires, especially once the summer gave way to fall. The main problem with Montevideo was that it simply did not have a big enough year-round population of jazz devotees to sustain a band that preferred laying down fat riffs at late-night jam sessions to playing for distracted revelers at a dance hall. When the vacation gigs dried up, the Swing Stars caught a ferry back to Buenos Aires, thankful for the experience even if financially worse off than when they arrived.[27] Still, the strangely bucolic urban landscape of Montevideo stuck with Booker as a point of reference and possible future destination. The city possessed a pace and flavor that agreed with him and a pungency that only the ocean brings. Maybe it was that simple. Whereas Buenos Aires seemed to almost hide itself from the Mar del Plata that defined it, Montevideo was the opposite. The Atlantic Ocean was so omnipresent that it was useless to deny it. Around practically every corner Booker turned, there was the water, staring at him, talking to him, talking *over* him.

In an article in *Síncopa y Ritmo* from February 1938, a critic calling himself Acede describes the pleasant surprise of encountering the genius of the Swing Stars. It was not the first time Booker had played in Buenos Aires, obviously, but since forming the band, he had spent relatively little time in Argentina, which meant that Buenos Aires still was not used to Booker the bandleader and featured soloist. Acede had already heard of Booker's name before he saw him with his own eyes, likely having read about him in a translated excerpt (published in *Síncopa y Ritmo* a year earlier) of the widely circulated and cited book by Hugues Panassié, the one declaring Booker one of the top alto sax players in the world.[28] But Acede's astonishment at Booker's virtuosity is surprising by itself. It suggests that the American had passed under the radar during the greater part of his initial tenure in Argentina, so much so that even a magazine as attentive to the fluctuations of the local jazz market as *Síncopa y Ritmo* had not really paid his live performances much notice until that point.

When Booker began to grab the attention of the porteño public, however, he really grabbed it. Having in some sense discovered him, Acede quickly became the city's most assiduous observer of the American's style. Booker, he said, was creatively restless and unpredictable, ardent and emotive in temperament, at once sublime and subtle in tone. The journalist even captured something of the contradictions of Booker's personality through the prism of music criticism, praising the musician's humor, but also questioning his frequent reliance on vaudeville antics. Acede acknowledged the inconsistencies of Booker's performance, especially his occasional lapses in energy. But he blamed most of this on the indifference of the crowd—caused, he said, by a general ignorance of jazz music's complexities. It was understandable that someone of Booker's caliber would lose interest and focus from time to time; he needed a knowledgeable and respectful audience to thrive. When the American sensed the careful attention he craved, his mood changed and the cloying clown receded. The payoff was immediate: "When he closes his eyes and gets serious, everyone's hair stands on end."[29]

## BOOKER PITTMAN'S BOYS

The time was ripe for Booker Pittman to make a record; everyone could agree about that. At the end of the 1930s, the Argentine branches of Odeon and RCA had stepped up their production of local artists, with jazz orchestras such as those of Héctor Lagna Fietta, Ken Hamilton, and Dante Varela leading the charge. During 1939 and 1940, Booker recorded at least four sides for a small independent label.[30] He was no longer accompanied by his old bandmates from the Black Stars and Swing Stars, who had headed off on their own. David Washington would soon be leading his own combo along with the precocious young pianist Enrique "Mono" Villegas. The nucleus of his new band, Booker Pittman's Boys, consisted of the pianist Ernesto Boero, the guitarist Jorge Curutchet, and the drummer Jorge Cistari.[31]

Booker Pittman's Boys recorded a grand total of four numbers: three standards and one jam session. Listening to the tracks today, even through the haze of technological precariousness and the inconsistent quality of his bandmates, is to witness Booker Pittman at the peak of his powers. His solos on "Margie" and "Tuxedo Junction" are less hurried than those of the Parisian sessions of Freddy Johnson several years earlier. At last the undisputed leader of his outfit, recording without the inevitable commercial hindrances of Odeon or RCA, Booker takes advantage of his newfound freedom to impose greater acoustic spaciousness on the sessions. The recording room is *his* space, finally, and he knows exactly how to fill it; his tone and phrasing sound impetuous yet controlled, complex yet deeply rooted in the blues. At times, his playing reveals a carefree, whimsical approach; other times, a defiant, lashing, almost insolent attitude toward his instrument. And he rarely repeats himself. Despite what critics like Acede said about the uncomprehending masses of Buenos Aires, Booker's resistance to the easy allure of garden-variety improvisation was seductive to discriminating porteño jazz audiences. His playing was enough: Booker did not need to sing to win people over. But still he sang, in live performances and now on records. He sang because he liked to and, now that he had his own combo, because he could; and he sang because audiences no doubt wanted him to. When Booker sang, he echoed the beguiling hoarseness of Louis Armstrong, though not the contemporary Armstrong: the *throwback* Armstrong, full of the jocular semi-vulgarity of the mid-1920s. The Satchmo of yesteryear.

## KING OF THE SOUTH

By the time Booker Pittman's orchestra reappeared on the radar of *Síncopa y Ritmo* in February 1941, it had morphed once again into something else. For one thing, the band had left the Confitería Adlon, where it had been in residence for a year, for the Odeon Bar. The "Boys" combo of the recording sessions gave way to a new set of musicians, including Adrián Russo again. But this was not the only change. Booker's orchestra had grown larger, a shift that reflected Russo's ambitions to lead a true big band and Booker's desire, most likely, for glossier venues and a larger spotlight. While Booker was the focus of the band, Russo's return meant the American was relieved of most of his administrative duties. This new division of labor, even if it meant giving up on his grandiose dreams of being a bandleader in the mold of Duke Ellington or Benny Goodman, freed up Booker to indulge his longstanding fantasies of being a multi-instrumentalist. No longer did he play only alto sax or clarinet; now, he played trumpet as well. The

Booker Pittman. *Síncopa y Ritmo*, February 1941. Booker's appearance in the pages of *Síncopa y Ritmo*, one of the world's first dedicated jazz magazines, signaled his prominence in the Buenos Aires jazz scene. Public domain/fair use.

orchestra's revolving door was somewhat worrisome, a sign of fickleness and unpredictability, two of the very qualities that made Booker's playing so riveting. The size and inexperience of the band's new configuration—several of the newcomers had just graduated from Gene Poole's Academia Americana—lent a certain precariousness to the mood and makeup of the orchestra.

According to another colorfully monikered critic, Pee Wee, Booker's team of saxophonists lacked discipline and the band's repertoire needed freshening up, specifically by injecting it with the compositions and arrangements of Booker's old friend Count Basie. Still, Booker's performances as a soloist were as fresh and impeccable as ever.[32] The disparity between Booker's skill and technique and those of his orchestra likely led to such ambivalent reviews. The drummer Juan Duprat wrote later that other musicians in Argentina tended to treat Booker "like a god."[33] Another profile from *Síncopa y Ritmo* declared Booker "the most extraordinary jazz figure that the Buenos Aires public had seen on a consistent basis up till now." As was often the case, however, the critic praised Booker at the expense of local audiences. "It is rare that musicians of his level choose to live among us, since the difference in atmosphere is so great that when [the musician] doesn't run the risk of being misunderstood, he feels beaten down and diminished."[34] If the pinnacle of Booker Pittman's career in Rio de la Plata had arrived, in other words, his reign came with its share of problems and contingencies.

## SLEEPLESS

Early Sunday mornings, the Buenos Aires clubs would finally, slowly die out like beach embers. One by one and sometimes couple by couple, the audiences filed out, followed sometime later by the musicians. Tired but not at all sleepy, Booker must have enjoyed strolling the narrow streets that ran parallel to the river until he reached the outer margins of the Centro, perhaps heading south toward the San Telmo neighborhood, and when he was especially wound up, going as far as the docks in La Boca. Other Sundays, he might have walked in the opposite direction, perhaps heading toward the train station or veering left toward la Recoleta, letting inertia sweep him across the ocean-like expanse of Avenida 9 de Julio, past the cold stone mansions of Retiro, until he suddenly sat face-to-face with the long, high wall of the cemetery, then turning around and walking into the yellow light of La Biela and ordering a café con leche and churros.

On his way back home, Booker may well have stopped at the Plaza San Martín, grabbing a park bench to soak in the morning sun if it was cold or the shade of a rubber tree if it was already hot. The rest is not difficult to imagine: still sustained by the residual intoxication of the night, the deep sadness that bedeviled him had still not kicked in. His melancholy remained lyrical and delicious. Freed from the tight cluster of nightspots in the Bajo, staring inconspicuously at the diurnal denizens of Buenos Aires— the families and dogs, jugglers and vendors, clowns and beggars—Booker must have thought often about his childhood, especially his mother and sister. He apparently did not feel obliged to write to them much, if at all.[35] His life in South America was an ongoing adventure, a nonstop party, and a high-wire act. Perhaps he was within his rights to isolate himself from his blood relatives for months or years on end. Maybe he needed the isolation and even the chaos to be able to focus.

And it had worked, hadn't it? Booker could finally call himself a bandleader, a real one. In a moment of pride, he had even written to tell his mother, who shared the news of his success with a New York reporter.[36] Local fame had shined on him obliquely and world fame, he reckoned, was just around the corner. With renown, he could begin to contemplate the Return: the triumphant tour of the United States, in the prime of his career, no less. And just like that, his friends and fellow musicians from Dallas and Kansas City to Chicago and Harlem would become wise to his remote whereabouts and his staggering feats all at once and in the most spectacular way possible. The front-page stories in the *New York Times* and *DownBeat* would double as postcards. But the vague certainty that he was on the road to success no doubt coexisted with something else: the pressure to always be a star, to excel without fail, to shine immaculately. And together with this weight, the sweet poison of a sleepless, chemical-fueled night, and the constant menace of bodily collapse, of imminent implosion.

## THE COMPETITION

To say that Booker Pittman's showman/jazzman ambivalence, his awkward blend of modern impulses with old-fashioned reflexes, was a simple byproduct of the frivolity of the Rioplatense music scene is, at best, a lazy explanation. By the beginning of the 1940s, there were plenty of imported records and foreign radio broadcasts in Buenos Aires. But the paucity of imported musicians of Booker's caliber created in him a sense of slow starvation. It also seemed to spur a shift in his ambitions. The fact that he increasingly took up new instruments suggested a certain impatience with the level of available talent and, at the same time, an inflated sense of his own musical vocabulary and skills.

As luck would have it, at this precise moment, another truly outstanding jazz musician arrived on the scene: long-lost native son Oscar Alemán. That the guitarist's return to Argentina from war-torn Europe was a somewhat reluctant one did not make it an unnoteworthy event. At the time, Alemán was still the only Argentine jazzista to have won international acclaim. When the exalted refugee washed ashore in 1940, he promptly wowed local audiences with his unique talent and Parisian pedigree in a country that had long venerated France as the source of excellence and authority in all things modern, even when it came to the music of Black Americans. As if that were not enough, Alemán possessed every bit as much charisma and showmanship as Booker. Four months after his reentry, Alemán and his new quintet opened the Gong nightclub on Avenida Córdoba. By the end of 1941, the combo already had a long-term contract with Radio Belgrano.[37] Now it was official: Booker was no longer the only jazz oracle in Buenos Aires. What was worse, Booker had not lived in Paris long enough to acquire the same celebrity or cosmopolitan sheen as Alemán, whose only major flaw, according to the perverse logic of Argentine audiences, was being a native of Argentina.

It was not just a question of the returning hero's local celebrity or Parisian panache that left Booker Pittman in the shadow of Oscar Alemán. In reality, the guitarist was hardly Booker's nemesis. The two virtuosos of the Buenos Aires jazz scene had been friendly enough during their years together in France. Booker's most fearsome enemy was his drug and alcohol addiction, which had become more evident to those around him since his move from Brazil. In this sense, his story echoed those of so many other friends and colleagues of the same era. Booker had found considerable renown since catching a boat to the Rio de la Plata. Yet his memoirs suddenly become skeletal when he describes his years in the region, almost as if his writing were mimicking the vicissitudes of his body. There is only one elliptical sentence touching on the issue: *Introduced to drugs*.[38] It is clear the American had received minor initiations before his arrival to Argentina. The musical circles of Kansas City, Harlem, and Montmartre were not exactly abstemious societies, and Booker was never someone to avoid the parties and dive bars that made up his world or turn down small bohemian pleasures, especially prior to a show. Even if, as we have seen, he had been given to bouts of drinking since his days in Kansas City, in a later interview, he mentioned New York as the place where he first tried marijuana. "Everyone—with few exceptions—used it to fuel their great improvisations in the New Orleans style." And so it was that Booker caught reefer madness himself, though he explains that of all the drugs he tried, marijuana was the "most inoffensive."[39]

Booker thought pot to be so harmless, apparently, that he smoked it openly around other musicians in Buenos Aires. The drummer Juan Duprat later recalled that the American's "special" cigarettes drew plenty of attention. While younger players associated Booker's marijuana consumption with the jovial, joke-telling side of the musician, his growing drug abuse led to notorious bouts of deep depression and despair. While in public Booker could be infectiously joyful and confident, behind the scenes "he considered himself absolute trash."[40] What Duprat wrote off as mood swings caused by reefer madness only told part of the story. By the end of the 1930s, Booker Pittman began to abuse cocaine as well, a habit that quickly led him to other hard drugs. Perhaps it was not surprising that drug pushers pushed their wares so aggressively in Argentina. Buenos Aires may have been provincial, but its vices were not. Already in 1933, there were more than two hundred brothels in the federal capital, and the drugs and organized and unorganized crime circuits that thrived on prostitution only intensified over the course of the decade. During this time, cocaine was simple to find in the Bajo Porteño, especially in the kinds of night spots that Booker haunted.[41]

Even when high and emboldened, Booker was the kind of person who disliked taking unnecessary risks in back alleys. But by the beginning of the 1940s, cocaine had become his all-purpose flour, his daily sustenance. It got to the point where he needed coke to go on stage; because he would drink after hours, the next morning, he used coke to treat his hangovers. The problem, Booker told a Brazilian magazine decades later, was that cocaine initially *worked* for him, lending him the illusion of energy that he wanted and felt he needed. The drug's efficacy faded over time. Gradually, Booker began to feel the insidious, corrosive effects of cocaine on his brain and on his playing. Later, he learned that his experience was not at all unique. Meanwhile, dealers circled the clubs like friendly vultures, peddling substances that would help him recover the lung power he had lost due to his abuse of cocaine. But these drugs—morphine, heroin—were even more potent and addictive than cocaine. For anyone familiar with substance abuse, it was an all-too-familiar story: for the drugs to work well enough for him to play, he had to take higher and higher doses.[42]

To make matters worse, paying for his increasingly expensive fixes sapped Booker's always precarious finances. He knew something drastic had to be done. Rather than borrow money from a dubious acquaintance or a common loan shark, he asked trusted friends to lock him in his apartment. But when a couple of them paid him a visit one night, they discovered that he was as high as a kite. As it turned out, his long-time dealers had been secretly visiting his building, leaving Booker just enough of their product under the door to ease his pain and retain their services for another day, another week, another month.[43]

### THE PRETEXT

As far back as February 1940, Booker Pittman told the Argentine magazine *Sintonía* that he was opting out of his long-term contract with the nightclub La Chaumière because, simply, he needed to rest. The journalist probed deeper. "What's the reason?" he asked.

"*Misterioso, misterioso,*" Booker responded evasively.[44]

It took him a year and a half, but by September 1941, Booker was finally free of the vicious circle of Buenos Aires and back in Montevideo. His friend Juan Rafael Grezzi had organized a jazz concert at the Teatro Trocadero, and Booker was the main attraction. Grezzi had sold him to local audiences as *jazz negro* incarnate. When Booker arrived, though, he found himself performing in front of a distracted ballroom crowd.[45] He should not have expected anything better. The early 1940s witnessed the apex of big band jazz, and not only in Rio de la Plata. By the beginning of World War II, swing dancing had even invaded the less likely corners of the globe. Jitterbugging was all the rage among the same populations that only years before had rejected the shimmy and the Charleston as lewd and decadent. Whereas in 1937, jazz in Montevideo was still a curiosity and niche market, now it was a mainstream pursuit. It did not help that Booker was trying to go cold turkey, each step a chore, each note an imposition. Though the event's organizer, Grezzi left the Trocadero show bitterly embarrassed by the performance of his guest of honor. The magnificent concerts that the Swing Stars gave in Montevideo four years earlier had stuck in the Uruguayan's mind as the platonic ideal of genuine modern jazz. After a haggard Booker took the stage, selling his music with the gimmickry of vaudeville and the conventionalism of commercial swing, Grezzi, in a scathing review for a local magazine, blamed the corrupting influence of Buenos Aires nightclubs, whose public expected bands to place their technique "at the service of cheap and bombastic playing."[46] It was perhaps the harshest written criticism Booker had received in his career up to this point, and coming from someone whom he considered a friend, it must have cut him to the quick.

Regardless, Booker remained in Montevideo well beyond the disastrous show at the Trocadero. He had other reasons to set anchor in Uruguay besides music. Like Grezzi, he treasured his memories of his first visit to Montevideo. The unassuming elegance of the Parque Rodó neighborhood, the sleepy vitality of Ciudad Vieja, the pleasantness of the people, the lovely *orla* and the nearly white sands of the city's beaches: it was the anti-Buenos Aires. And for Booker, there was likely another important detail. Montevideo was still apparently a city without easy access to street drugs. *Una ciudad sana*. A healthy city, a sane city, a wholesome city.

## THE SLOW ESCAPE

These are the simplest explanations for Booker's escape to the north shore of the River Plate delta. But there were others as well. For one, Montevideo resembled Rio de Janeiro enough to rouse Booker's nostalgia for the Marvelous City. And it was not just the beaches and the hills, smaller versions of the carioca landscape, or that the wavelets from the Mar del Plata seemed like the Atlantic surf in miniature. It was the cordiality of the people and the slower rhythms of the city. Also, there were many other Black people besides Booker, doormen and trash collectors, housemaids and small businessmen, distant cousins of his whose familiarity perhaps softened the American's solitude, even if it sharpened his creeping sense of privilege, of his fundamental difference from Afro Uruguayans and everyone else in South America, for that matter. From the early nineteenth through the early twentieth centuries, Uruguay experienced many of the same demographic patterns as Argentina had, though with a few notable differences. The waves of European immigration and the concomitant whitening campaign were somewhat less intense, and the visible eclipse of Afro-descendant denizens was not nearly as absolute as it was in Buenos Aires by the 1930s. From lowly city workers to world-famous soccer

Rambla República del Perú and Playa Pocitos, with Hotel Casino Rambla on the left. The Rambla was one of the venues where Booker played during his first stay in Montevideo. Intendencia de Montevideo, 1944. Centro de Fotografía de Montevideo. Public domain via Wikipedia Commons.

stars like José Leandro Andrade and Isabelino Gradín, Black Uruguayans stood out in ways that the much smaller minority of Black Argentines generally did not. Carnival season, meanwhile, prominently featured Afro Uruguayan candombe music and *comparsas*, some comprised of a mix of both Black and white bodies in blackface. With a greater presence of Black and mixed-race urban dwellers also came greater racial discrimination, a trend chronicled in *Nuestra Raza*, a Black-owned newspaper that began publishing in Montevideo in 1933.[47]

Booker Pittman doubtless paid closer attention to the distinguishing nuances of Montevideo culture now that he found himself mostly alone, with ample time on his hands. The city had charms all its own, and Booker was clearly susceptible to them. But perhaps its appeal lay not so much in the *comparsas* and the beaches. Maybe it was that day-to-day *montevideanos* struck him as *simple* in their ambitions, content with a loving companion, a modest-sized apartment, enough money to pay for an occasional lunch at the Restaurant Municipal, and afterward, popcorn and candy apples for their children as they watched the sunset from the grassy knolls of Parque Rodó, slowly sipping their *maté* as the sky gradually darkened. But the seeming simplicity of this life must have pained the musician as well because he feared he would never find this modest paradise for himself, either because he could not or because he did not want to.[48]

## THE DEEP FUGUE

In the end, Montevideo was not as innocent a city as it first appeared. Booker was clearly looking for something besides candy apples and scenic sunsets. Sooner or later, in the squares and dives off the city center near his *pensión*, the American found what he hated himself for seeking: inconspicuous sources of the same illicit drugs that had plagued him in Buenos Aires. Before he knew it, he was back to square one, as if he had never crossed the wide river delta in the first place. Performing at the cabaret El Royale Pigalle, drugs and whiskey became his main sidekicks again.[49] Booker's playing was likely more inspired for a short spell, and then it was not. Then it surely got worse. His body weakened; his energy ebbed and flowed, but mainly ebbed. Booker needed another way out—a more definitive retreat, a great escape. Someone, possibly Grezzi, had told him about a new casino in the remote border town of Rivera, hours overland from the capital.[50] Perhaps it was Grezzi who spoke by phone with a representative of the casino, reaching a contractual arrangement on the American's behalf.

In any event, Booker left Montevideo and never looked back, following a centrifugal itch to flee the city and the cities that had long mistreated him. It was the opposite of his flight impulse from early adulthood when he lived dreaming of escape from small-town life for the metropolis—each one bigger, more modern, and more dangerous than the last.

As the bus took him northeastward across low hills and seemingly endless, undulating grasslands, Booker must have felt an invisible burden slowly melt away. Hours later, he found himself in a different century. He would have been astonished to see flesh-and-blood gauchos not just in the distant fields but also boarding the bus, with their fine hats and heavy boots and dusty layers of wool and leather. Arriving at the Casino Hotel Rivera, Booker was shown a spacious, elegant, and comfortable room. For the first time since he had toured the Midwest with Jap Allen's orchestra over a decade earlier, stopping in places like Des Moines, Sioux Falls, and Omaha, Booker soaked in the stillness of a small town.[51]

Rivera was so small that when Booker roamed beyond the main commercial streets, he suddenly found himself in the red earth and perfumed air of the countryside. Walking in the other direction, he wandered into Brazil. Not only was there no border guard, but there was also no border: the dividing line, as far as he could gather, was either a treeless park or an unpaved street patrolled by men on binational donkeys. When he crossed the invisible line, though, he noticed the differences almost immediately. He had already heard the cadences of Brazilian Portuguese on the bus and in the casino, but once in Santana do Livramento, the language would have immediately begun to predominate. Ducking into a small market, he saw to his delight that the products—the handmade sweets, the bottled drinks, the *salgadinhos* (salty snacks)—were not the same ones he had consumed over the last few years. But mostly, it was the people who were different, their habits and rhythms, the way they greeted one another in the street, their penchant for smiling, for gratuitous celebration, for complaining and swearing while they smiled and celebrated. It was all enough to warm his heart. He had forgotten how much he missed the little things in Brazil.[52]

## ROCK BOTTOM

Booker started spending more time in Santana do Livramento than in Rivera, in part, no doubt, because he yearned to immerse himself in the deep pool of Brazilian conviviality that he so missed, but also because good cachaça was much cheaper than the acceptable brands of whiskey.

*Cachaça, coringa, pinga.* Whatever one called the liquor, it had a taste the American had long associated with his beloved Brazil.[53] He would spend hours in the afternoon drinking and talking to whoever happened to sit down next to him at his favorite boteco. Sometimes, perhaps, he took his sax with him and jammed with other barflies sporting *cavaquinhos* and *cuícas*, two typical Brazilian instruments. The word spread of his presence, and musicians came to expect the odd American and his unbridled musicality. But Booker did not abandon Uruguay entirely. What kept him tethered to Rivera besides his work in the casino was a woman he met there named María Fernández (or Fernandes), who happened to be the single mother of a young boy.[54] It seemed like an unlikely time and place for Booker's paternal instincts to finally emerge. Presumably, it did not matter to the boy that the American sounded funny when he spoke Spanish (or Portuguese) or that he was dark-skinned and dressed differently or that he lived in a hotel. If Booker felt the stirrings of something new and powerful inside him, he would hardly have felt like he deserved María or her son or that he could return their affection in his present state. Nonetheless, Booker and María apparently would stay together on and off for several years.[55]

As always, drinking helped Booker to overcome his shyness with strangers. It also helped him to convince himself that he was conquering his other vices and, even more improbably, that by drinking, he was giving his body a rest from all the cocaine. The optimism of mirth-making and the insidiousness of addiction took hold of him to such a degree that he began to abuse alcohol more than ever before. It did not matter where he was or with whom. On both sides of the border, he drank day and night with devotion and discipline, as if he were a diabetic injecting cachaça into his body instead of insulin. Things got so bad that within a few weeks, by his own estimation, Booker was drinking six bottles of cachaça a day.[56] Naturally, his relationship with María must have suffered. At a certain point, he likely felt too ashamed to see her or the boy anymore; he just could not, not like this. Their increasing, albeit temporary, absence from his life must have driven him to drink even more. The rest is easy enough to imagine. His musical performances at the Casino Rivera devolved into a pathetic vaudeville act. Each night, he played and sang less and shouted more in a slurred argot of English, vestigial French, and Portunhol. If the crowds did not grow sparser, it was because the serious jazz fans gave way to bored gamblers or rubberneckers gawking at Booker's ongoing self-destruction. After weeks of this bizarre spectacle, no one quite understood what the American was babbling about. His playing became punch-less and erratic when it happened at all, and even the other musicians likely lost their patience with him.[57]

It was not surprising that when his contract with the casino expired, Booker was not offered a new one. Because he did not know what else to do, the day he received his last payment, he packed his one trusty suitcase and moved to Santana do Livramento, leaving his semi-luxurious hotel suite for a small room at a friend's house in what amounted to a *favela*. To chip in with the rent, he accepted an invitation to play at two small cabarets, Tosca and Balão.[58] He felt freer this way, more dignified somehow. But the owners ended up paying him with cachaça; the customers, too. It was as though the whole world were conspiring to get him to keep blowing his horn, whatever the cost.

## THE WELL

The cost turned out to be very high. The first ominous sign of trouble was a light numbness in his fingers. Booker wrote it off as the biting winter chill of the region or maybe the first hint of a cold. To furnish heat to his body, he threw down even bigger quaffs of coringa. When he could no longer feel his feet, he grew worried, the fear piercing the emotional blubber of his drunkenness. As he walked slowly and unsteadily to the hospital in Santana with the help of a friend, Booker could hear the crunch of pebbles and dirt on the ground without being able to feel them through his shoes. It was as though he was outside himself, like part of him had left his body. By the time Booker was transferred to the hospital in Rivera, the pain and discomfort would have been unbearable. The parts of him that were not numb were in agony. He could not walk and had trouble swallowing and chewing food; even breathing was becoming difficult. After carefully observing the American for several interminable days, the small team of Uruguayan physicians diagnosed the condition he suffered from as polyneuritis.[59]

Perhaps two weeks later, ambling slowly along the commercial streets of Rivera and Livramento, resting on a bench in the Plaza Internacional, Booker saw that people's first reaction to his recovery was astonishment. The rumors of his imminent death had been circulating through the main arteries of the two border towns for some time. The false news of the musician's death had reached the eager ear of a local journalist, except that by the time the piece was published, Booker was already out of the hospital.[60] Once he had fully recovered, it made little sense for Booker to keep holing up at the end of the earth. If he had not managed to protect himself from his own vices here in the middle of the pampas, after all, what more did he have to fear from the big city, where at least he could count on old friends, steady work, and anonymity when he needed it? Booker once again felt his old homing instinct, his cosmopolitan urge, and with it came a yearning to play the saxophone again, a desire that for months had been eclipsed by his tyrannical compulsion to drink, to be unconscious, to hit rock bottom. *Pra chegar ao fundo do poço,* as the saying went in Brazil. To sink to the bottom of the well. Only now, his only desire was to climb toward daylight, to feel again.

## THE THIRD RETURN

Finally recovered from his frightening illness, temporarily sober for the first time in years, Booker Pittman caught a bus downriver and then a ferry to Buenos Aires with a Uruguayan pianist and a couple of other musicians from the border area. Though he does not mention them in his memoirs, it is likely he traveled with María and her son as well.[61] He had gotten some of his strength back, and after another couple of short hospital stays, felt ready to triumph once again in the South American jazz capital. But wary venue owners and bookers would have been unsure about which Booker had crossed the river this time. Was Booker truly healthy yet, and more importantly, was he clean, *really* clean? Also, who were these musicians he brought with him from the pampas? After looking unsuccessfully for work in his old haunts—the Odeon, the Richmond—Booker and his chums landed gigs in some of the newer confiterías willing to take a chance on the American. But as his technique and energy returned, he doubtless realized, now painfully sober, that his bandmates were not musically at his level. What was more, they seemed blinded by the big city lights and diminished by the stone-faced scrutiny of porteño enthusiasts.

In the wake of his illness, it dawned on Booker that he had neither the ambition nor the energy to lead a professional orchestra, that he simply did not react well to the pressure that came with the job. Still, word spread quickly about the American's riveting individual performances. Club owners, journalists, and fellow bandleaders and musicians soon saw that Booker seemed more like himself again as a player and as a person. By June 1944, he was blowing solos at the swanky La Cigale with the Cotton Pickers, a relatively new combo led by guitarist Mike Ratip. The excellent orchestra featured soloists of the caliber of the tenor saxophonist Felix

Williams until the musician's untimely death that very summer. But that did not stop the Cotton Pickers. By the beginning of 1945, Ratip had hired several Brazilian musicians, including the up-and-coming clarinetist Isidro Rocha.[62] If the Cotton Pickers were not led by Booker in name, they might as well have been. It was as though the orchestra had been tailor-made for him: international, biracial, loaded with swing. Unlike most Buenos Aires ensembles of the era, the Cotton Pickers were dedicated not to sweet scores and slick arrangements but rather to the chemistry and improvisation of its members, a jam band writ large. It was an ideal situation for Booker. As the critic Pee Wee wrote in *Síncopa y Ritmo*, "We trust now that Booker will stay with us for some time. His influence is highly beneficial [and] the satisfaction he gives us when we hear him play is something that we never want to give up."[63]

*Chapter Five*

# SOME NEGLECTED SPOT

I hope when I am dead that I shall lie
In some deserted grave—I cannot tell you why,
But I should like to sleep in some neglected spot
Unknown to everyone, by everyone forgot.
—JESSIE REDMON FAUSET, "OBLIVION"

BOOKER PITTMAN'S EXODUS FROM BUENOS AIRES IN THE AUTUMN OF 1946 was not just a byproduct of artistic restlessness or abject addiction. It was also a direct consequence of Argentine politics. Three years earlier, after a period sometimes referred to as the Infamous Decade marked by corrupt politics, mostly ineffectual economic policies, and increasing income disparity and poverty, the general Juan Perón participated in a coup d'etat that brought an end to the government of Ramón Castillo. Serving as labor secretary until being elected president in 1946, Perón—along with his charismatic wife Eva—implemented pro-union labor policies and more inclusive social programs that benefited the nation's fast-expanding, urban working class. The movement they led was also anti-communist, corporatist, and highly nationalist, with the state assuming the role of "moral guardian," a self-designation used to justify censorship of foreign, overly commercial, and otherwise unwholesome influences on Argentine culture. As a result, the military regime and later the Perón presidency made sure that *música criolla* ruled the nation's stages and airwaves.[1] The country that had needed Booker's presence and influence now demanded his absence. And not just Booker's. The only viable option for an orchestra such as the Cotton Pickers, so loyal to jazz and at the same time so dependent on expat talent, was to look for engagements in neighboring nations.

In March 1946, the orchestra embarked for the Cassino Atlântico de Santos in the Brazilian state of São Paulo. A posh beach hotel in what was, at the time, an important port-of-call for transatlantic ocean liners with a cosmopolitan clientele accustomed to well-rehearsed orchestras but hungry for top jazz talent, the casino was the ideal venue for the Cotton Pickers. Ratip's motley crew of Argentines, Americans, and at least one Brazilian dabbled in rumbas and sambas in addition to jazz. But the heart of the orchestra remained open-ended improvisation. Booker, as happy and energized as he had been in years, played better than ever. A Brazilian journalist who caught one of the Cotton Pickers' shows remarked that the "protean" saxophonist had his way with his instrument to such a degree that he seemed "made of another substance entirely."[2]

Booker's hard-earned musical bliss lasted less than a month, and not because the band's contract expired. The casino closed suddenly. In fact, *all* Brazilian casinos closed, thanks to a federal decree issued by the nation's new president, Gaspar Dutra, caving to political and religious pressures. As chance would have it, at the conclusion of World War II, Brazil had its own political turmoil to contend with. The change in the world order also saw the end of Getúlio Vargas's Estado Novo (1937–1945), a regime that had grown increasingly more authoritarian and nationalist as the war raged on, even after Vargas declared his support for the Allies. Such sentiment inevitably spilled over into the cultural realm. In ways that echoed debates about jazz's perceived threat to the integrity of tango in Argentina and Uruguay, by the 1940s, samba had hardened its role as a synecdoche of Brazilian culture; influential magazines like *Diretrizes* were filled with impassioned defenses (and apologies) of samba's putative eclipse by commercial big band swing.[3] When members of the Brazilian military intervened in 1945 to prevent Vargas from remaining in office, it signaled a tentative return to democracy. Yet remnants of moralistic nationalism remained. Dutra's puritanical mandate may have been aimed at gambling, but its main collateral victim was the nation's professional music scene, long centered on prestige venues like the Copacabana Palace, the Urca, and the Atlântico. The collapse of Brazil's casinos, writes the historian Zuza Homem de Mello, was not simply an economic catastrophe for the nation's tourist sector. It was also a cultural blow that "left the musical world half orphaned, forcing it to find a new path forward."[4]

## STATELESS

Victimized by ill-conceived government policies for the second time in a year, Booker Pittman lay low in Santos, picking up the pieces and playing where he could, and tried to figure out his next move. Even after the prohibition of gambling, the city remained the most important seaport in Brazil, regularly hosting ships full of tourists and soldiers, American whiskey, and Italian wine. Erstwhile gambling casino Monte Serrat rebranded itself a "Night Club," and Booker continued to find work there for a time, headlining alongside ballet dancers, opera singers, comedians, and tango orchestras.[5] Increasingly, though, the coastal city's nightlife moved to smaller cabarets and boates, attracting a more democratic clientele than the Atlântico, the Monte Serrat, and their competitor Parque Balneário ever did. In these less elegant but often more animated venues, Belgian businessmen hobnobbed with local stevedores, accountants hooked up with their *amantes*, and soldiers on shore leave got into fistfights with *paulistanos* on weekend getaways.[6]

Booker was also still ostensibly committed to María and her young son at this time, though perhaps only intermittently. Once Ratip and the gang left the hotel and returned to Argentina, Booker briefly shared a room with a waiter he had befriended.[7] Their life revolved around jazz records, bars, and *futebol*. Booker, still managing to control but not fully slake his thirst for alcohol, had struck an uneasy balance between insecure self-control and precarious cockiness, sociability and unhinged excess. He met new musicians, dock workers, and prostitutes, and in no time, he forged an intimate circle of provisional friends whom he found at once comforting and cloying. Even though he missed his bandmates, he felt relieved to be back in Brazil, deeply so. Booker was adaptable. He knew he could make new friends and collaborators wherever he went, and when he did, he could manage to live without his old ones. María and her son notwithstanding, Booker was not the kind of person who became easily attached to anyone or anything. Instability was the price one paid for perpetual novelty, for constant renovation.

Still, Booker suddenly knew now that he did not want to be anywhere besides Brazil. Although it is unclear whether he and María ever formally married, the Santos newspaper *A Tribuna* announced María's birthday in January 1947, identifying her only as the "spouse of Mr. Booker Pittman."[8] Nonetheless, he was done with Argentina and done with Uruguay, too. The sheer trauma of his hospital stay in Rivera must have extinguished whatever fleeting illusions he had of making a permanent nest in Rio de la Plata. But Brazil was a vast country and Santos was a small, isolated city, larger than Santana do Livramento but considerably smaller than Montevideo. Gigs for musicians, even good musicians, were relatively few and far between. For a time, Booker bounced back and forth between Santos and nearby São Paulo, apparently playing regularly at the club Oasis and occasionally a concert at the Teatro Municipal.[9]

When the cultural remains of the sunken casinos dried up, though, Booker felt the familiar tug to return to his beloved Rio de Janeiro. The move was inevitable, and he had one more motive than usual. He needed to go to the United States Embassy to renew his travel documents, which he had left in Buenos Aires, apparently by accident.[10] Now that World War II had ended, Booker no longer feared presenting himself to the authorities of his country and risking being drafted into the military. So, as soon as he had saved up enough money (likely in early 1947), he caught the next boat he could up the coast. It is unclear whether María and her son joined him there.

## RECARIOCA

Copacabana had changed noticeably in the ten years since he had left. In the 1930s, the area was still mostly a hodgepodge of mom-and-pop businesses, windswept mansions, small apartment buildings, empty, sandy lots, and a smattering of grand hotels. Now, the neighborhood had gained density, verticality, and urban flavor, emerging as a full-fledged residential *bairro* and not just a vacation destination for foreign tourists or a weekend wonderland for downtown denizens. The fall of the casinos had spelled the end of the rival urban outpost of Urca as a nighttime destination. But in Copacabana, with more space for growth than Urca, this same collapse gave birth to new constellations of bars and boates. No longer the bucolic getaway of a decade earlier, Copa had, by 1947, been transformed into a rather convenient place to live and work. Nearly all the music venues were grouped together in the same stretch of the beachside neighborhood, between Rua Barata Ribeiro and Avenida Atlântica, in Postos 2 and 3. One of the boates, Meia-Noite, located in the Copacabana Palace next door to the venerable Golden Room, was his old friend Jorge Guinle's new pint-sized jazz club. At the Meia-Noite, Booker quickly reunited with other friends, including fellow expats like the entertainer Louis Cole and the pianist Claude Austin.

In many ways, Cole and Austin had helped to fill Booker's shoes when he left for Argentina in 1936. In the late 1930s, Cole formed his own orchestra at the Cassino Atlântico, their performances regularly broadcast on Radio Ipanema. Cole's background before moving to Paris with Booker lay in vaudeville more than jazz, and he quickly took to the carnival and casino–driven peculiarities of the Brazilian entertainment scene, embracing marchinhas and the sambas of Noel Rosa in particular, though continuing to perform dance-based jazz, blues, and rumbas as well.[11] Cole and his orchestra recorded a few sides on Columbia in 1940, including a "rumba-marchinha" composed by Ary Barroso.[12] Throughout the rest of the decade, in spite of his many talents, Cole maintained a "discreet" presence in Copacabana, as one reporter put it, and mostly as a singer, tap dancer, and general showman rather than as a bandleader.[13]

Though many assumed he had come to Brazil with Booker, Cole, and Pratt on the SS *Siqueira Campos* in 1935, Claude Austin had, in fact, arrived some years later, in the early days of World War II. Early reports of his presence on Brazilian soil made out Austin to be a jazz legend—Duke Ellington and Cab Calloway's arranger and the person who taught Mae West and Pat and Rosemary Lane to sing—who had come to Brazil with the sole purpose of studying Brazilian popular music.[14] A Rio de Janeiro daily declared Austin the "absolute master of jazz" who had been celebrated by Eleanor Roosevelt at the White House.[15] Austin's pedigree may not have been quite as lofty as advertised, but his abilities as an arranger and pianist were considerable. In fact, he did arrange for Ellington for a time and had even penned the first commercial version of "St. James Infirmary Blues."[16] What was more, his musical appetites were omnivorous, his repertoire constantly updated to include the latest hits from Brazil and the United States. With his solid though unexceptional skills on the piano, agreeable presence, and reputation as a very capable bandleader, Austin soon found his niche in Rio's casino and nightclub circuit. By 1944, the American was headlining a prime-time slot on Rádio Cruzeiro do Sul and performing during the summer holiday season at the palatial Poços de Caldas casino in Minas Gerais.[17] Austin flourished in plusher settings such as the Golden Room at Copacabana Palace, Night and Day Club in the Hotel Serrador, in Cinelândia, and the even more music-centered Meia-Noite.

Booker's dear friend Bibi Miranda, meanwhile, was also still part of the scene when Booker took his first stab at a Brazilian comeback. At the end of the 1940s, Bibi was looking and playing better than ever, gigging not just with local combos but also occasionally with foreign-based orchestras such as saxophonist Bud Freeman's touring big band.[18] With Booker's rather short-lived return to Rio in 1947, Booker and his old gang quickly gravitated toward another, even hotter venue, a nightclub called Vogue. Housed in a new, imposingly elegant hotel of the same name in Posto 2, Vogue was a vestige of the upscale atmosphere and clientele of the newly bygone casinos. And like the casinos, Vogue paid musicians handsomely. Only the space was much smaller, so small that Vogue's famously fastidious manager made Booker muzzle his sax with flannel so as not to annoy the hotel guests with his wailing solos.[19]

Years later, several of these same guests perished in a massive fire that brought down the Hotel Vogue. Newspapers the next day reported that an up-and-coming and fatally unlucky American crooner, Warren Hayes, had leaped to his death from his tenth-floor room. To musicians and clubgoers, the grotesque defenestration scene seemed like the culmination of a musical curse. Another boate that Booker haunted in 1948 was the Mei Ling on nearby Carvalho de Mendonça. The club was named after the first lady of China, Soong Mei-ling, who had spent four months in Rio de Janeiro in 1944.[20] The Mei Ling proved a huge success, attracting the top jazz talent in the city. More than that, it was the type of venue that Booker invariably preferred, with forward-looking management that let the musicians call most of the shots. According to one account, during a memorable jam session organized by Jorge Guinle and his brother Carlinhos, Booker stole the show, wowing enthusiasts with his renditions of "Honeysuckle Rose" and, with the help of Louis Cole, "Walls of Jericho" and "How High the Moon."[21] Once again, Booker had found his groove in Rio de Janeiro.

## BIRTHDAY MAN

And just like that, he lost it again. The red-hot Mei Ling went up in literal flames just a few months after its inauguration.[22] Booker does not mention the fire in his memoirs, but he must have been deeply disappointed by the club's demise and doubled over from the serial turns of fate that seemed to always beset him personally. It was as though he was not supposed to make a living playing music. But jazz-dominant venues in Brazil were usually small, always precarious, and frequently short-lived. They began, they shone brightly, they flamed out, and then they vanished, only to be reborn in another place and under a different name. In their way, they mirrored Booker's own cycles of evanescence and resilience.

In October 1949, Booker T. Pittman turned forty years old. To commemorate the occasion, or perhaps to bury it, he made another move, this time for São Paulo.[23] He hit the road again knowing that he was no longer a young man. Alone in his hotel or walking the streets of the city, he must have reflected on all the things he had done and all the things he had not done in the two decades since he left Dallas: how many records he had made, how many orchestras he had led, how many countries he had set foot in, how many women he had seduced. Even though he knew he should not, Booker likely compared himself with his friends and colleagues in the United States, his peers, or at least people he considered his peers: Ben Webster, Clyde Hart, Johnny Hodges, Budd Johnson.

Ten years earlier, on his thirtieth birthday, this same exercise may have struck Booker as good fun and even given him hope for the future. At that time, his star was on the rise in Buenos Aires and anything seemed possible, even a triumphant return to New York City. If the siren song of addiction was already growing too loud for him to ignore, Booker still looked and felt fit and had plenty of time to right the ship, or so he thought at the time. Now, the same *balanço* had lost its luster. Now Booker punished himself with measuring sticks he had always convinced himself were unimportant and conventional: marriage, children, wealth, fame. They represented the same blindly bourgeois values that he had long despised in others, and still, privately, Booker no doubt berated himself for not having these very same things. What was worse, he had still not fully conquered his addictions, and while he could claim a few records to his name, who had actually heard them? The few journalists and promoters who knew he existed and mattered were Brazilians, Uruguayans, and Argentines who tended to cite the same book by Hugues Panassié, written fifteen years earlier, to argue that Booker was one of the best alto saxophone players in the world. But was Booker really that person anymore?

Lurching from gig to gig, fed up with the repetitiveness of his life and mostly fed up with this present version of himself, Booker tired of São Paulo the same way he had tired of Rio de Janeiro, only more quickly. By 1950, Sampa had become almost as big a city as Rio, but it still lacked the deep musical scene and circle of friends that the capital offered. It was urban without yet being fully cosmopolitan; it was too big, and it was not quite big enough. Booker yearned for something else, something more intimate and comforting in ways he could not quite define. It was the same blind desire that had driven him out of Montevideo into the unknown expanse of the pampas. But this time, the itch to errancy felt different somehow, less provisional, more open-ended and desperate. One day, he and a friend—the young musician, arranger, and composer Waltel Branco—decided to catch the next train for Branco's home state of Paraná.[24] It was beautiful there, Branco must have told him, and there was money and work to be found. A perfect place to find the low-key adventures Booker was looking for. If he wanted the easy life, Paraná was the place.

The party started on the train to Londrina. The two men got so drunk in coach class, their faces so flushed and swollen from cachaça and their voices so loud, that the other passengers thought it best to keep their distance, their collective stare unsettling Booker to such a degree that he began to the play the saxophone as if it were an amulet instead of a mere instrument. He was giddy to be on the road again, far from the *boates* and *cabarés* of the big cities, from clubs full of posers and petty formalities, stiff dress suits and cloying managers, with endless demands to play fashionable boleros and tacky *samba-canção*. Maybe train coaches were the ideal musical venue for Booker in his present state of mind. They gave him the chance to play and travel at the same time; they rolled his two favorite activities into one. And not just that. The sound of the train moving leisurely over the tracks, it occurred to the American, could *swing* better than any human drummer.[25] The Londrina-bound passengers may have paid train fare, but since they had not forked out a cover charge for this impromptu performance, they had low expectations: Booker could play anything he felt like. The collective evil eye soon vanished. Booker's solo and small-format performances almost always worked like that. First, he disarmed the audience, then he seduced them outright. The taciturn passengers had stopped speaking in hushed tones; they lowered their newspapers and put away their crochet needles and began to pay attention to the unexpected virtuosity of this strange and probably crazy man blowing his instrument in the aisle. Booker invited them to participate in the show, at first furtively, then openly. As if the pop-up performance was nothing out of the ordinary, Booker took requests, enthralling his mobile audience with a potpourri of sambas, blues, jazz, marchinhas, and other sonic surprises. The drunk, ecstatic foreigner and his Brazilian sidekick played with feeling, abandon—and as Booker wrote later—*with truth*. Playing truthfully never seemed to hurt.[26]

## TERRA NATAL

When he awoke still half-loaded in a strange house, Booker Pittman discovered that he was in Oklahoma. Or at least that is what his eyes told him. Walking through the streets and down the alleyways of Londrina, he observed that the earth of Paraná was the same chalky red hue as the rolling plains north of Dallas. The earthen dust left its pigmentation in everything: clothes, hair, his sax, even his money. And that was not the only thing about Londrina that reminded him of his native land. After lunch, Waltel took the American to a local boate that doubled as a gambling house. Badly hidden in the second story of the building, the illicit den reminded Booker of the nightclub where he first heard live jazz: the Tip-Top, in the Dallas neighborhood of Deep Ellum. Londrina's gambling joint was more

Texan than Texas itself. At the entrance of the *cabaré* there was a room full of weapons where the gamblers—the better part of them *fazendeiros* (farmers) in boots and oddly contoured cowboy hats—left their pistols while they threw away their money on the second floor.[27]

Booker's first impression was that he had landed in a place so exotic that it seemed vaguely familiar to him. In truth, Londrina in 1950 was a great deal more pastoral than Dallas, or at least the Dallas of the present. By the 1920s, Booker's hometown had been modernized to the extent that he saw fewer and fewer horses in the streets as he grew older and hardly any cows, though goats and chickens were not uncommon. Londrina in 1950 was a new city of just over 30,000 that, only two decades earlier, was a small village of several hundred, a mid-nineteenth-century version of Dallas.[28] Perhaps because of this, Booker was smitten by Londrina from the outset. It reminded him of a tropical version of the dusty frontier cities to the west and north of Fort Worth, where Big Pitt may have taken the family on day trips in his Model T in his younger, happier days, though it was more likely that his first encounter with the Paraná evoked an image of Texas that predated Booker's lived experience of the place, an image that he had likely gleaned from picture books and from the silent Westerns of Hoot Gibson, Tom Mix, and William Hart. The big difference was what drew people there. The rough-and-tumble pioneers of northern Paraná had struck it rich not with oil or gold but with coffee, as plantation owners, fueled by English capital, had savagely stripped the region of its native rainforest over the course of less than two decades. Londrina in 1950 was a city under construction, a half-finished boomtown.[29] With its mixture of new automobiles and old horse-driven carriages, men and women dressed immaculately in the latest fashions alongside grimy farmhands and mendicants, Londrina seemed like a city cycling through a century of progress in the space of a decade.

That very same night, Booker Pittman started blowing his alto sax in Londrina's gambling club. No doubt inspired by the Wild West atmosphere of the venue, the Texan's first number was "Pistol Packin' Mama."

> Oh, drinking beer in a cabaret
> Was I having fun
> Until one night she caught me right
> And now I'm on the run

Recently popularized by Bing Crosby and the Andrews Sisters, the song expressed a kind of urbane country irony that Booker, for some reason, found irresistible. To prepare his audience for the number, he used the curved neck of his saxophone to mimic the classic pose of the gunslinger. Ever since his time in Argentina, Booker had been cultivating a performance style that punctuated freewheeling technical flourishes with vaudeville humor. In truth, it was a return to the spirit of 1920s hot jazz when clowning, shouting, ambient noise, and instrumental novelties were commonplace. As a young lion in Kansas City and Harlem, he had had little patience for all the fashionably corny gags of the period. To his mind, they diluted the limpid essence of the music, the liquid core of it that he was always trying to tap into. But now, four decades into his life, he realized that he missed the tomfoolery, longed for the funny sounds and stories and the gimmickry, the humor of jazz.[30]

The success of "Pistol Packin' Mama" was immediate. How could it not have been? Suddenly before audiences stood a first-rate Black American saxophonist, dressed up like a Texas cowboy, singing hillbilly music as if he were some odd amalgamation of Louis Armstrong and Hank Williams. A provincial if ambitious backwater, Londrina was a more apt place than Buenos Aires, Rio de Janeiro, or São Paulo for Booker to practice his odd throwback approach to jazz. The city and the venue recalled Booker's fun-loving and ill-fated stint at the Hotel Casino Rivera several years earlier. Except Londrina was flusher with money than Rivera; Londrina was a frontier town, not to be confused with a border town. The city's casino-cabaré was cheaper and more informal than the pretentious São Paulo clubs Booker had run away from. The pay was nearly the same, but the Texan felt at home in the dark, vaguely dangerous room, with its small bevy of chorus girls overseen by a poker-faced owner. The loquacious customers regularly invited Booker to their table to sip good whiskey with them. If that was not tempting enough, the bar on the first floor was open but seemed only lightly frequented. It was a place where Booker could quietly collect his thoughts while downing pinga before his next set. All in all, the perfect spot for someone like Booker, who wanted little more than to drink and play in a place where nobody expected him to stay for long.[31]

## INFRA-EXILE

Londrina turned out to be the last outpost at the edge of another dangerous abyss. Booker's whereabouts grew especially nebulous between 1950 and 1953 and were not completely clear again until 1957.[32] It is likely that he stayed in and around Londrina for about a year and that, at a certain point, he abandoned the city. In any event, he did not go far. If Londrina already represented a place of exile within the larger escape pod of South America, his new home went one step further: it was an even deeper refuge, an infra-exile. The map of Booker's activities and escapades during these years was quite small. An eight-hundred-square-kilometer circuit of provincial towns, hamlets, and farms, his nomadic terrain was a relatively tiny piece of Brazil, a patchwork strung together by a loose network of friends, acquaintances, and small-time bosses. Booker's restlessness was typical of the time and place. Long neglected, the immediate inland regions of Brazil were increasingly attracting workers and families in search of land and opportunity, a trend that would continue for several decades. The northern half of Paraná and western portion of the state of São Paulo, with their fertile lands and booming coffee industry, were among the first regions to draw masses of skilled laborers from elsewhere in Brazil and overseas, later to be followed by the states of Goias and Mato Grosso, especially after the foundation of Brasília in 1960. By the time Booker arrived, growth and development in Paraná had reached fever pitch; upward of half of the state's residents were migrants.[33]

Yet, as an American musician struggling with addiction, Booker was no ordinary migrant. His first full stop in Paraná after Londrina was an abandoned *fazenda* outside the city where he fled to escape what had become his biggest vice once again since returning to Brazil: cachaça.[34] There he stayed for several months with his dog Tex, a stray that he had found (or who had found him) shortly after he arrived.[35] Booker cherished the peace and calm of his new abode, so remote from the perilous world of boates and casinos. It spoke to something deep inside him that he had long neglected, a proximity to the colors, smells, and cycles of the earth and to animals, whether wild, tame, or feral. When Booker was drinking, it would have been easy to convince himself that he did not need anything else besides what he already had. But when he was not, he must have realized he was too old to continue abusing alcohol but too young for retirement, and anyway, it was hard to feel like he had moved to paradise when he was hungry half the time.[36]

For a while, Booker survived in part by hunting and selling frogs and sometimes eating them.[37] As for his beloved cachaça, there was always a farmer, a laborer, a musician, or a musician's wife who took pity on the man giving late-night soliloquies in four convoluted languages from the depths of the barn or toolshed or servants' quarters he called home. With his skin color, accent, talent, and eccentricity, Booker became known in the region as the *baiano diferente*. The moniker was likely rooted in local demographic trends, as something like three-quarters of the migration to Paraná in the period came from the States to the south rather than from the generally darker-skinned laborers from the Brazilian Northeast, including Bahia.[38] In any event, as a Black American in rural Paraná, Booker certainly would have been a novelty, if a somewhat pathetic one. For his friends and sympathetic neighbors, it would have been hard not to ease Booker's pain with the same substance that they all knew was prolonging it. Better a "different" Bahian than a dead one, they must have figured.[39]

Booker's first rural repose may have given him some much-needed rest, but mostly all it accomplished was to make his addiction less visible to others. Eventually, desperate for cash, he began to work again, albeit in piecemeal fashion. He did not dare to go back to the big city or even to a big town like Londrina or the slightly larger Curitiba in coastal Paraná. Wary of the temptations that would find him there, he continued wandering from one small town to the next. He spent a few weeks in Rolândia until the owner of the cabaré where he performed was murdered. Next, he moved to Jacarezinho, having signed a contract in a boate there, until the woman who had hired him landed in jail.[40] He found more work in Marília, a boomtown in the state of São Paulo just across the border from Paraná, but the boate was soon shut down by the local police.[41] Booker was rarely picky when it came to paying his rent. He worked in almost any venue no matter how empty, squalid, or paltry. He must have seen a certain advantage in the very inconsequentiality of the provincial dives where he played, a secret weapon against the dullness that permeated the larger, better-paying venues. There was a comfort that came with plying his trade in the hinterlands of a remote country, at the margins of the margins.

The problem was money: Booker was desperately in need of it. Life in rural Paraná may have been dirt cheap, especially when he was not paying rent, but it was rarely free. And if he ever wanted to go back to the city, even a modest-sized one like Curitiba, Booker knew he needed cash to travel and establish himself once he arrived somewhere else. He began to accept other work besides long-term gigs in boates and cabarés. He did not limit himself to jazz. If he was called on to play marchinhas, he played marchinhas, and the same thing went for choros, sambas, mambos, and boleros; he even joined up with a marimba band for a spell. When opportunity knocked, he took work in religious processions, high school dances, wedding parties. For a brief time, he worked as a bandleader in one of the many circuses that toured the Brazilian hinterlands in the 1950s.[42] In other words, Booker accepted work from anyone in need of music and musicians and quickly found himself in the same position as before: dependent on the same venal, frivolous gigs that had driven him away from Rio de Janeiro and São Paulo to begin with.

Eventually, he settled in Cornélio Procópio, a small city folded into the verdant rolling hills of northern Paraná, a patch of concrete and exposed red earth amid long stretches of rainforest and coffee plantations. Hours away by train or car to Londrina or Curitiba, Cornélio Procópio was as good a place as any to get lost. It is not difficult to imagine how a typical day went.[43] Booker would likely have rolled out of bed late, his head dully throbbing, and reached for the bottle of cachaça that lay close at hand. Tex may have rustled when he awoke, growling ever so slightly. The dog knew his day had begun only after Booker wetted the reed with his tongue, fastened on the leather mouthpiece, and pushed a few notes out of his mottled saxophone. Perhaps the owner of the nightclub where he played happened to have an empty shack on his property where Booker slept off his long nights, and he would have known not to expect the musician for work until late morning at the earliest. The man did not pay the American just to blow his horn at the bar. In fact, he likely would not have paid him at all had Booker not also done odd jobs for him: feeding the chickens, scrubbing the floors, picking up groceries, painting houses.

Of these sundry tasks, the one Booker minded least was painting houses. This kind of labor did not require the same level of physical exertion that working on a coffee plantation did, and it lent him a sense of accomplishment once he was done; even the pungent fumes seemed to finish what the cheap alcohol had started. By midday, though, the sun began to make his job harder. The paint ran, the mosquitos bit. Booker reached inside his overalls and pulled from his flask, not so often that anyone would notice, but enough for him to make it until lunchtime. After eating a meal of leftovers, he changed into his night attire. His dusty yet elegant clothes were those of a drifter who had not always been one. When he played his alto saxophone at a small nightclub that doubled as a bordello, Booker imagined that the customers did not care what he looked like any more than they cared about the mold on the bathroom tiles or the stench of ammonia and baking soda rising from the concrete floors. The audiences were sparse, their expectations low: local fazendeiros and merchants having a few drinks after work, a smattering of businessmen from neighboring towns like Bandeirantes and Santo António da Platina, slipping upstairs with one of the young women (or men) when no one noticed.

What Booker liked most about this kind of bar was that he could play anything he wanted. Usually, it was cachaça that kept his head clear and warm and his lips wet, but in warmer weather, he would sometimes begin with cold beer to cut the heat. When he blew his horn, he imagined that he shook off a layer of exquisite sadness that seemed to envelop him whenever he drank. As usual, he turned most of the melodies that he remembered into blues tunes. It was simple with old standards like "St. Louis Blues" and "Summertime," less so with the Brazilian, French, and Argentine compositions he had gleaned from years spent in other climes, melodies like "La vie en rose," "É bom parar," "El día que me quieras," and "Aquarela do Brasil." Booker, though, had a way of making adaptations seem effortless and personal, even inevitable, remaking songs with grace and verve, making them his own.

## NECROLOGIO

Proper music gigs, though, were hard to come by in towns like Cornélio Procópio. The combination of the scarcity of work and Booker's tendency to spend what little money he had finally drove him to pawn his sax, likely more than once.[44] Bereft of his livelihood and off the grid, Booker fell into full radio silence for the first time since his hospital stay in Rivera, Uruguay. It was at this time the rumors first surfaced in Rio de Janeiro and São Paulo that the down-and-out virtuoso was sick and dying, or worse, that he had already died. The rumors were credible, just as they had been in Buenos Aires a decade earlier. Booker *was* sick; he *was* killing himself; in some sense, he *had* died. Regardless, it came as a great surprise to Booker Pittman to hear for himself the confirmation of his demise. The news came from a foreigner, a traveling French perfume salesman named Philippe Corcodel. Not just any businessman, Corcodel was a jazz enthusiast and amateur musician who had likely first heard Booker during their years together in Paris in the 1930s. One version of their fateful encounter, published years later in the Brazilian magazine *Cruzeiro*, was that Corcodel found Booker Pittman playing in the tiny red-light district of Santo Antônio da Platina, located ninety minutes east by car from Cornélio Procópio.

"You are not alive," Corcodel told him.

To make his case, the Frenchman showed Booker a recent obituary from the magazine *Manchete*.

"Boy oh boy," Booker responded, incredulous. "We need some sauce to celebrate."

Later that day, the story went, Booker put down his paintbrush and picked up his saxophone. A few musicians and a smattering of spectators began to gather in the same building that Booker had just painted. The musicians drank, played, drank some more, and performed what Booker later called a *jam-session de morte*.⁴⁵

According to another subsequent account, Corcodel discovered Booker in the bathroom of a hotel in Curitiba, though Booker admitted that it could well have been "any other drinking hole" in Paraná.⁴⁶ The scores of articles and interviews published years later inevitably passed through four unreliable filters: the rumors spread by physically distant friends and acquaintances, the sometimes fanciful imagination or carelessness of journalists of the period, Booker's occasionally precarious memory, and time itself. Even so, the most credible account of Booker Pittman's rediscovery can be found in two fragments of his memoirs. According to Booker, local acquaintances of his had spoken of him to Corcodel when he passed through Londrina. His interest piqued, the perfume salesman drove to Cornélio Procópio, where he found Booker in the city's even smaller red-light district around noon, painting the walls of a brothel.⁴⁷ After introducing himself in English, Corcodel showed him an issue of *Manchete* dated February 14, 1953, and asked the musician if he read Portuguese. "I do," Booker replied.

Actually, *Manchete* published two obituaries for the price of one. The first was written by Sérgio Porto, author of the first Brazilian history of jazz, a modest tome whose first edition was published that very year. Porto's account was rife with errors besides the central falsehood of Booker's death. It said, among other things, that Booker had grown up in Washington, DC, where he had "learned how to play and drink" and recounted Booker's long voyage to Brazil without mentioning that he had spent an entire decade in Argentina and Uruguay.⁴⁸ Also published in the fateful issue of *Manchete* was the account of the journalist and composer Fernando Lobo, father of the later-to-be-famous musician Edu Lobo. Lobo's piece was, at turns, more accurate and also more fanciful than Sérgio Porto's obituary. Lobo did manage to steer clear of biographical errors related to Booker's life in the United States. He also shared new information about Booker's latest stint in Rio de Janeiro, when Aloísio de Oliveira, a member of Carmen Miranda's venerable Bando da Lua and Miranda's one-time lover, allegedly remarked that "something was amiss with the saxophonist's body and soul." According to Lobo, Booker himself had asked the journalist not to write about him as if he were an American musician. He did not want news about him to reach the United States. "I would like to be from here," he said.

Yet Lobo's *crônica* ultimately consisted of more speculation than reporting. He said that he had heard of Booker's death from an "errand boy" who,

Lobo revealed later, was actually the musician's old friend Louis Cole.⁴⁹ The rest of the story, however poetically written, was pure conjecture:

> He is a Negro with his eyes shuttered, like the one we might see in the crime pages, a silent Negro, without a voice, without anything. Who was by his side when they came looking for him? Who knows? His own people were far away, marooned in a cotton plantation in Virginia or in one of those terrible tenement houses in Brooklyn or Harlem. The moment he closed his eyes for the last time, other musicians in other worlds played his instrument, as if they were black cherubs who instead of blowing their clarions played their trumpets and saxes with the tone of a funeral procession, but to the rhythm of jazz.⁵⁰

## POSTMORTEM

Black cherubs from Harlem notwithstanding, Booker was moved by the ardent evocations of his own passing. "I must say [the obituaries were] very neatly done," he wrote in his memoirs.⁵¹ In an interview published years after the episode, Booker gave a plausible but also suspicious explanation for the misunderstanding that led to the fake news of his death. In the countryside of Paraná, he said, they had found the body of a Bahian man who resembled the American physically and who also happened to play the saxophone. The newspapers and magazines took it from there.⁵² As for the legendary first encounter between Booker Pittman and Philippe Corcodel, most likely it happened weeks or even months before the publication of the twin obituaries in *Manchete*. Once he had been outed as a living person, Booker could not pass up the chance to poke fun at the credulity of his admirers, starting with the music critics. "What is this nonsense, my friends? I'm the one who drinks too much, but it's all of you who seem inebriated."⁵³

Booker's strange punishment for the ultimate falsehood was for him to be the object of more lies. In December of the same year, another article appeared in the pages of *Manchete*. The American, it was announced, had simply tired of life in the metropolis and was now happily married with three children, his "internationally-acclaimed [*sic*] sax pawned off for 600 cruzeiros."⁵⁴ While Booker had, in fact, sold off his sax, the bourgeois touch about fathering three children was a complete fabrication, this time aimed squarely at resurrecting his life instead of the contrary. His "marriage" to

"Boocker [sic] Pittman vivo, casado e pintando paredes" ("Booker Pittman alive, married, and painting houses"). *Manchete*, December 12, 1953, 4. Public domain/fair use.

María Fernández was, by all other evidence, firmly behind him. As Lúcio Rangel would later put it, Booker had, by this time, become a "perfect vagabond."[55] But whose lie was it, then, the musician's or the journalist's? Booker viewed most interviews partly as performances, and in this case, he seemed to be having fun with journalists who themselves often relied on fabrication whenever it suited them. But there was another more serious side to his subterfuge. Because he was often worried about his image, Booker did not want to be seen in his present state, least of all by people he knew in other climes: Rio de Janeiro, Buenos Aires, New York, Washington, Dallas. In either case, a photo shows the errant musician posing next to an empty birdcage, the bird escaped, his supposed family nowhere to be seen, and his lips puckered into a whistle as if he himself were a happy-go-lucky canary recently freed from captivity.

Typically, the popular tales and official biographies of jazz musicians are full of supposedly transformative narratives, according to which the artist abuses his body to a prodigious extreme until one fine day, suddenly, he pulls himself out of the gutter. And from that day forward, baptized by a miraculous experience or circumstance—sometimes aided by a close friend or relative—he rises up and slays the beast once and forever: the heroic triumph of the recovered addict. The truth, in most cases, is not so simple or so linear. In this sense, musicians and other celebrities are no different from other addicts who hit rock bottom eventually and inevitably, but then, almost invariably, they hit it again. They nosedive, they get up, they learn, they forget, they have relapses, they learn another lesson, they fall again. And so often, crumpled up in the abyss that they are supposed to crawl out of, they never rise up. They die there, and that is where their story ends.

Booker Pittman had the good fortune of dying a literary death instead of a literal one. But not even the news of his untimely death could end his suffering. Booker's rediscovery and resurrection in the final months of 1953 fell far short of rescuing him from his protracted state of hibernation. Part of the problem was that he *enjoyed* many aspects of his life in Paraná, or at least that is what he liked to tell people. In an interview with *Jet* magazine in the next decade, when asked exactly what he was doing all those years in the Brazilian hinterlands, Booker responded, "Drinking rum, living the good life, and playing and singing Brazilian folk music."[56] It was a line he fed several journalists in his later years. Clearly, though, the good life was not always so good to him. To pay off his debts and support his bad habits, Booker could not limit himself to painting houses or pawning his sax. He also labored in the coffee plantations in exchange for food, pinga, and a pittance. Usually, he had a roof over his head, but he moved frequently from shack to shack, farm to farm, with Tex his only constant companion. And so the one-time third best alto saxophonist in the world became a kind of super-vagrant, a foreign hobo or itinerant laborer who never seemed to get very far: half exposed, half hidden from view, never quite catching up to the train that would take him away from it all.

In later interviews and memoirs, Booker Pittman himself was either unwilling or unable to recall much about this period with any certainty or precision. When putting together their joint memoirs, Ofélia must have sensed that there were many holes in Booker's narrative of the Paraná years. To lend more cohesiveness to his story, she added a note (apparently based on her later discussions with her husband) in which she describes how an unnamed friend of Booker's invited him to stay at his family's *sítio*. Ofélia says the isolated farm lay a full three hours by car outside the town of Santo Antônio da Platina. Booker took with him his trusty Tex, two blankets, a big bottle of cachaça, and salt. Once they arrived at the farm, the young owner (Ofélia refers to him as a "rapaz," or boy) promptly went away for two months, telling a farmhand to keep an eye on Booker and giving the struggling musician access to all the potatoes, corn, and papaya that he could eat. It was not quite enough. Tex hunted down a chicken and dutifully brought it back to his keeper. It turned out that this was not allowed. The farmhand soon caught wind of Tex's innocent thievery and shot the dog dead.[57] Although Ofélia does not dwell on the subject, it must have been devastating for Booker to lose his steadiest companion at the time. The musician now found himself truly alone, caught in a downward spiral of alcoholism and malnourishment in as remote a place as he had ever seen. It must have seemed to Booker as though he had finally reached not just the nadir of human solitude but also the limits of errancy itself: *o fim da picada*, as Brazilians say, the end of the trail.

Years later, in a candid and insightful profile on Booker Pittman, the American observed how his Paraná phase had left its mark on him. And not just physically. Paraná, the story went, had left sunspots in the musician's *mind*, recesses and scars, gaps in his memory.[58] What the anonymous reporter described was trauma and its aftermath. But what was it about Paraná that captivated Booker for so long, that held him spellbound despite his misery, despite the punishment he doled out to himself under the guise of pleasure, leisure, and freedom? Maybe the similarities between Paraná and Texas or Oklahoma, so often drawn by the musician when he talked about the Brazilian hinterlands, were not just accidental. Maybe *this* was his trip home. Perhaps this earthen wild place riven by floods and droughts, greed and ambition, somehow stood for Texas in Booker's mind. Perhaps Paraná represented a home that he could experience by proxy, lose himself in, even, all without going to Dallas in person, without facing the familiar ghosts that still waited for him in the dives and alleys of Elm Street. A home without the echoes of Blind Lemon Jefferson, without the Tip-Top Club and the shoeshine stand. A home without his mother or his sister or his brother. A home without the Grand Temple of the Knights of Pythias, a building and a name he could not think about without also thinking about the grandiosity of his father and its flipside: his cruelty. A home without Big Pitt, though, for all he knew, his father was long dead by now. Even so, there was so much in Texas that Booker did and did not want to see again in person. The same was true for other key coordinates of his past: Kansas City, Harlem, Paris. But mostly it was Dallas that haunted his long delirium, his endless fever dream.

It was all too raw for him, too real for him, too etched with the sounds of the past, like a stack of old shellac records he no longer wanted or needed: heavy memories that weighed down his luggage. Booker felt ashamed. In his mind, he had not achieved nearly enough to earn the trip home, to expose himself to the full beauty and judgment of going back. But when he drank enough, he found that he could travel to these places inside himself, safely and cheaply. It was not so hard to do. When he filled his glass with booze and filled the air with "Black Snake Moan" and "St. Louis Blues," he found that he could slither back unannounced, under cover of pinga. To drink was not just to forget; to play was not just to play. Both meant traveling with a mask on. They were the quickest and most efficient ways to make a carnival of the return.

## DIXIELANDER

If Booker Pittman's resurrection happened at the end of 1953, it was not until two years later that his true comeback began. In the meantime, unbeknownst to Booker at first, a Dixieland and hot jazz revival was underway in São Paulo. Devotees were inspired by traditional jazz movements in Europe, the United States, and Japan. They read about Booker's peers—Louis Armstrong and Fats Waller, Count Basie and Bix Beiderbecke—in Brazilian publications such as the *Revista da Música Popular*, the first important venue for jazz writing in the country's history. In December 1955, a group of amateur musicians calling themselves the Paulistania Jazz Band caught wind of Booker's ghostly presence in Paraná, most likely from Philippe Corcodel. They sent word to invite Booker to play with them at a boate on the outskirts of the city, an event attended by an audience of roughly two dozen hot jazz aficionados and draped into the characteristic mist of the region, which lent the event the aura of film noir. Booker made his way back to the big city. "With an old clarinet, defective and kind of rusty," wrote the pianist Eduardo Vidossich, one of the players assembled for the occasion, Booker enthusiastically played tunes from his youth, mixing in a dash of bebop for good measure, and promised to make a definitive return to São Paulo.[59] Booker did not mind the smallness of the venue or the modesty of his bandmates' skills. "I haven't played with such an appetite in fifteen years," he told a reporter. He liked to play with amateurs because, though possessing inferior technique, they left him ample freedom to create in an atmosphere of "intimate and healthy happiness."[60]

When he returned to São Paulo in May 1956, Booker stayed at the house of the jazz sleuth Corcodel, joining Vidossich's amateurish but earnest orchestra made up of like-minded players, all of them devoted to the sacred cows of the Jazz Age. Now calling themselves the São Paulo Dixielanders,

Booker Pittman playing the clarinet. *Revista da Música Popular*, February 1955, 39. Public domain/fair use.

the band consisted mostly of immigrants and the sons of immigrants. Vidossich had arrived in Brazil only three years earlier from Switzerland and had already created a program devoted to hot jazz at the São Paulo station Rádio Nove de Julho.[61] The drummer Hank Wackwitz was born in Holland, the scion of a Jewish businessman who had fled to Brazil during World War II; later in life, Wackwitz would emigrate to the United States, retiring decades later to the north of Texas, near Dallas.[62] The trumpeter and arranger Masao Ukon, to whom Booker Pittman would remain closest throughout his later years, had recently arrived as a fully formed jazzbo from his native Japan, where he had led and recorded with an orchestra called the Dixieland Heartwarmers.[63] As for Corcodel, he became so immersed in the São Paulo Dixielanders that he began more and more to resemble a Brazilian jazz artist and not just a jazz-mad French perfume salesman. Seeing an opportunity, he taught himself the trombone, insinuated himself within the orchestra, and began referring to himself as Phil Phillipe.

Inspired by the almost miraculous arrival of a musician of Booker's stature exactly when they needed him, the São Paulo Dixielanders wasted little time in parlaying their good fortune into a creative and commercial leap. Led by Vidossich and Corcodel, they chased down work at social events, small concert venues, and boates, including a gig at the opening of the Ilha do Jazz (Jazz Island), so called because it was located on an artificial island in the middle of the lake at Parque Ibirapuera in the heart of the city.[64] In July 1956, the Dixielanders made a record with the idea of pulling together the funds necessary to buy Booker a new alto sax. But he still did not have one, so on the record he sings and plays his rusty clarinet on the two tracks: "Darktown Strutters' Ball" and "Bugle Call Rag."[65] The band cut only three hundred copies, reportedly all signed by Booker.[66] In a review of the record later in the year, *O Globo*'s critic Sílvio Túlio Cardoso, while acknowledging the considerable talent gap between Booker and his bandmates, praised the ensemble for its feeling and general sturdiness of ideas. Cardoso also rightly identified the group's 45 "as a pivotal foundational recording of the on-going [sic] jazz revival movement in Brazil."[67]

Midway through 1956, the São Paulo Dixielanders appeared on the local television channel Canal 7.[68] It was the first time Booker Pittman had appeared on the small screen, still something of a novelty in Brazil. Local radio stations of the time, meanwhile, found the band's retro sound not only passé but something worse: not commercial or current enough for the airwaves in the era of samba-canção, rock and roll, mambo, and bolero.[69] Nonetheless, a certain buzz surrounded the traditional jazz movement in São Paulo as long as Booker Pittman was part of the scene. The Dixielanders knew that local success would come sooner, though, if the band could raise its national profile. It was inevitable that the Dixielanders would take their show to Rio de Janeiro, and in November 1956, off they went. First, the orchestra popped in for a Dixieland and cool jazz jam session at the Rio de Janeiro Country Club.[70] On this same trip, Booker reconnected with his old friend Claude Austin in a televised jazz show at the Golden Room at the Copacabana Palace, an event promoted by the ascendant media giant Globo and attended by the likes of Dick Farney, Paulo Moura, and Fats Elpídio, with whom Booker had jammed upon his arrival to Brazil two decades earlier. The show drew a full house, and Booker was greeted with an unexpected homage rendered by the musicians and fans who had never forgotten the American, even if many thought he had died. Still under the influence of cachaça, the dragon he had never quite managed to slay, Booker's feeling of gratitude merged with the urges of a born-again showman. He was half-drunk and moved to tears; as one reporter wrote, "[H]e wept, shook his head, and then laughed in rhythm."

The afterglow of the Golden Room show lasted for some time. On his return to São Paulo, Booker played with the same unbridled enthusiasm for audiences there. At a show at the Caxingui nightclub, wrote Vidossich, Booker did not stop for so much as a second. In his solos, in his accompaniment, whether on the clarinet, on the sax, or singing, "this man with lungs of steel" bowled over everyone who had come to hear him. He played from nine at night to seven in the morning, at one point managing to play sax and clarinet at the same time.[71]

## FOLKLORE

Early in 1957, the São Paulo Dixielanders founded the Associação Brasileira de Amadores de Jazz e Folklore. The idea was to celebrate traditional jazz alongside analogous idioms: blues, spirituals, *samba de morro*, and so on. Booker Pittman already felt at home playing samba. In fact, according to Vidossich, the famed sambistas from the Morro da Tijuca neighborhood remarked that Booker was the only *gringo* who knew how to play samba the right way.[72] But even if he now aspired to be a Brazilian musician, Booker never limited himself to Brazilian music. Perhaps tainted by the purism of the Dixielanders, he criticized rock and roll as a mere adulteration of boogie-woogie, which had emerged decades earlier. Alongside the *Paulista* banjo player Dudu (Francisco Eduardo de Souza Pereira), Booker played a concert dedicated to American Negro spirituals.[73]

Soon enough, though, the American's old anti-commercial reflex came into conflict with his weakness for sheer entertainment, not to mention his taste for the high life. For this reason, Dizzy Gillespie's visit to Brazil in July 1956 was especially transformative. The famous trumpeter brought with him the modern, uncompromising style of bebop mixed with an unwavering showmanship that recalled an earlier era, that of Fats Waller, Cab Calloway, and a young Louis Armstrong. Dizzy's traveling spectacle was, in other words, simultaneously young and old, complex and formulaic. One journalist, writing in *Revista da Música Popular*, bemoaned the fact that someone of Gillespie's talent and innovation resorted to "circus feats" and "pointless noise" in order to satisfy Brazilian live audiences.[74]

The Dixielanders were split in their assessment of Dizzy Gillespie. He may have been the summit of popular vanguardism, but the effusive bebopper flummoxed diehard revivalists like Vidossich. Conversely, the didactic fundamentalism of the São Paulo Dixielanders puzzled Booker. Above all, Booker wanted an audience and yearned to entertain and inspire more than teach. In Dizzy, he likely saw something of himself, or at least how he imagined himself. What was more, Booker realized that *he* was the flavor of the month, not a group of throwback amateurs, as endearing and sincere as they may have been. When creative differences and squabbles arose between members of São Paulo Dixielanders, Booker Pittman lost his patience and left the group without saying a proper goodbye. In the short term, Booker fell into the hands of the city's predatory empresários, seduced by the prospect of steady work at São Paulo's swankiest clubs. Vidossich and Corcodel understandably felt betrayed by Booker's sudden departure. Being the eldest members of the orchestra, they saw themselves as the protectors of the younger musicians who, during the depths of Booker's misery, had taken him in with open, reverent arms and served as his "launching pad for new glories."[75]

But if escape was one of Booker's most consistent impulses, striking it rich never was. Ever since his most recent triumph in Rio, Booker felt confident that the sun still had not set on his career. He sensed the time was ripe for one last comeback. But he also worried—correctly, it turned out—that he lacked the sobriety to seize the moment. In his aching bones, he once again felt the curative womblike pull of the countryside. Or maybe it was the opposite. Maybe what he felt was an ailing cat's instinct to slink out into the woods to die. In either case, while playing at a basement club located in a button factory on Rua Frei Caneca in the São Paulo neighborhood of Consolação, Booker resolved to travel back one last time to Santo Antônio da Platina. He had left hastily the last time, and he now missed the people and the familiar landscape of Paraná.[76] If he had not bid farewell to the Dixielanders as he should have, at least he could show more grace and gratitude to the hospitable *paranaenses* with whom, after all, he had spent a great deal more time. When he finally did return, with all the press and radio exposure he had received in São Paulo, Booker was greeted as a homegrown hero in Santo Antônio. Suddenly, as if by magic, he was no longer the musical novelty act or the amusing barfly, the painter of bordellos or the field hand, the frog hunter or the weird, wayfaring *baiano*. Now, he was the Great Booker, the masterful Booker, *seu Buca*, and he had begun his rebirth only after having been buried alive in the red earth of the Brazilian hinterlands.

## AIRPORT DIVE

More than flattering him, the celebrity treatment Booker received in Paraná made him feel that maybe he had not wasted all those years after all. But it also tightened the pressure for him to stay on the path toward success. Perhaps because of this, when he returned to São Paulo, Booker took what may have been his deepest dive of all. By now, he could not deny that his long bucolic pause had not solved his drinking problem. If anything, his years of infra-exile had made his addiction worse, and he needed to solve it now—it was too big of a problem to keep putting off. If he did not, he simply could not continue playing at music venues that revolved around the consumption of alcohol, which was most of them. The problem was just that simple, and at the same time, it was devilishly complex. The need to remove alcohol from his bloodstream and his life, forever, had more urgency now that he had the prospect of acclaim in his sights for the first time in years. But this was also what made his quest for sobriety so difficult.

To scrape together some money while he tried desperately to pull himself together, Booker took a gig at a bar near the airport, returning each morning to sleep at Corcodel's house. Instead of weaning himself off booze as planned, though, Booker did the exact opposite, poisoning himself almost methodically, day and night. At the airport dive, he drank pinga with no restraint whatsoever. Just as in the worst days of Rivera and Santana do Livramento prior to his hospitalization, the musician found himself in chemical freefall. His playing became erratic again, with more bellowing and ranting and spitting than blowing. When he managed to stay awake on stage, Booker began to experience hallucinations, which likely led to tics and antics that went far beyond the eccentricities that crowds had grown to expect from him. He was deeply unwell.[77] Perhaps slow or reluctant to recognize the seriousness of the American musician's struggle, the empresário Jordão de Magalhães began to take an interest in Booker since his return from Paraná. Then, one night in August 1957, to his shock and horror, Jordão discovered the musician at death's door. He drove the American from the airport bar directly to a hospital, where the attending physician told Booker Pittman he had exactly fifteen days to live.[78] More than a death sentence, the doctor's words echoed and amplified what had already been rattling around in Booker's addled mind for some time. Maybe he just needed to put himself in a position to hear them from someone else, and now, finally, here they were: the cold, dispassionate words of a stranger, echoing down to the bottom of the well.

*Chapter Six*

# THE REVIVALIST

That's why there was this music in them; music was all they had to forget with. Or they could use it for a way of remembering that was as good as forgetting, a way that was another kind of forgetting.

—SIDNEY BECHET, *TREAT IT GENTLE: AN AUTOBIOGRAPHY*

THE INAUGURATION OF THE NEW, RECONSTITUTED BOOKER T. PITTMAN took place at a club in central São Paulo called The Cave, Jordão de Guimarães's latest confection, on September 6, 1957. The band was a far cry from the Dixielanders. The stylish quartet made up of alto sax, piano, bass, and the electric guitar of Baby Santiago bedazzled the audience with tinges of rock and roll, shades of cool jazz, and hints of samba, all under the hot sign of Booker. The opening show was not just well attended; it was a media event promoted, filmed, and photographed—according to one journalist—like no other boate opening in the history of São Paulo. Even celebrities showed up: the singer Sílvio Caldas, at one point, jumped on stage and crooned with the band.[1] Booker had played with countless stars in his casino days of the 1930s and 1940s. The same was not true anymore, though what distinguished the 1957 Cave shows from prior Booker Pittman comebacks was the musician's sobriety. The sheer length of the American's season of inebriation had begun to tarnish one of his main strengths: his technique. Once out of the hospital, his beaten-down body slowly recovered, and as it did, the blood returned to his cold fingers, warmed his numb lips. If saxophones could slur, his had been slurring for years; he knew because he had never lost his ear. Back with his full arsenal of blue notes and obbligatos and arpeggios, basking in the rapt gaze of the crowd, there must have been moments when Booker hardly noticed that he was playing raw for the first time in a decade.

## SATCHMO, THE MATCHMAKER

Far from being isolated events, the Louis Armstrong concerts of November 1957 were part of a coordinated Cold War strategy on the part of the US State Department to counter the Soviet Union's longstanding criticism of what the communist superpower saw as the fundamental hypocrisy of the United States' rhetoric of freedom and democracy when Black Americans were still fighting for their basic civil rights at home. What better way to blunt the Soviet Union's attacks, Dwight Eisenhower's administration reasoned, than by showcasing abroad the towering figures of the nation's most famous musical export while also building cultural bridges in what were widely viewed as vulnerable populations in Africa and Southeast Asia? While less urgent attention was paid to Latin America since the defeat of fascism in World War II, an abiding paternalism in Washington implied that the region's leaders were either "pawns or potential pawns of the Soviets."[2]

In some ways, Armstrong's jazz tour was the opposite of Booker Pittman's long tenure in South America. Whereas Booker had insinuated himself slowly and painstakingly into various local music scenes in Argentina, Uruguay, and Brazil, winning over fans and critics night by night, club by club, barely scratching out a living and sometimes disappearing altogether, Armstrong's tour was a flash conquest and celebrity spectacle condensed into weeks instead of decades. The watershed encounter between Satchmo and his old acquaintance was no accident. Jordão de Magalhães was not the main force behind bringing Louis Armstrong to São Paulo—that work fell mostly to rival empresários Dante Viggiani and Paulo Machado de Carvalho Filho, from Rádio and TV Record.[3] But the supposedly chance meeting between Booker and Satchmo, announced in the newspapers as early as October, was meticulously prearranged by Magalhães in coordination with the tour's promoters. Frequently touted in newspapers as Booker's savior and resuscitator, Magalhães was now his go-between as well. Looking beyond the reunification, he even speculated whether Satchmo might end up whisking Booker away and taking him back to the United States at the conclusion of the tour.

The event did not quite go as planned. After a delayed arrival from Montevideo, Armstrong was visibly fatigued as he emerged from the airplane at Congonhas Airport. He was met on the tarmac by an ecstatic but pushy throng of admirers and reporters and an equally jumpy police force. With the help of his wife Lucille, the American legend was trying his best to field questions from reporters when an overly zealous cop inadvertently

CHAPTER SIX: THE REVIVALIST    133

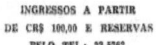

Newspaper advertisement for Louis Armstrong's shows at São Paulo's Paramount Theater. *O Estado de São Paulo*. November 17, 1957. Public domain/fair use.

knocked a microphone into the musician's face, reinjuring his lower lip and abruptly putting an end to the press conference. The accident cast a pall over his entire visit to the city.[4] It was as if everyone knew Satchmo's weak spot. And perhaps they did. A photo emerged from the Argentina mayhem of the American donning a catcher's mask to protect his chops from rapacious fans. Armstrong later admitted in an interview that he was superstitious about his lips; if they were injured in any way, he feared that even greater calamity would befall him. In any event, captured by *Life* magazine and reprinted elsewhere, the catcher's mask image comically evoked the game of baseball for many American fans.[5] Never mind that for Brazilians, particularly older Afro Brazilians born under bondage (slavery was not abolished until 1888), Satchmo's look held another connotation entirely: the disciplinary masks often imposed on errant enslaved persons.[6]

Irked by the injury more than the chaos, Armstrong either did not notice or did not recognize an ebullient Booker Pittman who yelled out "Pops!" the minute his friend emerged from the Varig jetliner.[7] Even farther from earshot, the São Paulo Dixielanders, recently reunited with Booker, played their revivalist hearts out. It was a sweet and apparently ignored tribute to the brand of music Satchmo had helped to invent. Armstrong later claimed that he had noticed Booker and the band, but the nervous policemen entrusted with his protection violently controlled his every movement.[8]

In any event, why should Armstrong have been expected to play his part in this half-manufactured media event gone awry? Jordão de Magalhães wanted to make believe that Satchmo and Booker were somehow equals, that he had staged the long-awaited Pan-American summit of two jazz titans. But even if the reunion had gone as planned, the empresário's assumption of symmetry between the musicians was simply untrue. The years of artificially built-up aura, mostly by Brazilian music journalists, with their persistent obligatory references to Hugues Panassié's outdated ranking of the world's greatest alto saxophonists, suddenly yielded to brutal reality: whereas, in November 1957, Louis Armstrong was still Louis Armstrong, Booker was at best an obscure virtuoso, virtually forgotten outside of a clutch of writers and aficionados in a handful of South American cities and friends and family in Europe and North America with long memories, starting of course with his mother and siblings.

A few days later, when the two Americans finally met again face-to-face, Armstrong was effusive in his praise of Booker. When a reporter asked him if he remembered Booker, Armstrong replied, "Do you think I could forget the face of one of the greatest alto saxophonists I've heard in my whole life?"[9] A photo of the two published in *O Cruzeiro* seemed to confirm that Armstrong was sincerely moved by this second encounter, and no doubt he admired Booker's enduring talent. But there was also something calculated about his praise, something that smacked of gracious hyperbole. Satchmo's words were likely a sign of pragmatism more than a candid assessment of Booker's current stature as a musician. Although Armstrong saw that Booker Pittman was a *local* treasure more than anything else, he cleverly gleaned from the Brazilian press corps that his best way of praising the adopted native son was to pitch his transcendence as a jazz artist of global stature.

Of course, when Armstrong invited Booker to jam with the All Stars, Booker obliged. How could he or anyone else refuse? It was not as though he were Armstrong's equal. What Booker Pittman had done the last two decades in South America paled in comparison to what Satchmo achieved in three days and nights in São Paulo. The celebrity aura of the All Stars' tour, which included a meeting with Brazilian President Kubitschek, made a mockery of Booker's countless boate performances and bordello jams, casino contracts, and society gigs over the years. Armstrong possessed peerless gravitas and, though nine years Booker's senior, a still admirable tone and technique on the trumpet. It did not help that Booker had been singing more and more as of late and that his painfully hoarse voice sounded like a worn-out version of Satchmo's.

Despite all this, the fateful Paramount show allowed the Texan expat to briefly upstage the King of Jazz and shine on an international stage for the first time in decades. It also introduced him to his future wife. When Ofélia Leite de Barros had read about Booker Pittman in *O Cruzeiro* months earlier, she began to ask herself whether the fortune teller from the São Paulo neighborhood of São Judas might have been right after all. Ofélia was a skeptic when it came to soothsayers and *macumba* (black magic). But just maybe, she thought, this elegant musician was the foreigner whom the fortune teller foresaw in her cards. The foreigner who would pull her out of economic hardship and let her see the world. The foreigner who would make her happy. A thirty-five-year-old seamstress semi-separated from her husband Orlando, Ofélia needed something new in her life, but she was not sure what. One thing she knew about herself was that she was not lacking in intelligence, much less *garra*, nerve. She asked Orlando to come with her to the last Louis Armstrong show at the Paramount. "Take your mother," he said. "Because I'm not going."[10]

Ofélia did go with her mother and brought her nine-year-old daughter Eliana, too. During the show, it struck Ofélia as odd that she could feel nervous for someone whom she had never met. "Would he be ready for the spotlight?" she found herself wondering, almost fretfully. "Would he feel behind the times after all these years out of contact, off the map?" That was the first sign of something serious on the horizon: that she cared about someone so unnecessarily and so precociously.[11] And then in the dressing room, after the show, she knew. While Satchmo was being mobbed by journalists and autograph-seekers, Booker stood off to the side in a white flannel blazer and black pants, suddenly diffident and unassuming, intimidated in a way that he had not been on stage.

"I came to talk to *you*," Ofélia said, looking him straight in the eyes, dead serious. "I know your whole story. I'm a fan."[12]

Booker was incredulous and also a little circumspect. What did this person want from him? At first, he pretended he did not understand Portuguese; this trick sometimes worked whenever he felt shy or out of sorts.

But then he began to wonder who this woman was, this audacious fan who did not fit the profile of club groupie or society floozy. And anyway, he thought, what kind of woman comes onto a man in the presence of her mother and daughter? She had to be either insane or insanely bold.

"So where are you hiding out?" Ofélia asked. At The Cave, Booker told her. She did not know where that was, she said. She did not frequent the nightclubs.

"Near the Church of Nossa Senhora da Consolação," Booker said, as if to compensate for the dubious reputation of The Cave or any other boate.[13]

## THE PURSUIT

Even all those years when pinga swam in his veins so thick his body ached from the poison, Booker's strange wariness of women abided. He did not know why exactly. Some of his friends saw in the sentiment the telltale sign of a confirmed *mulherengo*, a womanizer. Why settle down with someone when he still had the magic touch with women? His charming demeanor had mellowed elegantly with age, and now that his head was clear and his pockets occasionally flush with cash again, he surely could have milked the bachelor's life for a few more years. Secretly, Booker feared that if he let someone in too close, he might be tempted to let them stay, and if they stayed, they might never leave; and that once he had gotten used to their company, he would fear the solitude as much as he had once feared captivity. If time had dulled this old reflex of his, he did question (especially *now*, as he fought hard to stay dry) what good the reflex had done for him all these years. He began to wonder whether his instinct to stay alone and independent, which he had always jealously protected, was actually a treacherous impulse, an emotional malfunction as grave as his instinct to drink.[14]

In November 1957, Ofélia encountered a different Booker Pittman from the one she would have known if she had met him even a few weeks earlier. The new Booker was still evasive, but he was also trying on sobriety for size, and this turned his evasiveness a different color than ever before. One night in early December, he and Ofélia agreed to meet at the movies. Booker did not show up. Later, he invented a cover story that was in itself revealing. He told her he did not trust himself with money, so he had his friend Toti's wife hide it from him. Since he could not find her that day, he had stayed home rather than leaving the apartment empty-handed.[15]

The explanation did not fool Ofélia. Booker's problem clearly went beyond money. Everyone said his playing was fine, the best he had sounded in years. But off-stage, he was unsure of himself to the point of panic. As Ofélia would later recall, he was "unable to go outdoors unless someone held his hand." Fortunately for Booker, Ofélia was only too happy to play this role. They began meeting at the Riviera Bar, at the Corner of Avenida Paulista and Consolação, where Ofélia sipped martinis and Booker drank Coca-Cola. They listened to Nat King Cole's songs on the jukebox so many times that the owner finally gave them one of his records as a present, perhaps out of generosity or maybe so he would not have to hear the tune ever again. The couple stuck to a strict routine. Just before nine o'clock, Booker would kiss her dryly on the lips, and Ofélia would take a cab home. On the nights when he worked, Booker would catch a bus or walk down Avenida Conceição past the cemetery to his boate near the church.

For a few months, it went on like this, sweetly, ritualistically, almost like courtly love. Ofélia was smitten by Booker's gentleness. But this same gentleness made her perplexed and impatient. *Puxa*, she thought, was it ever going to happen? So she made it happen. Booker was slowly putting the loose parts of life back together. As someone who was starting over, the banal routines of daily life meant everything: folding socks, chatting with the custodian about *futebol*, taking in the sun on a park bench. For now, Booker was content to be living, breathing, blowing his sax, and strolling the avenues and streets of São Paulo. Not that he didn't enjoy his regular rendezvous with Ofélia. He appreciated her quick mind and her expressive eyes, her roughhewn vitality, and especially her unwavering belief in herself and in him, the new him. They talked about their childhoods, including even the stories they had half forgotten.[16] Left to his own designs, Booker, she felt, might remain in this pleasant stasis indefinitely until, suddenly scared blind, one day he might stop coming to the Riviera and stop playing at The Cave, and he would be nowhere to be found. Suddenly, he would be in Paraná again, or Rio, or Buenos Aires. She knew this in her bones because she already knew him or thought she did. Sensing her window may be closing, seizing the initiative as always, Ofélia invited Booker to carnival in Jundiaí, a small town between São Paulo and Campinas, next to a deep green sliver of virgin rainforest, ideal for strolling and sometimes more than strolling. He said yes.

On the morning of the outing, both were apprehensive. Ofélia was nervous that nothing would happen and nervous that Booker would not have the money to pay for their hotel. But something did happen, almost in the blink of an eye. "It was not an overwhelming passion, that kind that makes you lose your senses," Ofélia wrote later. "It was about the calm and security that I needed and never had, the certainty that I would never be betrayed." Her second fear turned out to be unfounded, too. When Booker slipped into the bathroom after their first night together, Ofélia frisked his clothes and found sixty cruzeiros, more than enough to cover the cost of their secret honeymoon.[17]

## ON RECORD

Booker did not run away with the All Stars, as most people expected, as though it were preordained. In fact, he did not even join Louis Armstrong's orchestra for their swing through Rio de Janeiro, probably because Armstrong did not invite him. But there was also Ofélia to take into consideration and the fact that Booker suddenly had too many commitments in São Paulo. He was now a star in his own right within the still small-time world of *paulista* popular entertainment, the Satchmo of Sampa. Besides his nightly gigs at The Cave, Booker frequently performed live on TV Tupi. He even made one cameo appearance on the silver screen, playing a brief solo on the alto for Anselmo Duarte's comedy *Absolutamente certo*. In the space of a few months, he had become not just a nightclub and media phenom but also something of a local expat curiosity for visitors. Touring bands like The Platters and Bill Haley and the Comets, tipped off by local promoters, regularly paid homage to Booker at The Cave.[18] He shared the boate stage with a number of artists, including the singer Maysa, whose star had begun to rise in São Paulo.[19]

Booker stayed at The Cave for a few months, finally tempted by a higher offer at a rival nightclub called Michel. Before he left The Cave, though, Booker paired up artistically with another Jordão de Magalhães discovery, Morgana, recording a B-side with the young vocalist, "Let's Fall in Love." The 45 shows Booker in top form on a new instrument for him, the soprano saxophone. Given the suppleness of his technique and the confidence of his tone, it is no wonder he would stick with the soprano—without giving up the alto entirely—for much of the rest of his life. The new instrument allowed him to bridge the melodic range of the alto and the clarinet in a way that appeared seamless, giving voice to the higher-pitched runs and jumps he had always heard in his mind. The record also hints at coming limitations. The warble in Morgana's voice, combined with the poor technical production of the recording and the superannuated sound of Booker's soprano, and especially his Satchmo vocal stylings, lends the record an almost uncannily throwback feel.[20]

*Booker Pittman Plays Again*, RCA Victor, 1959. Fair use.

This was not quite the case with the RCA Victor long play that followed in the footsteps of the Copacabana sides. Recorded in the quartet format, *Booker Pittman Plays Again* was Booker's debut long-playing record as a featured musician. The LP does not sound modern, or at least not what critics and listeners meant by "modern" in the late 1950s. Yet Booker's technically sound backing musicians—the drummer Paulinho, the bassist Luis Marinho, and most notably, Fats Elpídio on piano—lend the record a breezy, bluesy feel that sounds something like the 1950s small-format recordings of Booker's erstwhile contemporaries Johnny Hodges and Budd Johnson. Despite its use of local musicians, *Plays Again* makes no attempt to include Brazilian compositions, rhythms, or instrumentation. It is, rather, a traditional American jazz record made in Brazil.

On the album cover, Booker stares daringly into the camera while he blows on the alto, resting his right foot on a stool on which a soprano sax lies: a pose of vitality and sobriety and a promise of musical versatility. The album's liner notes from three prominent South American jazz critics—Jorge Guinle, Lúcio Rangel (a highly respected Brazilian gatekeeper of popular music at the time), and the Argentine Néstor Ortiz Oderigo—strenuously make the case for Booker Pittman's induction into the jazz canon. The tactic of consecration most often employed by music journalists of the time was citation, building their arguments on the words of earlier kingmakers like Hugues Panassié. Guinle, Rangel, and Oderigo chose to draw connections between Booker's upbringing and foundational experience in Kansas City and Harlem with the formal virtues and innovations of his playing. Guinle acknowledged the debt Booker owed Armstrong, Bechet, and Waller. But he singled out the Texan's blues pedigree and credited it to his early personal encounters with Blind Lemon Jefferson and Ma Rainey. "In his instrumental solos," Guinle wrote, "[Booker] uses anticipations, lags, and dynamic nuances in his phrasing to produce a kind of trance that reminds one of the black protestant [sic] preachers from the American South, where he comes from."[21]

*Booker Pittman Plays Again* as a musical statement is not a manifesto or even a christening of an innovative new arrival onto the jazz scene. It does not pretend to break new ground. Rather, it is something like a former castaway's proof of survival, a sobriety test, and also a purity test. Like the commentary of Guinle and Ortiz Oderigo, the album makes an oblique statement about the past, an insinuation that musical history was incomplete without Booker Pittman in it, that it was remiss; that the jazz world had overlooked Booker because it never thought to look for him in a global outpost like Brazil. If, in its soft-spoken way, *Booker Pittman Plays Again* stands as a plea for critical reparations, it also doubles as a showcase for the American's formidable range of talents. Rising to the occasion, Booker performs confidently throughout, alternating almost imperceptibly between alto and soprano. Of the album's twelve tracks, almost all are American standards: "St. James Infirmary," "Oh, Lady be Good," "Sweet Georgia Brown," "All of Me." The warhorse "St. Louis Blues" fittingly opens the record just as it had inaugurated Booker's life in jazz as a teenage clarinetist in Dallas three decades before. Booker's soprano solo captures something of the fire of the 1920s, all done with a slight Bechet-style warble, though he seems to be holding back from the propelling lilt of his famous live performances. By contrast, his solo on "Darktown Strutters' Ball" summons Booker's slightly later hot-swing style perfected in the nightclubs of Paris and Buenos Aires, unleashing lacerating stop-and-go runs that never spin out of control, even as they constantly threaten to.

Perhaps the record's most interesting track is the sole original, "Blueing with Booker and Elpídio." Since their first meeting in Recife in 1935, Booker had likely jammed with Fats Elpídio on several occasions. The Pernambuco native's experience and stature as one of his country's most swinging pianists made him an attractive partner for the *Plays Again* sessions. Not only was he an excellent accompanist, but when asked, he could improvise capably in the hot style that Booker preferred, and he knew his songbook top to bottom. "Blueing with Booker and Elpídio" is playful, sassy, full of fat blue notes on the soprano grounded by Elpídio's measured, feathery striding on the piano. It features vocal references to places where Booker had lived over the years—Texas, Oklahoma, Kansas City, São Paulo, Copacabana—the closest the record gets to an autobiography.

*Plays Again*'s other tracks are most effective when Booker resists the temptation, fast becoming a reflex, to mimic Louis Armstrong's signature singing style. His rendition of "My Melancholy Baby" evokes fragility and understatement, for instance, and "Summertime" likewise benefits from a less-is-more approach that becomes George Gershwin's lyrics. Still, a pattern that would plague Booker's subsequent records emerges. Ostensibly providing a rough counterpoint to the bell-like clarity and adroit vitality of his sax lines, the record's vocal tracks end up as awkward translations of the same strategies that had generally worked well on the stages of Brazilian boates. In person, Booker's vocal stylings denoted authenticity, a passable simulacrum of Satchmo thousands of miles from New York and New Orleans. On vinyl, they amounted to charming but derivative redundancy.

## THE FUGITIVES

Still, the *Plays Again* recording sessions gave Booker Pittman a much-needed shot of confidence. Perhaps now, he thought, he would not have to depend so heavily on club contracts. As was the case with the Dixielanders, Booker left The Cave without warning. And like Eduardo Vidossich before him, Magalhães naturally took offense, telling anyone who would listen that he had saved Booker's life and rekindled his career, not to mention bought him the alto sax with which he was winning over audiences and critics alike. Could it be that one of small-market celebrity's fringe benefits was that it allowed Booker to act like a big-market celebrity—the late arrivals, the no-shows, the sudden vanishings—without the burden of moral hangovers or the fear of lasting consequences? Perhaps, although in a newspaper interview while still in São Paulo, Louis Armstrong himself revealed that Booker could have stayed with Armstrong's Paris-based orchestra in the mid-1930s but had simply decided not to: "He left us, and we didn't know why."[22]

Booker might have been the Harry Houdini of South American jazz performers, but he did not vanish on Ofélia. Ofélia would not let him, for starters. She knew how to thread herself into his life in ways that would make easy escape difficult. One way was to become his personal manager. Another way was her daughter Eliana, who was just as forceful as her mother and, as it would turn out, just as musically inclined as Booker. Ofélia had a sense that they might take to one another, knowing the personalities of each. Still, how was she supposed to convince Booker to take the giant leap of moving in together and becoming Eliana's stepfather all at once? Having been married before, Booker was susceptible to monogamy even while it terrified him. His relationship with María had introduced him to stepparenting, at least to a degree. But he had little interest in *creating* a family, let alone supporting one. Ofélia knew that she needed to get Eliana and Booker in the same room to see if their arrangement would work. So, one Sunday, Ofélia, Booker, and Eliana walked to the movies together. Afterward, they stopped by a pizzeria on Rua da Conceição. At a certain point, Booker turned away to chat with the waiter. Ofélia saw her chance. Lowering her voice, she asked her daughter what she thought of Booker.

Eliana pondered the question for a brief moment, then she said, "Let's give it a try."[23]

There was another complication. Ofélia still lived in Orlando's house, and they were still legally married, *casados* if no longer a *casal* (a couple).[24] For a time, Ofélia worked around the problem by keeping Booker a secret. After spending her evenings with him, for appearances and for Eliana's sake, she would come back to the house on Rua Santa Cruz in Vila Mariana every night at 10 p.m. Even so, whispers of her separation from Orlando reverberated throughout the neighborhood. Not only did the charade grow tiresome, but it was also hurting her livelihood. Her customers sought her services less frequently, or they stopped coming entirely. Even if Brazilian laws and mores in the 1950s prevented her from seeking a divorce, Ofélia was determined to end her marriage to Orlando in every other way.[25] On Good Friday 1958, as though part of the Easter procession, Ofélia and Booker strolled openly along the Largo do Paissandu in the heart of the city, Ofélia's arm slipped 'round the American's bony waist. The performance achieved its desired effect immediately. Neighbors and acquaintances who happened to be there watched the new couple closely and gossiped loudly. By the time Ofélia got home later that night, word of the spectacle had already reached Orlando, even if nobody knew who Booker was. Orlando grew furious. He burst into the apartment and demanded that Ofélia and Eliana move out immediately. Both mother and daughter were terrified.[26] But then it dawned on Ofélia: this might be just what she needed, a chance to make a clean break with Orlando and get Booker to commit to a new life with her in one fell swoop. Orlando did not know it, but he was doing her a favor. It was Booker she wanted. How could he possibly refuse her now?

## THE DIRTY AXE

He could not. The three of them found a very small two-bedroom apartment in Bosque da Saúde, a neighborhood somewhat removed from the city center. And here their new, more insular life began, with Booker playing late nights and early mornings as before, returning home around the time Ofélia would wake up. While her new husband slept, Ofélia would see customers in her bathroom, since the living room was too small. Booker was determined to be discreet, to keep up at least the appearance of propriety. He kept his distance from the handful of Ofélia's friends who dropped by on a regular basis and made sure never to let Eliana see the two of them together in the twin-sized bed they shared. Ofélia was puzzled by Booker's wish to be an invisible companion. It was almost as if he were trying to convince himself that their love was still illicit. But either way, she found his chivalry and discretion captivating, and she wanted to return the favor somehow.

One day, Ofélia decided that Booker's sax was altogether too dirty and proceeded to scrub it with soap and water until the brass gleamed like new. Booker went into a quiet panic. Before his gig at a boate that night, he spent several hours scrambling to get the ruined keys replaced, testing the tone repeatedly until he could be sure it sounded and felt like the same old instrument, even if it did not look like it. The next day, he told Ofélia, "I'm not angry with you, because I know you didn't do what you did in bad faith, that you were only trying to help. But you must understand something. The dirtier the sax, the better the sound."[27]

Little by little, Booker realized that he needed Ofélia and Eliana, truly needed them. Once he gave in to this feeling, he found he wanted to spend as much time with them as possible and missed them when they were not home together. Even on weekends and late nights when, as a married male musician in mid-century Brazil, Booker had a moral license to poetic solitude and bohemian selfishness, he often opted to stay home. It was as though without knowing it, he had exhausted his urge to be undomestic; to haunt bars and boates long after he had stopped playing; to wander the streets with impunity.

By now, he knew only too well what clinging to bachelorhood had brought him. Not only was he happy staying home watching television, blowing his sax softly, teaching Eliana, making love to Ofélia. He also began to lean on Ofélia to resolve conflicts, to negotiate contractual terms, to stand up to discrimination and abuse in the workplace. The outside world, now that he had to face it while sober, terrified Booker, so he avoided it whenever possible. Ofélia haggled with empresários for higher pay, and she put an end to her husband's pro bono work. Booker felt at once irritated by and grateful for her efforts. He had a long-standing habit of playing at private parties and jam sessions for free. She convinced him to stop his regular popcorn-and-whiskey sessions with the São Paulo Dixielanders during his free hours on Saturdays, going with her instead to the movies so that he would arrive rested at his nightclub gigs.[28]

One Sunday afternoon, Booker was invited by the American owner of the Club Michel to play at a party at his fancy home on the Viaduto Maria Paula. He brought Ofélia with him because he usually brought Ofélia with him. But Ofélia was not content simply to make sure that her husband arrived on time or to silently nurse a beer and admire his playing. She paid close attention to how Booker was treated. She noticed that he was not offered anything to eat while he played, and by the time the party ended at 2 a.m., there was no food left and no feasible way to get home. After trying to catch the bus in the rain, Ofélia and Booker returned to the fancy house.

"What are you still doing here?" the owner asked curtly.

Soaked and tired, speaking loudly and deliberately, Ofélia demanded that the wealthy man pay for their taxi ride home.[29]

They were tiring of São Paulo, both of them. It pained Ofélia that, despite his renown, Booker was still often treated like a second-class citizen in the city's party-and-nightclub scene. By extension, so was Ofélia, perhaps even more so. She was darker-skinned than Booker and lacked the patina of male foreignness to protect her from white upper-class insolence. But it was not just a race issue or a class issue. There was the problem of *geografia* as well. São Paulo in 1959, while a far cry from the backwaters of Paraná, was still not quite on the same level as Rio de Janeiro in the Brazilian cultural circuit and could be a hard place for a musician to make a living. It still had fewer venues than Rio, which meant fewer gigs, and when the work came, it sometimes did not pay as well.

When the chance came to ditch Sampa, Booker and Ofélia took it. First, there was the second annual Concerto de Jazz held at Rio de Janeiro's prestigious Teatro Municipal. Organized by the radio disc jockey Paulo Santos, the show would not be televised, though even so, it promised plenty of exposure, proof of just how far jazz had come in Brazil in recent years; a live recording of the parts of the show was released the following year on Prestige Records. The concert showcased several newly established and emerging Brazilian artists. The nimble Brazilian Jazz Quartet featured the pianist Moacir Peixoto and the saxophonist Casé (José Ferreira Godinho), both fresh off two recordings with Columbia Records, including on LP with Jimmy Campbell and Major Holley called *The Good Neighbors Jazz*. Then there was the young clarinet and saxophone virtuoso Paulo Moura, who would arrive on the scene that same year with his cool-tinged album *Paulo Moura interpreta Radamés Gnattali*, on Continental. Though uncredited on the Prestige LP, Booker would also share the stage for the first time with the established crooner-pianist Dick Farney and his trio, an encounter that would soon lead to other collaborations between the two.[30]

## BIBI AND CO.

The Teatro Municipal concert also reunited Booker with his first Brazilian friend and one of his closest, the drummer and percussionist Bibi Miranda.[31] Bibi had traced his own circuitous route through the music world since they had last seen each other. In many ways, Booker soon found out, their lives had mirrored one another's. After following Romeu Silva back to Europe in the mid-1930s while Booker remained in South America, Bibi latched onto a series of odd projects. The first was a Portuguese fascist propaganda film, *A Revolução de Maio* (1937). Scripted by the jazz aficionado António Ferro, the film featured a big band piece demanding touches of jazz and samba and Bibi obliged, throwing in a kind of Brazilian scatting for good measure. The film proved highly popular and spawned a small tour of the orchestra featured in the film, led by the Chilean singer Rosita Serrano. The ensemble would perform in Germany for some time, and while Serrano would stay in Berlin, becoming an unlikely fixture of Nazi revue films during the war, Bibi returned to Paris.[32]

There, Miranda met up with another globe-trotting bandleader, the Peruvian-born Ciro Rímac, whom Bibi had first met in Rio at the Cassino Atlântico. An unsung pioneer of the global "rhumba" (commercial rumba) craze, Rímac appreciated Bibi not only for his wide-ranging drumming and percussion skills but also for his ability to sing material in Portuguese. With Rímac's orchestra, Bibi played some of the same countries he had likely toured with Romeu Silva and Booker Pittman earlier in the decade: Belgium, Holland, Luxembourg, Denmark, Italy. In a 1938 side with the Berlin label Telefunken, Bibi Miranda can be heard not just drumming but also quite capably scatting and singing the words of a Noel Rosa tune

("É bom parar") that might as well have been intended for Booker Pittman: "Por que bebes tanto assim, rapaz? / Why do you drink so much, boy? / Chega, já é demais! / Enough already, it's too much!"[33]

Back in the United States for the first time since playing there with Romeu Silva, during what was to be a short stay in New York, Bibi fell for the Big Apple much the way Booker had promised him that he would. He dove headlong into the Harlem scene and became particularly close friends with the dancer Freddy Taylor, whom he had known from their earlier days together in Montmartre, and Juan Tizol, Duke Ellington's Puerto Rican-born trombonist and cowriter of the jazz standard "Caravan." Tizol showed Bibi the best of what New York had to offer: Chick Webb and Benny Carter, not to mention Ellington himself. When they heard Papa Jo Jones play with Count Basie's orchestra at Midtown's Famous Door, Bibi's conversion to jazz drumming—hatched in Paris with Booker Pittman—was complete. When Rímac's orchestra was set to continue its international tour in Cuba, Bibi stayed on in Manhattan, bolting again only when enticing opportunities beckoned overseas: first an invitation to tour with the New Orleans-style bandleader Wilson Myers, and then Josephine Baker and Oscar Alemán, with whom Miranda recorded several sides in Denmark, including a memorable version of "Limehouse Blues" in a sextet also featuring the jazz violinist Svend Asmussen.[34]

While in Paris, Bibi Miranda rode the very end of the interwar jazz wave, performing in jam sessions at the Hot Club de France each Saturday with the likes of Django Reinhardt, Stéphane Grappelli, Bill Coleman, Coleman Hawkins, Benny Carter, Joe Turner, and even Freddy Johnson, who had recorded with Booker just a few years earlier, sessions that by now seemed like decades ago. By the time Bibi joined Russian-born French musician Bernard Hilda's orchestra in 1939, due to Nazi aggression, things had gone from risky to suicidal in Europe for Black musicians like Miranda, Alemán, and Josephine Baker, not to mention for Jewish musicians like Hilda.[35] Bibi only had the chance to play a small number of gigs with his new orchestra before he received word from the Brazilian ambassador to leave the country at once.[36]

Back in Brazil, now a seasoned veteran and one of the key drummers of both the small-format jazz and big band scene in Rio de Janeiro, Bibi Miranda finally cashed in on the prestige of the cosmopolitan prodigal son. After taking over the sticks for Fon-Fon's orchestra in 1940, he became a fixture at the Copacabana Palace, playing in black-tie affairs and jam sessions alongside Claude Austin, Frank "Big Boy" Goudie, Fats Elpídio, Aristides Zaccarias, and the city's slowly growing phalanx of jazzistas.[37]

Once Brazil's casinos were shuttered in the postwar period, after a stint at Vogue heading his own orchestra, Bibi foundered somewhat, for reasons that are not entirely clear. He finally headed back to Paris to perform once again with Josephine Baker's orchestra in 1951.[38] Like Booker in his more recent years, a spiritual crisis and mysterious sickness had kept Bibi mostly out of the public light. By 1952, it occurred to the weary middle-aged drummer and showman to do much the same thing that Booker Pittman had done. He decamped to a small plot of land, sold his drum kit for 20,000 cruzeiros, and announced that he was done with the music profession.[39] Bibi did not go as far away as Booker did, settling for the then sparsely populated Western outskirts of Rio de Janeiro—where he was determined to raise chickens—rather than the deep cover of northern Paraná. Still, it was as though he and Booker ran by the same internal clock, with the same urges to move and flee within Brazil and away from it: the same homing instincts—and rambling instincts—and only occasionally did the two coincide.

Two people who were not at the Teatro Municipal concert were Louis Cole and Claude Austin. After his appearance with Booker at a jam session at the short-lived Mei Ling nightclub in 1948, Cole became a fixture at Vogue much as he had at the Cassino Atlântico, often playing there with Claude Austin and Fats Elpídio. By 1952, he was recording again, this time on Continental.[40] A year later, he played in a massive jam session at the Beduin nightclub in the Hotel Glória along with Dick Farney, Cipó, Zaccarias, Fats Elpídio, Dolores Duran, Johnny Alf, and a host of others.[41] In 1955, Cole and his sextet recorded the live album *Uma Noite no Vogue* on Discos Rádio before moving to the new nightclub Fiesta after the Vogue burned to the ground. A year later, he traveled to São Paulo and performed at The Cave just months before Booker Pittman made his triumphant return to that city.[42] It would be his last trip. First came the premature whispers about Cole's death. While the journalist Míster Eco was quick to quell the first wave of rumors and even chastise the journalist who spread them, the news turned out to have had more than a little basis in fact: Louis Cole had cancer of the larynx. Like Bibi Miranda, Louis retreated to a *sítio* in Mesquita in the state of Rio de Janeiro. In dire financial and bodily health, he would never sing again, Míster Eco announced.[43] In fact, Louis Cole would die little more than a month later.[44]

Claude Austin would soon meet a similar fate. After the memorable jam session at the Mei Ling and the demise of Vogue, Austin entered not so much a worrisome slowdown as a holding pattern. Working for some time at the Bambu and then the Hotel Excelsior, often alongside Cole, the always elegant Austin paid the bills by playing at numerous benefits, weddings, birthdays, diplomatic events, and private parties, frequently traveling to gigs in São Paulo but rarely beyond. He often appeared on the radio, too, interpreting swing classics, carnival hits, and everything in between, playing and singing, as one columnist put it, "sambas in English [and] foxtrots in Portuguese."[45] By the time he too fell ill from cancer in 1957, Claude Austin had become more than just a nightclub fixture; perhaps to his surprise, he had found himself a beloved figure in Brazil. And he did not stop working. Until just a few months before his death in June 1958 at age fifty-five, the American still began each show at the Excelsior with his signature performance of the Johnny Mercer/David Raskin song "Laura":[46]

> And you see Laura on the train that is passing through.
> Those eyes, how familiar they seem.
> She gave your very first kiss to you.
> That was Laura, but she's only a dream.

During the last South American act of his life, Claude Austin married a Brazilian woman and fathered four daughters, the youngest just one year old at the time of his death. For all intents and purposes, Austin had become a respectable Brazilian gentleman and family man; the first lady herself, Sarah Kubitschek, privately reached out to the musician by telegram as he lay dying. When Austin passed away a short time later, she publicly grieved the American's death and even offered his widow to pay for funeral expenses.[47]

Throughout his Brazilian years, something had seemed to elude Claude Austin, a kind of plenitude that lay just beyond his reach, like Laura on the train. He was not alone in this. Booker Pittman, Bibi Miranda, and Louis Cole had spent relatively little time together since Booker's first year in Brazil, and Booker and Claude Austin did not cross paths until Booker's second stint in Rio in the late 1940s. Yet there was an invisible bond that tied the men together, something besides the horror of disease, the thrill of novelty, and the dread of economic precarity. All of them were talented Black expats and shared not just a sense of lingering nostalgia for their faraway friends and families but also a sense that music, and jazz in particular, supplied a passport to something ineffable and lacking in the world they were born into. It was not just the regular work in swanky clubs and seaside penthouse apartments that would likely have been off-limits to them in the United States. For the three Black Americans, Brazil, with all of its social and racial inequities, must have at least lent them the illusion that they were not expressly prohibited from setting foot in certain hotels, bars, or neighborhoods as they would have been in mid-century Dallas or Baltimore. As the Brazilian journalist Lúcio Rangel noted with a dab of irony, though, for Black American musicians in Rio de Janeiro, there was no "sunny side of the street."[48] In their adopted country, Booker and his compatriots breathed rarefied tropical air. But this air also seemed to suffocate them over time, to smother them with its conditional privilege and boate glory, with its chimera of loftiness and quasi-fame.

1958 proved a fateful year for another person central to Booker Pittman's past, namely his father, William Sidney Pittman. Big Pitt's unraveling had begun in earnest two decades earlier, with the apogee and sudden demise of his Dallas newspaper, *Brotherhood Eyes*. Abandoned by his wife and three children and increasingly combative professionally, Sidney used his tabloid as a battering ram against all whom he imagined stood against him: two-faced preachers, philandering businessmen, corrupt politicians, and any other "evil doers [sic] within the race."[49] Booker's father's comeuppance was not just predictable; it was almost as though he wished it upon himself. He directed his ire not just against the Black elites of Dallas but against perceived rivals and antagonists from other parts of Texas and beyond: *Brotherhood Eyes* sharply criticized what Sidney saw as the Tuskegee Institute's divergence from its original moorings since the death of its founder, reporting on alleged prostitution and bootlegging operations near the Alabama campus.[50] The elder Pittman's mudslinging met its match in an insurance executive who responded to the attacks by having him arrested on trumped-up federal charges of extortion and obscenity rather than mere libel. In February 1937, at the age of sixty-one, Sidney Pittman was convicted by a grand jury and sentenced to five years at the Leavenworth Penitentiary. In many ways, he was a broken man upon his early release in 1939. As part of his parole agreement, he renounced his career as a newspaperman and took work as a solicitor for a Dallas tailor, later supporting himself by doing carpentry work. Booker Pittman's childhood home at 1018 Liberty Street was sold, and his father, one of the nation's truly pioneering Black architects, spent his final years morally dejected, economically destitute, silenced, nearly blind, and mostly forgotten, bouncing around from address to address until his death from coronary thrombosis on March 14, 1958.[51]

## FULL CIRCLE

Thanks to the Teatro Municipal concert, which convinced Booker Pittman of the growing vitality of Rio's jazz scene, and despite the recent absence of Cole and Austin, the saxophonist caught the *carioca* bug once again. Later that year, he was invited by the theatrical promoter Abelardo Figueiredo to play on TV Rio's holiday special *Noite de Gala* alongside Maysa, Elizeth Cardoso, and others. The next morning, Booker and Ofélia discovered that Figueiredo had returned to São Paulo somehow without remembering to leave the Pittmans' return tickets or pay for their hotel. Booker stepped outside to smoke, and at that very moment, an old friend of his, Renato Pacote, appeared seemingly out of nowhere, took a long look at Booker, and said, "What the hell are you doing there?" It was a good question. What *were* they doing in São Paulo? And why weren't they *here* in Rio, Booker's first love and Ofélia's, too? What precisely was keeping them from moving? Back in São Paulo, watching television, listless and still broke, the Pittmans prayed for deliverance. It came in the form of a phone call from a promoter whom Booker knew from his last stay in Rio a decade earlier. He had seen Booker at the Noite de Gala and was impressed enough by his performance, and no doubt by his newfound sobriety, to offer him a contract to open a new boate, the Plaza, next to the Hotel Plaza Copacabana. When Ofélia negotiated the price with the promoter, she lied a little. She told him that Booker fetched thirty cruzeiros per night in São Paulo, when in truth, he made half that. The promoter said thirty cruzeiros was perfect. And so, one day later, on New Year's Eve 1959, Booker, Ofélia, and Eliana moved to Rio de Janeiro.[52]

After the Pittmans settled into the city, in the posh beach neighborhood of Leblon, Booker sought to refamiliarize himself with the ever-changing Copacabana, where the work was still to be found.[53] Gone were most of the music venues from his previous stays in the neighborhood—the Atlântico, the Vogue, the Mei Ling—not to mention a number of restaurants and botecos he had once haunted. But the Copacabana Palace remained, and scores of new bars, clubs, and restaurants dotted the mushrooming built environment of the grand avenues—Nossa Senhora de Copacabana and, of course, the beachside Avenida Atlântica. The smaller streets of Posto 2 still abounded with the kind of intimate conviviality that Booker had missed the most. From Praça Cardeal Arcoverde, Booker ambled slowly along Rua Barata Ribeiro, turning right up Rua Ronald de Carvalho toward the ocean.[54] Reaching his beloved Praça do Lido, he would have been surprised at how much it had not changed in a decade and also how much it had.

The restaurant inside the park was closed; the children's slides had been upgraded. A new generation of cariocas drifted in from the beach, mostly children, fair-skinned boys and girls tied invisibly to their nannies, teenage pranksters in sneakers, shopkeepers in hats and horn-rimmed glasses, occasionally solemn street vendors and old men reading newspapers. The housewives and nannies bared more of their shoulders and their calves than he recalled; everywhere there was a shade less formality and modesty. The trees had grown, but they were the same trees, at least. Booker sat down on a bench and remembered having stared at these same trees decades prior when they were saplings, thinking then how they reminded him of the Texas riverbeds of his childhood lined with sycamores and bald cypress—the Red River, the Trinity, the Brazos. Now larger and mottled, the trees of the Praça do Lido stood orphaned in a briny and dusty urban garden, seemingly healthy despite the ever-taller buildings around them. The park's shadows had grown longer as well.

In ways that he could not fully grasp, Booker had treasured this little square ever since he first stumbled upon it in his first year in Rio de Janeiro in the mid-1930s. In that first glimpse, he had imagined himself staying in this corner of the city forever, returning always to this same sun-kissed spot, a stone's throw from the beach. It was as if the first taste of the place had contained a free glimpse into his future, and it was a surprisingly conventional one: a wife, a child or two to care for, stability, domesticity. At that time, he was a Brazil-struck twenty-five-year-old who presumptuously saw an inexhaustible abundance of time ahead of him. The foretaste of his future life, born of his first euphoric weeks in Rio, allowed him to savor his first contact with the city all the more. The same was not true now, a quarter-century later. Booker was beaten down by self-abuse more than by circumstance and finally robbed of the privilege of endless imagining. But now he had within his grasp the very things he first saw so clearly while sitting on this bench staring at the young trees. His wife may have been legally married to another man, his ideal progeny a willful stepdaughter. But his vision, if he could call it that, had not been wholly inaccurate.

## NEW LIFE

The work came quickly and in bunches. By the end of January 1960, Booker was playing at a boate called Alfama in the Botafogo neighborhood, in addition to the Plaza.[55] By the end of February, he was performing live on TV-Tupi on Monday evenings.[56] He even performed capably in the made-for-television movie *Tensão em Xangai* on the same channel.⁵⁷ In late March, Booker headlined at the third Grande Concerto Brasileiro de Jazz. Organized by his old friend Jorge Guinle and others, the concert also featured pianist and vocalist Dick Farney and the young saxophonist Paulo Moura.⁵⁸ A short time later, Booker began performing at the Little Club, a tiny boate on the Beco das Garrafas, an unassuming dead-end alley near the Copacabana Palace that had recently established itself as ground zero for a circle of musicians associated with jazz and bossa nova.⁵⁹

Booker was now advertised primarily as a soprano sax player and secondarily as a clarinetist. But it hardly mattered. As in Paraná and São Paulo, the American was no longer just a jazz musician. He continued to blow at high society parties and galas. The difference now was that he simply played more often: the sheer density of musicians in Rio de Janeiro generated new opportunities every week. And musical hybrids, despite the hostility of nationalist, orthodox music critics, were taking Rio by storm in 1960. Booker's base was the Little Club, where he could play jazz in the jam session format he preferred and almost anything else he wished as well. One reporter called Booker's well-attended late-night show "quite noisy, but extremely enjoyable after a few shots of whiskey."⁶⁰

Still, the Pittmans' money problems persisted, and the Little Club contract alone could not pay the bills. Booker had long before ceased to be a purist in terms of musical genres, so the moment suited him; besides, Ofélia convinced him that anti-commercial snobbery would only lead to starvation. All the years spent in different regions and countries had turned the American into a kind of musical polymath. The fact that Booker could play straight jazz, Dixieland, swing, boogie-woogie, and rock and roll, and blend them at will with samba or bossa nova, bolero or cha-cha-chá, only increased the demand for his services. And he was not just versatile; he was mobile. He happily took short trips to gigs in São Paulo and Salvador and even inaugurated a new club (Candango) in the new capital of Brasília.⁶¹ Booker was, in short, ready at a moment's notice to play almost anything, almost anywhere.

## THE FABULOUS BOOKER PITTMAN

With the new decade also came something that had long eluded Booker Pittman: an international major label debut as the featured artist with the album *The Fabulous Booker Pittman: The No. 1 Soprano Sax in the World* on the French-based Musidisc label. The LP's conceit rather absurdly linked

*The No. 1 Soprano Sax in the World: The Fabulous Booker Pittman*, Musidisc, 1960. Fair use.

Booker's return with this supposedly unrivaled mastery of the soprano sax, when in fact it was the alto sax, and to a lesser extent the clarinet, that had defined his sound in all of his various heydays—from Kansas City to Harlem, Paris to Buenos Aires. Still, the album did manage to revive something of Booker's old form, even more so than his previous long play. It had been over a year since the recording of *Booker Pittman Plays Again*, and by now, Booker was even more comfortable on the soprano sax. The opening track, "Petite Fleur," takes on one of Bechet's signature numbers from his later years in Paris. As such, it is a statement piece, and Booker does not pass up the opportunity. With his measured phrases and lovely lilting obbligatos, his performance is a study in immaculate tension and tone, in slow-burning control instead of barn-burning virtuosity. In "When the Saints Go Marching In," with its up-tempo swing, Booker's soprano perhaps never sat so well into a groove on record, showcasing the best of his abilities as an always eloquent, sometimes swaggering blues interpreter. Musidisc's cavernous production lends the record a light, spacious quality. It is a less intimate and grounded recording than *Plays Again* but also more airborne, almost ethereal at times. Booker's command of the soprano is augmented by his doubling on the tenor sax and sometimes the baritone, as in his swinging rendition of Cole Porter's "Love for Sale."[62]

Booker sings more sparingly on *The Fabulous Booker Pittman* than he had on his last LP. But when he does sing, as in "Lonesome Road" and the closing "Nobody Knows the Trouble I've Seen," his voice seasons the rich instrumentals instead of overpowering them. *The Fabulous Booker Pittman* is a balanced and vigorous *outing* in more than one sense. Advertisements in publications like *Billboard* echoed the thrust of the album's title and liner notes: "Booker makes his sensational comeback as the recognized no. 1 soprano sax."[63] But the hype was misleading. The LP was not really a comeback album, not just because he had already cut a record as a leader but also because Booker Pittman had never fully arrived internationally in the first place, as evidenced by his smattering of recordings until the late 1950s. Even his early notoriety was based more on his nightclub pedigree, the critics he impressed, and the exalted company he kept than on any substantial archival evidence. In the age of the stereophonic long play, records were the ultimate arbiters, the main vessels of musical prestige.

More than anything else, *The Fabulous Booker Pittman* strives to give Booker a seat at the table of the global jazz scene, one long denied to him not by the Basies and the Armstrongs of the world but by Booker himself, who, for decades, had stayed as far away from the northern jazz banquet as humanly possible. And the record mostly succeeds. Booker might not have been able to stake a claim to the "best of" sweepstakes. The album, even if it garnered generally favorable reviews in *Billboard* and *High Fidelity*, did not win him widespread coverage or place his name in the *Playboy Magazine* jazz rankings. But the gloss and prestige of vinyl put him on the world map of jazz for the first time in decades. It reminded his old friends, colleagues, and fans in Paris and New York, Chicago and Buenos Aires that he still existed and that, given the opportunity, he could still swing like mad.

The timing of the album and its titular boast owed a large debt to Sidney Bechet, who had died earlier that same year. In some ways, Bechet's life ran parallel to Booker Pittman's, though, in terms of personality and visibility, the two diverged wildly. Bechet had first arrived in Europe in 1919, his first gig with the Southern Syncopated Orchestra was at the Royal Philharmonic Hall, followed a short time later by a command performance in front of King George V at Buckingham Palace. In Paris, the orchestra headlined at the Théâtre Apollo in Montmartre before heading back to London, where after a night's debauchery, Bechet was accused of raping an English prostitute and promptly deported.[64] Later in the decade, he returned to

Europe, only to be tried and convicted for the attempted murder of a fellow American musician, serving eleven months in a French prison. Yet Bechet would not be kept away from Europe forever. Despite prevalent racism, xenophobia, and court systems that he claimed were unkind to him as a Black foreigner, he felt perpetually drawn back to the Old Continent and particularly to France and its abiding enthusiasm for Dixieland and hot jazz. In the 1930s, aging fast, half-forgotten, and reduced to running a laundromat in New York, he plotted ways to make himself relevant again. Recording a series of successive sides with Hugues Panassié and Mezz Mezzrow after the war, Bechet moved back to Paris for good in 1949, living his final years in a crepuscular glow of expat glory.

## THE MANHATTAN AFFAIR

Booker Pittman lacked the patina of New Orleans Jazz Legend that Bechet had in spades. But in many ways, Booker was a more likable man and more fitting phoenix of a bygone era—a genteel lover rather than a rash fighter—and his amiable character no doubt spared him from serious brush-ups with the law and deportation. What Booker lacked in viciousness he made up for in vice, of course, but just as Bechet's mean streak ebbed over time, so too did Booker's dependency on booze, drugs, and dealers.

And still, Booker's renaissance was not without problems. In November in Copacabana, he had a run-in with bigotry as unpleasant as he had experienced since leaving the United States nearly three decades earlier. It started with a visitor named Joe Bible, a Black American electrical engineer on a pleasure trip to Brazil. Booker and Ofélia decided to take Joe out for a Tuesday night on the town, and they began with one of the newest and fanciest boates, the Manhattan Club, on 34 Rua Carvalho de Mendonça, just around the corner from the Little Club. Owned by a white American named Frank Firzlaff, the Manhattan Club sought to cull its clientele from the most elite circles of the city. The "most elite circles" in racist code meant well-to-do white people, only the *cearense* doorman at the Manhattan Club did not speak in code. When he flatly denied Ofélia entrance to the club, she called her husband aside. When the bouncer got a good look at the elegant Booker, he recognized him and grew nervous. He was just following orders from his boss, the doorman said apologetically, "but between you and me, Senhor Frank doesn't want to see any blacks in his club." An assistant of Firzlaff's was summoned to the door.

"Senhor Frank will see you inside to clear up the situation."

Ofélia would have none of it. "We're not looking for any favors. Have him come here to explain it himself."

When he found himself face-to-face with Booker, Firzlaff backpedaled. "The rule was never meant for all Negroes. You and your friends are free to come in."

At this point, Joe Bible spoke up. "Are you from the North or the South?"

"From Minnesota," Firzlaff hissed, adding that there was no such thing as racial prejudice where he came from. "You have to understand that here in Brazil, the presence of Negroes in a bar drives away white customers."

Bible could barely contain himself. "If I were Brazilian, I would smash your face in."[65]

The episode made news in all the major newspapers the next day, and later, many of the magazines. Instead of damage control, Firzlaff only managed to make a mockery of himself, his boate, and Americans generally. It did not help matters that his Brazilian wife, Neuza Peixoto Firzlaff, while pretending to defend the club's policy, spoke openly to a reporter from *Última Hora* about how better off she thought the club was without Blacks. "I know it's a little racist of me," she admitted, "but I don't like black people. If it were up to me, no black man or woman would be allowed into the club. But my husband is very sentimental."

Neither Booker nor his friend Joe Bible ever formally testified against Firzlaff, apparently.[66] The two were almost certainly fearful of reprisals. Civil rights activists in the United States were in the pitch of battle against legal racial discrimination and segregation, a fight they still had no certainty of winning. Perhaps Booker and Joe expected no better outcome in Brazil. Booker Pittman was practical when it came to race; as a young man, he had seen what trouble his own father's outspoken rage had gotten him into. Firzlaff, likely under legal advice, denied any wrongdoing and admitted only to having denied entry to guitarist Bola Sete for having an unpaid tab. But everyone knew this was a lie. And Booker was not without his connections, beginning with the press. In direct response to the Manhattan Club incident, the formidable Afro Brazilian activist, writer, and artist Abdias do Nascimento took up the cause against boate racism.[67] Inspired by events in the American South, he organized what amounted to a sit-in of Black Brazilians at the Manhattan Club: shades of Carolina in Copacabana.

## IN DEMAND

Meanwhile, Booker Pittman was not just getting work. He was turning it down when it did not pay enough or when he or Ofélia smelled a rat. The born-again saxophonist still had his regular gig at the Little Club, and the sold-out shows led to other work at places like O Crepúsculo on Rua Toneleros, the Plaza, and Bottles Bar, right next door to the Little Club in the tiny Beco das Garrafas. But Booker did not limit himself to boates; he never did. He played in private parties and led jam sessions at after-hours clubs, blew his sax at benefits and catwalks, and occasionally hob-nobbed with visiting celebrities such as Lena Horne, Nat King Cole, and the bandleader Ray Anthony and jammed with touring jazz heavyweights like Roy Eldridge.[68] Frequently, he was invited to civic and political events as well: on one occasion, he gave a send-off at Galeão Airport for the outgoing US ambassador John Moors Cabot;[69] on another, he met a young preacher named Martin Luther King, visiting Rio for the 10th Annual Baptist World Alliance.[70] He even appeared in a fashion spread in *O Cruzeiro*, mock-serenading a local beauty queen with his soprano saxophone.[71] During his rare time off from the nonstop cycle of performances, family affairs, and social events, Booker could be found at the American-style fast-food

Booker Pittman with Nat King Cole and Elizeth Cardoso. Imagem do Fundo Correio da Manhã. 1959. Arquivo Nacional do Brasil. Public domain via Wikipedia Commons.

restaurant Bob's, having a chocolate-dipped vanilla ice cream with famed composer Heitor Villa-Lobos.[72]

Booker even began to be hired for theatrical productions. In March, he was cast in the Portuguese-language production of Jack Gelber's play *The Connection*, a heavy drama about jazz musicians and drug addiction. Booker was slated to play as well as act, though he never made it to opening night.[73] According to one account, he and a few other musicians left the rehearsal when the play's director, Jack Brown, perhaps worried that Booker's band was stealing the spotlight from the main actors, instructed them to play-act as bad amateur musicians. "Jazz is *my* thing," Booker said. "I get to choose what the band plays." He was fired on the spot.[74]

Urged on by Ofélia, Booker no longer felt he had to endure ill-treatment from American play directors any more than he did from nightclub owners and businessmen, drunk tourists and society women. Since returning to Rio de Janeiro, people had begun to talk about him differently. Before, he was known as an erratic and errant genius, inevitably described as "one of the best jazz alto saxophonists in the world," but almost always with a caveat, sometimes half-submerged, other times not. The phrase had become a ready-made jazz truism, passed on from writer to writer, from article to article, over the years: from Hugues Panassié to local music critics. But now, since *The Fabulous Booker Pittman* hit the record stores, Booker was simply "the greatest soprano saxophonist in the world." And it was not just the praise that impressed him; it was the proprietary lilt of the praise. In this sense, Booker was aided by the recent deaths of Louis Cole and Claude Austin. By skill, race, and birthright, he was now an elder statesman of jazz in Brazil, the torchbearer of Swing Era authenticity. By virtue of his nearly two decades in *our* country—or so thought many Brazilians—he was also one of *us*. Or almost. One journalist reminded readers that Booker was of "American origin, having played with orchestras of the stature of Blanche Calloway in his native land." But he was also "our only true jazz artist."[75]

Sensing national esteem sneak up on him and wary as always of being domesticated, Booker Pittman was no longer satisfied in performing solely for Brazilian audiences for paltry paychecks. He became restless again, and Ofélia's vicarious ambition and vigilance against exploitation only served to enhance Booker's natural tendencies. Increasingly, he took to the road as the feature act. At first, he did not venture far, headlining in Petrópolis, São Paulo, Belo Horizonte. Then, in June, he received an offer to inaugurate the new Hilton Hotel in Santiago de Chile. Booker was supposed to receive nearly two million cruzeiros for a three-month stint, a considerable sum at the time, though he ended up reducing his stay to twelve days after learning that he would not be able to travel with his family.[76] Already homesick, he was further shaken upon his return to Congonhas Airport when he got caught up in a Hollywood-style shoot-out between three armed Argentine fugitives traveling on the same plane and local police tipped off by Interpol. Never the fighting type, Booker survived the showdown by hiding under a chair cradling his saxophone, but the experience left him petrified.[77] From then on, he focused on shorter jaunts, and when he was forced to fly, he insisted that his wife and stepdaughter travel with him.

## EATING THE NIGHT

Later that year, returning to Rio from a brief tour to Montevideo, Booker Pittman played in a show at the prestigious Museu da Arte Moderna along with top-shelf pianist-crooner Dick Farney.[78] Born Farnésio Dutra e Silva, Dick Farney was one of the pivotal mid-century jazz figures in Brazil. He had experienced a frustrating flirtation with international fame in the 1940s. When his samba-swing single "Copacabana" proved a smash hit in Brazil, record executives in the United States came calling. He signed a contract with NBC Radio and was featured in an article in *Time* magazine on the new generation of jazz crooners. The sky was the limit, and it was no wonder. Farney was seemingly tailor-made for a career as a stateside crooner: white, handsome, debonair, with serviceable English, a Bing Crosby–like purr to his voice, and the feathery touch of Nat King Cole on the piano. But his career in the US never quite took off as promised. When big band orchestras took a nosedive after World War II, Farney did what any self-respecting Brazilian musician would have done: he retreated to Rio de Janeiro with a sheaf of records under his arm. Not satisfied to merely play and croon as usual, he put his record collection to practical use, herding together a group of young audiophiles at his house in the Santa Teresa neighborhood. What started as an informal gathering of eccentric jazz fans and yearling musicians taking in rare-edition Stan Kenton records turned into a laboratory of cool, a play space for airy sonic experiments in samba-canção, big band, baião, and West Coast jazz. The hybrid style still had no name in the mid-1950s. The gathering of musicians did, however: They called themselves the Sinatra-Farney Fan Club, a place where the likes of Paulo Moura, João Donato, and Johnny Alf routinely swung by to drink, smoke, listen, and snap their fingers together at Farney's scenic abode.[79]

By the beginning of the new decade, Dick Farney enjoyed the status of an elder statesman of the Rio music scene. If not exactly a role model for new bossa nova phenoms like João Gilberto and Roberto Menescal, Farney was a teacher and something of a touchstone for younger jazz fans and musicians. In this way, he was like Booker, only in reverse: Brazilian- rather than American-born; white rather than Black. Both men had invaded and cannibalized the other's homeland; both shared a weakness for jazz improvisation, sartorial style, and hard liquor. Yet while Farney had come back for good, surrendering to the consolation prize of hometown celebrity, Booker never did. This last fact said something about the secret character of each man. In the postwar period, Farney had sought out the global culture industry, took a good swing at conquering it, and missed honorably. Since taking the fateful ocean liner to Brazil almost three decades earlier, Booker had avoided the simplest route to jazz celebrity, preferring the ragged freedom of the margins to the pressure cooker of the Metropolis.

The Pittman–Farney album *Jam Session* was recorded at the auditorium of the venerable daily newspaper *Folha de São Paulo*.[80] Conceived as a back-to-back showcase of Brazil-based jazz titans rather than an actual collaboration between the two leaders, the record shows Booker in fine form. But his set is something of a throwback. Reunited with his closest friends from the São Paulo Dixielander days—Dudu on the guitar, Masao Ukon on trumpet, and Eduardo Vidossich on piano—Booker cuts loose in a way seldom heard on his studio albums, uncorking molten-hot arpeggios on the soprano and growling note-benders on the alto. His vocals on standards like "Sweet Georgia Brown" and "Am I Blue?" are done in jocular Satchmo mode, exactly what audiences expected of him at this point in his career. A novel twist is the self-composed "Cheese," with its memorable line: "Give me a piece, I want to eat the night."

It is a phrase that aptly describes Booker's own insatiable desire to push the tempo and his bandmates, lending the set a wanton, sometimes sloppy insistence on speed and spontaneity. Interestingly, Farney, the more accomplished vocalist of the two, opts for a straightforward instrumental trio, presumably to spotlight his tasteful chops on the piano. While Booker and his gang channel the rambunctious energy of their boate performances and jam sessions of yore, Farney's trio almost seems to approach the concert as an intimate chamber piece, subdued and refined. In this way, the record is a study in contrasts. On its two sides, *Jam Session* reveals two different types of performance élan and aspirational zeal. Each bandleader seems eager to peddle his own brand of authenticity: Dick Farney, knowing well how stiff the competition is, goes out of his way to exhibit his hard-earned jazz bona fides to a large Brazilian audience. For his part, Booker appears to bridle against the confines of the auditorium setting. True jazz, true *music*, he seemed to be telling the audience, was open-ended, unplanned, erratic, ecstatic. It was not the music that Farney thought he knew well, the jazz of martinis and showgirls, the slick anodyne sound of commercial big bands. Rather, it was music loosely tethered to sundry practices and traditions, not all of them American; the music of movement, *errant* practices, and traditions that nonetheless flouted the rules. The music of late-night clubs, of cabarés and boates, of spilled whiskey and cachaça, serious listening, and sometimes serious dancing: unrehearsed, unshackled, jumping and swinging as long and as hard and as well as possible.

Music that wanted to eat the night.

*Chapter Seven*

# SAXOPHONE, MICROPHONE, TELEPHONE

BOOKER PITTMAN HAD A DIFFICULT TIME EXPLAINING TO HIMSELF EXACTly what Eliana meant to him. The relationship was unlike anything he experienced before, and it surprised him profoundly. He had felt it from the day he met young Eliana in that pizzeria on Rua Conceição. He perceived an affinity with the girl that felt almost uncanny, a presence he felt but could not explain. There were always certain men who talked about feeling like strangers around their children, but with Booker, it was the opposite. Eliana was not *his* child, or at least that was his understanding at first. He noticed, simply, that he looked forward to their time together. Then, after they had moved in together, he discovered that he savored the meals they shared, that he felt comforted by the timbre of Eliana's voice and the rhythms of her habits and routines, even when she was in the other room doing her homework. Booker did not believe in destiny, exactly, but he always felt at home around Eliana in ways that made him think that they were meant to be in each other's lives. Their personalities were worlds apart. Eliana was irascible and loquacious yet pragmatic. Before his transformation into a husband and stepfather, Booker was more than just a bohemian; he was a *largado*, a veritable wastrel. Now that he was sober, as though compensating for his wild past, he had grown steady, methodical, patient, and prone to stay around the house. Despite their differences, there was an understanding between Eliana and Booker, an unspoken kinship and plenitude of emotion that went far beyond what was expected of them.

Even in the early years, Booker sensed he was preparing Eliana for something, even if he still was not sure what that something was. If it was not always clear that she would follow in his footsteps, she seemed to track him with her eyes wherever he walked, wherever he looked. And when he practiced, she really watched him, heard him, in a way that boate spectators usually did not. Eliana listened with the same intensity to the records he played, especially the vocalists: Ella Fitzgerald and Sarah Vaughan, Frank Sinatra and Nat King Cole. She also peppered Booker with more questions than she needed to about the United States: what it was like there, where he had grown up, what the food tasted like, how the people treated foreigners. Booker was reluctant to talk much about his family, but he knew instinctively that Eliana's questions were not just the idle curiosity of a prepubescent schoolgirl. He saw that she was painting herself into the scenes he described to her. Her mind was traveling, and traveling far, much as his did at her age.[1]

Booker sensed that something needed to be done. He suggested to Ofélia that they have Eliana enrolled in the Nelson School, an American institution, where Eliana could learn English from native speakers. Since there were no openings, Booker mentioned to the principal that he was Booker T. Washington's grandson. He did so with great hesitation: for much of his life, he had tried to conceal or at least play down his illustrious heritage with people he did not know closely for fear that the knowledge would color their impression of him, good or bad, that it would get him something he did not deserve.

At any rate, it worked: Eliana was immediately admitted to the Nelson School. Now fifteen, she was emerging as almost preternaturally headstrong. In the last year, Eliana's biological father Orlando had managed through legal chicanery to pull her out of the Nelson School mid-term and place her in a private high school in São Paulo, the Colégio Maria Imaculada.[2] Ofélia and Booker were angry and heartbroken. Eliana had grown so close to Booker that she now announced that she would stop calling him *seu Buca* and would now refer to him as *pai*, father. Ofélia had a part in this transition as well. "Seu Buca never had children of his own," she told her daughter. "If you want to call him Dad, he would appreciate it." Then it was Booker's turn to ask. One Christmas morning, he told her that if she wanted to give him a present, she should stop calling him *seu Buca* once and for all. *Pai* would do just fine.[3]

The small change in nomenclature seemed to bring them closer together, Eliana recalled later. Booker began to like the words *pai* and *papai* so much he began to refer to himself as such when reporters asked about this pretty, vivacious girl who increasingly showed up at his shows. When Orlando read a magazine article that identified Booker as Eliana's father without bothering to mention the "step" part, he became so furious that he refused to continue paying for his daughter's education. Eliana called in the middle of the night to plead with Ofélia and Booker to send money, and fast. Without a moment's hesitation, Booker took it upon himself to pawn his sax and pay for the rest of her tuition, though—her mother told her—she would have to find a way to feed herself for the time being: "We don't have enough money to treat you to so much as ice cream," she said. When Ofélia paid her daughter a visit the next month, she found that not only was Eliana well fed, but that she had managed to earn enough pocket money tutoring her classmates and giving them English lessons that she offered to lend Booker *back* the money he had spent on her.[4]

## HAPPY ACCIDENTS

Since his return to urban life, Booker Pittman had been exposed to more and more records, not to mention a whole assortment of performances on radio and television, the latter a medium that had just begun to take hold in Brazil's major cities. With this exposure came contact with new music idioms, including new forms of jazz. This was especially true in Rio de Janeiro, still a more cosmopolitan city than São Paulo, where Booker counted among his friends and acquaintances several jazz aficionados with open ears and vast record collections: Jorge Guinle, Sílvio Tulio Cardoso, Dick Farney, José Silveira Sampaio. These men were only too happy to share their newest vinyl with Booker. This was how he came to listen in earnest to Charlie Parker. When he first heard him, Parker's playing struck Booker's ears as a mad distillation of his sax heroes: a hyperactive Johnny Hodges, Lester Brown at the racetrack. Parker's vision was so radical it almost seemed disrespectful, as if he were burying his elders, turning his back on jazz. But soon, Booker began to appreciate Bird as something besides an insolent rebel. He slowed down his solos and began to hear the dexterity and subtlety of his phrasing, the urgent drive and eloquent pain beneath all that fast-talking: the blues of Bird.

Booker was not sure if Ofélia shared his newfound enthusiasm for bebop, and he had not even considered Eliana. Ever since she was a schoolgirl in São Paulo, Eliana was more inclined to dance than anything else. But he knew she enjoyed listening to his music, so he kept on playing the record anyway; he felt it would not offend anyone. Then something strange happened. One day, he heard what he first thought was an unusual instrumental accompaniment, an aural accident. He soon realized it was humming, and the humming came from the kitchen, not the back recesses of a recording studio. Complex humming, harmonically almost impossible, but there it was. And it was coming from Eliana's mouth. Booker tried to convince himself it was a fluke, rustling up a few musicians to try to work through the passage that Eliana had replicated effortlessly. They could hardly pull it off. "After one hour, one phrase," he wrote later, "and a headache."[5]

That was the first step, the moment when he became aware that his life was about to swerve again. The next one happened a few months later. Besides his regular gig at the Little Club, Booker also had an ongoing contract with Rádio Nacional's Programa César de Alencar and another with TV Rio on the program "Musical Carioca." He made sure to bring his wife and, whenever possible, his stepdaughter with him for the shows. Though Booker was the featured performer on TV Rio, his combo often included a female singer as well, a different one each time. One night, the scheduled singer called in sick. The show's producer, David Cohen, an American living in Rio de Janeiro, sensed from his limited encounters with Eliana that she possessed the looks, talent, and charisma for show business. He asked Booker and Ofélia if she could fill in for the singer in any capacity—as a dancer, for example. Cohen's mention of dancing was likely no accident. Eliana had already graced the pages of the national magazine *O Cruzeiro*, dancing photogenically while her stepfather assumed the stance of the virtuoso.[6]

"She can sing, too," Booker said.

"All the better," Cohen replied.

At first, Eliana resisted. "I'm afraid," she stuttered. Booker would have none of that. "É preciso cantar," he told her, a phrase that literally meant "to sing is essential" but also carried the connotation of personal agency, as in "you have to do it."[7]

So she did it. While her mother rushed home to pick out proper attire, Eliana remained on the soundstage to rehearse. She already knew the number she would sing, the traditional piece "Mama Don't Allow," since she had been rehearsing it for a private performance at the US Embassy that had been canceled at the last moment due to a plane accident. An extremely quick study, Eliana ended up singing shoeless in her television debut, shoes being the one article of clothing Ofélia had forgotten in her rush back to the soundstage.[8]

## ELIANA RISES

In April 1961, after her star turn on TV Rio, Eliana began singing regularly with Booker on television, radio, and even in clubs on weekends. She hit the ground running. At Rádio Nacional, she performed alongside established figures like Elizeth Cardoso and Linda Batista. "While still very young," commented *Diário Carioca*, "Eliana has all the tools to achieve an outstanding place in the artistic world, guaranteed the experience and the training of Booker Pittman."[9] *Radiolândia* marveled that as a singer, she showed "quite a lot of rhythm and *bossa*."[10] Within months of her debut, Eliana's star was rising to such an extent that offers to tour elsewhere in Brazil and Latin America began to arrive. In August, she accompanied Booker on tour to Recife.[11] A return to Brazil's Northeast must have made an impression on Eliana's stepfather: for a brief time, he referred to himself as Buca de Pernambuco, trying the nickname on for size.[12]

Recife was also where Booker and Eliana first laid down an LP together on the small Mocambo label.[13] Given the shoestring budget of the sessions, the album was surprisingly polished in terms of production, with crisp big band arrangements taking a back seat to the father-stepdaughter duo. Very much a transitional record between Booker's previous long plays and his later work, *Eliana e Booker Pittman* strikes a balance between US and Brazilian material, hot jazz and popular big band *à la* Sinatra, Armstrong, and Ella Fitzgerald with the newer modalities of samba and bossa nova. Eliana sometimes struggles with her English, and even Brazilian numbers such as "Bate que bate" occasionally challenge her rhythmically. Still, there are signs of brilliance throughout. She scats fluently, for instance, on numbers like "Mama Don't Allow," the number that first made her famous, cleverly spliced with a short reference to Jobim and Mendonça's "One-Note Samba."

If not yet featuring the accomplished and self-assured vocalist Eliana would be by the middle of the decade, *Eliana e Booker Pittman* showcases the arrival of a young, exuberant, and promising pupil, with the singer exhibiting little pretension beyond her present stage of development, no slick veneer of precociousness. Meanwhile, Booker's soprano is understated and elegant throughout, and not just on standbys such as "St. Louis Blues" or his brilliant turn on the 1960 Garry Mills hit "Look for a Star" but also in Brazilian numbers, beginning with his soulful instrumental take on Roberto Menescal's bossa smash "O Barquinho." For the first time in decades, Booker seems to approach his solos as opportunities not to stand out but to accent, not to dominate but to season Eliana's saucy debut in just the right ways. Even his vocal numbers sound less strained than his recordings from the late 1950s. More than just capturing the musical chemistry between the two—something invariably mentioned by observers of their live shows—*Eliana e Booker Pittman* channels something just as hard to fake: genuine joy and warmth.

In late 1961, Booker and Eliana flew to Argentina. The original invitation came hot on the heels of Eliana's first arrival on scene. An Argentine promoter invited the duo to perform at the Teatro Maipu for a two-week engagement. But then another draw emerged, the fourth Jazz Congress in Buenos Aires, organized by critic and aficionado Walter Thiers. Booker and Eliana were accompanied by the talented pianist Dom Salvador.[14] The nearly two decades since he had last graced the stages of the city, wrote the venerable Argentine jazz critic Néstor Ortiz Oderigo, had only broadened Booker Pittman's experience and deepened his musical maturity. Now focusing almost exclusively on the soprano sax, the one-time resident of Buenos Aires had managed to stitch together his previous mastery of the clarinet and alto "to achieve a vigorous style in which his agile fingering, the leaps and falls of his crackling sense of play, and his mercurial phrasing," Oderigo writes, "lend value and color to his vigorous lines, which translate his singularly measured sense of aesthetics."[15]

The visit was such a smash success that the Pittmans stayed much longer than expected, months instead of weeks. In addition to Booker's old stomping ground in the Microcentro of Buenos Aires, Booker and Eliana performed in Mar del Plata at the Confitería Paris. Eliana was impressed by how famous Booker still was in Argentina—everyone seemed to know him in the confiterías, and even in the streets. The family stayed so long and socialized so much, in fact, that Eliana met her first boyfriend, a rich boy from an elite porteño family, and learned her first lesson of the Artist's Life. When they finally left Buenos Aires in February 1962, the Pittmans stopped for a short engagement in Montevideo. But Eliana was so distressed by having to leave her boyfriend in Buenos Aires that she could barely contain her teenage grief, even when on stage. For the first time, her performance suffered. Booker took her aside at the hotel afterward: "Look, this is neither the first nor the last time in your life that you're going to have to leave someone you love," he said gently but sternly. "If you're going to fall apart like that every time you have to say goodbye to someone, you should just hang it up right now."[16]

## GIANT STEP

And then, in May 1962, came the biggest return voyage of them all so far. Booker had been talking for years about taking the giant leap northward back to his native country. The longer he delayed his return, the more daunting it seemed to him. When he was living in Argentina and Uruguay in the late 1930s and 1940s, Booker could still occasionally fool himself into thinking that he could go back to the United States without missing a beat. Surely, the scene had not changed enough for Booker Pittman's name and reputation to have been completely forgotten. So many of his friends and competitors were still headlining at the time—Ben Webster, Count Basie, Johnny Hodges—that Booker understood the scene to be ripe for the taking once he made his triumphant return. The swing scene was still a *hot* scene at its essence, even if big band had grown too large for his taste and sometimes a tad too sweet as well.

But then Booker had disappeared twice. And when he finally reemerged from his second hibernation, another world awaited. He had gone from promising to old in the blink of an eye. Little by little, he heard snippets of the new records: first Gillespie and Parker, then Monk, Coltrane. The sounds he heard incited something inside him. Was it envy? Admiration? Repulsion? He was no longer a young man; there was no denying that fact now. And these *were* young men, defiant young men speaking a strange new language he understood only because it was the familiar idiom of anguish and euphoria and searching, dressed anew. Returning now did not mean reentering the scene, did not mean rejoining the vanguard. He was twice the young lions' age; they would not have him. Rather, it meant returning as an old novelty act, a long-lost grandfather. A survivor and a former castaway, yes, but a curiosity as well, a pickled artifact of the early Swing Era.

Nevertheless, it was almost seen as inevitable in Brazil that Booker Pittman would go back to the United States, though for how long no one knew, Booker included. He simply had to go, he felt. Commercial air travel now made the trip not just feasible but also inevitable. It had become an embarrassment not to face the music of return. Still, it took some of the Rio scribes by surprise when the inevitable actually happened. What made the trip possible was the support of the People-to-People Program, an educational and cultural organization founded by President Dwight D. Eisenhauer in 1956.[17] Many Brazilian writers and fans were undecided whether to be proud or insulted, Booker's travel being either the final glorious consecration of his comeback from obscure misery or a betrayal of the country that had stood by him during his seemingly unending stream of tribulations. Maybe because the news of his departure was oddly disconcerting, a few journalists got the facts wrong. On July 24, *O Jornal* reported that Booker, Ofélia, and Eliana had participated in a music festival in Chicago and "recorded several LPs." *Jornal do Brasil* correctly wrote that Booker had attended the First International Festival of Jazz in Washington, organized by People-to-People, although the rest of the information seemed slightly dubious. Booker was said to have represented Brazil at the festival and had been sought after by promoters and musicians, including his old pals, who giddily demanded that he teach them how to play bossa nova.[18]

In Washington, besides blowing his horn at the festival, Booker played a gig with Booker Coleman's orchestra at the Hotel Charles. But everyone knew it was New York where the real action was. The journalist, photographer, archivist, and record producer Frank Driggs, whom the Pittmans met in Washington at the festival, encouraged them to add New York City to their itinerary. It did not take much to convince them. Booker knew he would be seeing more people he knew in Manhattan, and the Big Apple was still where most of the jazz clubs were, after all. With Driggs's help, Booker and sometimes Eliana played at the Shalimar in Harlem with Marlowe Morris's trio, with Buddy Tate at the Hotel Diplomat, with Edmond Hall and Jo Jones at the Central Plaza, and with Tony Parenti's band at Eddie Condon's.[19] In July, Booker performed with blues singer Jimmy Rushing at the MOMA's Jazz in the Garden Concert.[20]

The shows displayed Booker's still intact passion and chops, inventiveness and panache. He still stood out from the crowd, much as he had as a young musician at the Apollo Theater three decades earlier. But club gigs were not the main reason the Pittmans had taken the train up from Washington. A bigger draw was social: namely, rekindled friendships with Ben Webster, Budd Johnson, Jo Jones, and others. The Pittmans also made a trip to Newport for the jazz festival, where they were invited to attend as guests of honor. How could they refuse? Duke Ellington and Count Basie were there with their orchestras, and Johnny Hodges as well. When sober, Booker could be circumspect with people at first, but he quickly shed his shyness when hobnobbing with other musicians, and these were not just any musicians: they were super-peers, peers turned legends. Plus, there were younger stars in Newport that year as well—Oscar Peterson, Charles Mingus—and Booker felt that he should get to know them and that they should get to know him.

A series of photos backstage captures Booker pulling out all the stops. In one of them, he seems to assume temporary command of this luxurious ship of young guns or at least to want to. Everyone looks in a different direction. Eliana and Ofélia gaze at Booker, Eliana leaning on the shoulder of her mother while seeming to listen to an elegant Max Roach. Charles Mingus's face is distracted, taciturn. Perhaps it is because he cannot help being intrigued by Eliana's beauty and accent and at the same time bothered by her filial ties to this decidedly unrevolutionary figure, a

Eliana, Ofélia, and Booker Pittman, with Max Roach (second from right) and Charles Mingus (right). Photo by Jack Bradley. Courtesy of Eliana Pittman.

strange messenger from yesteryear who drops names like Sidney Bechet and Johnny Hodges and Willie "The Lion" Smith, who breathlessly breezes past thirty years of jazz history almost as though it had never happened. Max Roach, more cautious than Mingus, looks at Booker with diffidence mixed with curiosity. Who is this old aristocratic bushranger, he seemed to ask, this fancy Black expat who speaks in the tongue of another time? Meanwhile, Booker is confident, relaxed, a patient hero returning from a long war fought overseas, and at the same time, someone who skipped the war, who skipped many wars, because he slept through them, because he fell asleep and woke up decades later to a brave new world of hard bop and free jazz and civil rights battles. More than just a survivor, Booker looks like an unaccountably dapper, long-shipwrecked sailor. He points his gaze in Ofélia's direction, perhaps translating her words for the two American musicians. If Booker is a hero, he is also a former drunk and wastrel somewhat overcome by this sudden recognition, this sudden adulation and curiosity. He occupies a space of veneration that he did not always think he deserved.

## JET SET

Booker Pittman's first big trip down musical memory lane lasted several weeks, a trip amply documented by *Jet* magazine in a June 28, 1962, cover story. Despite its title, "Booker T. Washington's Grandson Exports Jazz to Brazil," the article said little about his illustrious grandfather. Instead, author Allan Morrison used Booker's triumphant return to the United States as a pretext to tell the musician's unusual story of expatriatism. Unlike most accounts, Morrison's story got the chronology and the facts mostly right. Since, as usual, the primary source was the musician himself, the article was a testament to Booker's newfound sobriety as well as the journalist's integrity. Morrison framed Booker as a jazz missionary: not an occasional ambassador such as Dizzy Gillespie or Louis Armstrong, but rather a deep, sustained presence in South America who spread the gospel of Black American music abroad. "He is still the leading jazzman in Brazil," Morrison wrote, "and probably has done more than any single individual to export the spirit of jazz into that country, to teach young musicians and to make converts to jazz." Morrison was also captivated by the Rip Van Winkle arc of Booker's story. Presenting him as a "noted jazzman of the 1930s" who had suddenly resurfaced in New York City three decades later, the *Jet* reporter wondered what Booker thought of the new generation of jazz performers. The question begged a hidebound answer, but Booker did not cave in. Instead of seeing nihilism and patricide in the young lions of hard bop and free jazz, Booker saw mostly quality and continuity. Or for the most part. Jazz had become more expansive, he said, "but I don't want to see it get too far out." [21]

If there was a negative side to Booker Pittman's first return voyage, it was that it did not lead to anything concrete in terms of future engagements. Booker was now hitting his stride in Brazil. He was finally making records on a regular basis for the first time in his life, and he had every expectation that the vinyl gods would shine upon him now that he had made it back to American soil, especially with the added feature of his young and talented stepdaughter in the mix. Driggs had long admired Booker's work and did his best to curry interest in Booker and Eliana. He even recorded a few demos, mostly at the club gigs themselves. But despite the series of successful live performances, the jam sessions in Harlem, and Booker's reactivated relationship with influential musicians, Driggs could not interest any record labels in either member of the unstoppable *dupla*. Maybe it was because Booker was too obscure, too much of a throwback, or maybe because Eliana was still too green and unpolished, too foreign

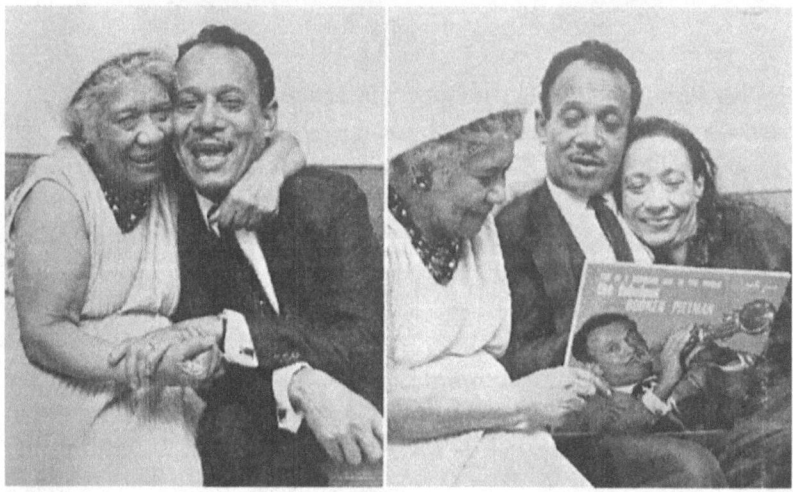

Booker Pittman, with his mother Portia Washington Pittman (left) and his sister Fannie Kennedy (right). *Jet* magazine. June 28, 1962, 59. Photography by Moneta Sleet Jr. Johnson Publishing Company Archive. Courtesy J. Paul Getty Trust and Smithsonian National Museum of African American History and Culture. Made possible by the Ford Foundation, J. Paul Getty Trust, John D. and Catherine T. MacArthur Foundation, Andrew W. Mellon Foundation, and Smithsonian Institution.

to be a jazz singer and too Black to be a pop singer. The triumphant return to glory was just a return, and a rather short one at that.

While in Washington, the Pittmans made sure to visit Booker's birthplace in the Fairmont Heights neighborhood. Sentimentally, though, the main event of the 1962 trip was undeniably Booker's long-anticipated reunion with his mother Portia and sister Fannie, a moment captured in the *Jet* feature. The family reunion almost did not happen. For all his devotion to Eliana and Ofélia, Booker did not talk much about his family in the United States. He had been away so long his immediate kin became almost like an abstraction to him, ghostly figures of the past rather than pillars of the living present. Ofélia was not like Booker in this regard. She knew that it was important for him to see his mother, whether he realized it or not, and that this might prove to be his last chance. When the meet-up did happen, Portia Pittman Washington was beside herself. In one of the photos published in *Jet*, she and Fannie stare admiringly at a copy of *The Fabulous Booker Pittman* while Booker looks on proudly. In another photo, Portia gathers her son in a loving chokehold, gripping his hand with her other fist as if her joy were cut with a dash of resentment over Booker's long silences.[22]

And who could have blamed her? Booker had apparently stopped corresponding with his family many years before. Portia never believed that her wayfaring son had died in exile, as was widely rumored. But she correctly sensed that something had gone seriously wrong in South America. So naturally, there was exasperation and not just euphoria and relief when she saw him again with her own eyes: the mother's mix of competing judgments and sensations. Her flighty Booker was now reformed, sober, dignified. He had achieved something like stardom in the Southern Hemisphere. He had also become, in his upside-down way, a family man. Portia later said that she took an immediate liking to Ofélia, whom she saw as a "solid person," even if she could hardly communicate with her without Booker serving as the translator.[23] As for his stepdaughter, she was something to behold: beautiful, lithe, full of talent. If she was not his blood daughter, and therefore neither Portia's granddaughter nor scion of the Booker T. Washington legacy, she might as well have been. Portia saw more than just a spark of energy in Eliana, more than just charm and vivacity: she saw unusual grit as well, and a love, admiration, and devotion to her Booker that struck her as miraculous.

## BRAZILIAN AGAIN

When the Pittmans returned to Brazil in August, things returned to normal, but they also did not. *Jornal do Brasil*, like many other Brazilian papers, reported proudly and hyperbolically that the voyage of return had reaped many benefits, accolades, and success but that Booker was nonetheless glad to be back in his real home: *A terra boa mesmo é aqui*, he was quoted as saying. "The really good land is right here."[24] The international successes reported in the local press were somewhat exaggerated, no doubt because the Pittmans themselves had fed their versions to starstruck reporters. But hyperbole aside, the trip had certainly done wonders for Booker's confidence as well as his renown. No longer limited to his regular gig at the Little Club, Booker, sometimes accompanied by Eliana, played a series of newer, larger clubs in Rio de Janeiro: the Cangaceiro, the Blue Angel, The Terrace, Fred's, Au Bon Gourmet. The two of them signed a four-month contract with TV-Record to do a weekly show.[25] In November 1962, Booker, Ofélia, and Eliana traveled to Belo Horizonte, where the family had a Keystone Cops run-in with the police that involved a car chase and a flat tire, supposedly over the question of their documents.[26] In April

1963, they went on a fifteen-day tour of other regional capitals: Manaus, Belém, Fortaleza, Recife, Salvador.[27]

The money was finally arriving in bunches. But Booker and Eliana's perceived comedown to the anything-goes cultural circuit and musical repertoire of Rio de Janeiro did not go unnoticed. *Diário Carioca*'s Míster Eco singled out Booker's performance in *Sonho em BG*, Flávio Ramos's musical "pocket show" at the Bon Gourmet, as indicative of a deeper problem. The columnist bemoaned the "many kilometers of distance" between Booker and the rest of the musical cast. But his criticism did not stop there. Why—Míster Eco asked—did Booker insist on spending his time and energy on countless boate shows, parties, and "little provincial fairs" (*festinhas interioranas*) when he could surely be paying the bills blowing with the likes of Louis Armstrong and Ray Charles two or three times a year? The journalist also pointedly questioned Eliana's supposedly "nervous" presence and ultimately secondary role alongside her stepfather. "She needs to free herself," he wrote bluntly.[28]

By this time, Booker's professional fate was securely tied to Eliana's and vice versa. Both seemed fine with the arrangement, though at times, their partnership led to certain misunderstandings. There was the question of the true nature of their relationship. One reporter published a story identifying Booker as Eliana's biological father, misquoting her as saying she had found her musical vocation because her "blood spoke louder" than her desire to study. Míster Eco saw fit to denounce the story as a lie, even if, he conceded, Eliana *considered herself* Booker's daughter. Eliana was talented in her own right, and her vocation as a singer was not a sanguineous one, he quipped, "unless it happened by osmosis."[29] A feature article in *Revista do Rádio* showed both Eliana and Booker posing together at the beach in their bathing suits while Booker blew his soprano sax or pretended to. As if the mild insinuation of incest were not enough, the magazine posed the awkward question, "Artistically speaking, who is better, father or daughter?" Questioning the legitimacy of their relationship and even spurring filial rivalry would have broken a weaker bond. But Booker was proud of how Eliana was blooming artistically, and Eliana was deeply loyal to Booker as a father figure and especially as a musical mentor.

And anyway, whatever the perceived dynamics of their partnership, their onstage chemistry was hard to deny. Booker had a saying in Portuguese that summarized the Pittmans' successful working relationship: *Booker, saxofone; Eliana, microfone; Ofélia, telefone*. Ofélia had, in fact, discovered her true calling as the duo's marketing whiz, consultant, manager and *crisis* manager, agent and *travel* agent, stage director and sometimes *artistic* director. If Booker and Eliana always seemed to be rehearsing or performing, Ofélia was constantly on the phone, smoothing out wrinkles in the itinerary, solving wardrobe issues, dealing with broken or missing instruments, and barking negotiations with nightclub empresários or television producers. As a bonus, her management skills worked to keep Booker's fan club at bay. Even after Eliana's rise to prominence, the elegant and charming "Buca" had a faithful brood of fans and suitors wherever he went. Ofélia implicitly understood how to set limits on their adoration without making them feel they were being rejected. Platonic seduction, after all, was good for business.[30]

Even in their trips abroad, monolingual Ofélia made herself understood, if not with gestures, then by grabbing the nearest bilingual person—sometimes Booker, later Eliana—and hurling them into the role of simultaneous interpreter. Despite her knack for multitasking, though, Ofélia was not adept at planning events in advance. In this sense, she was like Booker, a virtuoso improviser, her skills so sharp they not only made up for the chaos but also thrived off of it. But beneath her mask of uncouth anarchy, Ofélia was shrewd and fearless, a bedrock of advocacy and mediation, intuitively practical and unnervingly frank. The Pittman *dupla*, as both Booker and Eliana knew, simply could not have done what they did without her. Ofélia's hard-earned independence, her experience as a Black working-class woman in São Paulo, had trained her to confront racism, sexism, and injustice wherever and whenever they stood firmly in her way and to brush them off deftly when they did not. Over the years, she became less a stout defender of her own interests and more a stout defender of Booker's, and especially Eliana's.

## BOSSA

Something else played in Booker and Eliana's favor: fortuitous timing. In this sense, Booker Pittman's uncanny knack for arriving on a musical scene in full bloom remained fully intact. First Kansas City, then Harlem, Paris, Buenos Aires, and now Rio de Janeiro, where bossa nova had gone global since Eliana and Booker's first LP two years earlier. Honed by countless performances in Brazil, Argentina, and the United States, Booker and Eliana were by now fluent in the hot new bossa idiom, and the Pittmans rightly saw themselves in a unique position to bridge the gap between Brazilian popular music and jazz. The list of non-Brazilian artists who had either dabbled or dived deep into bossa nova was long: Stan Getz, Charlie Byrd,

Coleman Hawkins, Quincy Jones, Dave Brubeck, Herbie Mann, Shorty Rogers, Paul Winter, Eydie Gormé, Tito Puente, Lalo Schifrin, and Cannonball Adderley, just to name a few. The rapid expropriation of bossa nova took many Brazilian critics and musicians by surprise. Since its emergence in the last couple of years of the 1950s, bossa had already been deemed a diluted menace by cultural nationalists. And that was *before* the style took the world by storm. Practically before João Gilberto, Tom Jobim, Roberto Menescal, Carlos Lyra, and others could respond to the accusations, the bastard child of cool jazz and samba emerged as an emblem of *brasilidade* around the globe. So, in a sense, according to critics like José Ramos Tinhorão, samba had been twice corrupted, first by Brazilians listening to too much Chet Baker and second by Baker's countrymen, eager to make millions of dollars off the bossa craze.[31]

The anonymous liner notes of Eliana and Booker's next record *News from Brazil—Bossa Nova* bear traces of Tinhorão's nationalism if not his fundamentalism: "The recordings of Brazilian songs performed abroad are simply laughable."[32] *News from Brazil* is an "authentic" hybrid, on the other hand, at once a family act and binational one, each member bringing their national credentials to bear on the recording. The record also has a considerably more modern and seamless feel than the 1962 Mocambo LP. Backed by the capable Tamba Trio on several numbers, *News from Brazil* is less of a jazz offering than its predecessor and consequently, at least at first listen, somewhat less of a Booker Pittman affair. But if Booker sometimes takes a back seat to Eliana, his solos on both alto and soprano are just as pithy and punchy as ever, all the more impressive given that the only US standard included on the record is Duke Ellington's "It Don't Mean a Thing." The Brazilian accent should not be surprising. Booker was not new to the *batida* rhythm undergirding samba and bossa nova. He had, in fact, been playing sambas for decades. Since returning to Brazil in 1949, he had been compelled to play and even sing Brazilian standards at countless carnivals, fairs, and weddings. He soon took to sprinkling sambas into his boate repertoire as well.

For her part, on *News from Brazil*, Eliana sounds a great deal more mature than on her first record, rhythmically and tonally more self-assured. If she still had not reached the level of polish that she would achieve in her first solo record *É preciso cantar* (1966), it was understandable. She was still only eighteen years old. And as Eliana remarked in a television interview decades later, she was never a "supernatural" singer in the same vein as her contemporary Elis Regina. She may have been precocious, she admits, but never *that* precocious. By her own admission, Eliana was

Album cover of Eliana & Booker Pitman [sic], *News from Brazil—Bossa Nova!* Polydor, 1963. Fair use.

not born with The Voice; she had to *learn* how to sing.³³ Her growing confidence and technique and Booker's striking ease with samba-bossa modalities create moments of great synergy between the two, as evidenced by their interlocking solos in an energetic rendition of "Amor no Samba." Still, as the album progresses, it becomes apparent that it is still the *mestre* Booker who anchors the sessions. It is *his* bossa nova record. Early on, he flashes the leather on the soprano in "O Barquinho," nimbly laying down riffs that Eliana answers with nimble scatting of her own. Given more room to improvise on the alto on two instrumentals, Menescal's "O Passarinho" and Chico Feitosa's breezy "Festa na Floresta," Booker punctuates leisurely obbligatos with searing runs and fat blues riffs, adapting the up-tempo bossa nova *batida* with the same masterful yet unpredictable hot phrasing that defined his earlier records. In doing so, he became a logical exponent of bossa nova and also an unlikely one. A full two decades older than many of the younger bossa stars, Booker also stood in clear contrast—as an American-born, Brazilian-based Black man—to most of the new idiom's leading practitioners. Yet, in many ways, he was ideally positioned to serve as a bridge between jazz and samba in their different iterations. After all, few, if any, of the Brazilian *bossanovistas* could claim such deep knowledge of jazz. Conversely, none of the scores of US- or European-based converts to bossa nova could boast of such a long and deep-lived experience in Brazil, even if musical importers like Charlie Byrd and Stan Getz helped to make bossa nova "legible" to American jazz audiences, at times by simplifying the music rhythmically.[34] Boosted by a Brazilian supporting cast including his stepdaughter, the north-south musical hybrid of bossa nova came naturally to Booker Pittman. As the album cover of *News from Brazil* suggested, just as he helped to export jazz to Brazil, he was now intent on sending the music back to the United States, transformed into something else.

Or at least that was the idea. Judging from the lack of press it received, the record did not make nearly as big a splash abroad as the Pittmans would have liked. Clearly, Booker and Eliana would have to establish themselves in the United States if they hoped to join the ranks of Byrd, Getz, and others. Since the global rise of bossa nova, returning abroad was rarely far from Booker's mind or from Ofélia's. Booker had refreshed his contacts on their last visit, and increasingly, there were new offers. And when there were no offers, there were at least promises, and when there were no promises, there were *fofocas*, rumors. One paper announced confidently at the end of the year (1963) that a biography of Booker would be published in the US, with chapters to be written by journalists from the countries where he had lived and performed.[35] Whether or not the news fell under the category of a contract, a promise, or a *fofoca*, the biography never materialized. Nonetheless, Booker felt, justifiably or not, that he was one breakthrough away from international stardom. While Booker and Eliana continued to land work in and around Rio de Janeiro, they sustained themselves with short contracts at high-end venues, such as the Golden Room at the Copacabana Palace and the Oasis in São Paulo, as well as miscellaneous parties and social and cultural events. There were also frequent trips abroad: first, they went to Buenos Aires again, where they performed on television, at nightclubs, and in a concert at the Teatro Maipu.[36] Then, the *dupla* played for club and TV audiences in Montevideo, followed by a ten-day stint in the coastal Argentine city of Mar del Plata; shortly later, they jetted to Portugal before returning home.[37]

While they remained in Rio de Janeiro, both father and stepdaughter had to contend all too often with petty jealousies and bigotry. One egregious incident happened in July 1964, when Booker and Eliana were invited to perform on TV Excélsior by one of the station's sponsors. When the duo arrived at the studio to rehearse, the vedette Iris Bruzzi, with the backing of producer Carlos Manga, abruptly kicked the Pittmans off the set without bothering to offer an explanation. Another source says the real conflict was stoked by a simmering dispute between Manga and Ofélia, dating back several months.[38] Trusty ally Míster Eco blamed the ill-treatment on a nebulous "lack of respect," but clearly there were overtones of racial prejudice. *Tribuna da Imprensa* was more explicit. Journalist and friend Fernando Lopes lamented that "these things still happen in Brazil" and quoted Bruzzi as yelling, "I don't want to see these *pretos* [Blacks] here as long as I'm working."[39] True to form, Booker was graceful though cutting in his rejoinder. "That little blonde girl still thinks the instrument I play is the trumpet," he quipped.[40]

The racial tensions that occasionally boiled to the surface in such exchanges pointed to deeper-seeded inequities. In a pointed and telling article published in *Jornal do Brasil*, journalist Paulo Rehder proclaimed the nightlife of Rio de Janeiro in the mid-1960s as a cultural space increasingly dominated by Black performers. Based on a live show of and about Rio's nightlife broadcast from the studios of TV-Rio, the piece featured photographs of a number of Afro Brazilian performers, including Cartola, Nelson Cavaquinho, Elza Soares, and Booker and Eliana Pittman. The attitude of Rehder was outwardly one of tribute and celebration. "[S]ince our *crioulos* [Blacks] now occupy the greater part of nocturnal spectacles," he wrote, "Rio nights are blacker and more authentic when it comes to the popular arts ... proving once again the important influence of their race in Brazilian cultural history and civilization." To prove his point, Rehder wrote that after witnessing the talents of such figures, even a conservative white tourist from Dallas would surely be moved to "abandon his racial prejudice and tear up his John Birch Society card."[41] Rehder names Booker and Eliana as pioneering figures in this regard. He also evokes Booker's hometown to drive home his point. Just a coincidence? Booker had been integrating Brazilian nightlife for decades, but usually as a token performer and as a foreigner. Now, while paving the way for other Black performers in Rio's boates, he had settled into something resembling a stable, even bourgeois, Brazilian identity. When he flew back from the United States to resume his personal and professional life, it was not just proof of his loyalty to his friends and family or his preference for Brazilian soil ("a terra é boa mesmo"). He was enacting his true citizenship, a second homecoming.

It was also something of a trap. As a newly sober Afro Brazilian family man and not merely an impulsive and unpredictable expat, Booker

Pittman could no longer count on the social and racial protections sometimes afforded to Black travelers and exiles in Brazil. It mattered little that many Brazilians viewed the relatively light-skinned Booker not as *negro* but rather as *mulato*—a category with more durable currency in Brazil than in the United States by the 1960s. This was due in part to the military dictatorship's promotion of Brazil's *mestiçagem* or mixed-race heritage.[42] In this regard, the most influential intellectual of the middle decades of the twentieth century was the sociologist Gilberto Freyre, whose landmark *Casa Grande e Senzala* (1933), translated as *The Masters and the Slaves*, achieved wide readership in the United States and beyond. More than any other, Freyre's book popularized and even institutionalized the exceptionalist notion that Brazil was a "racial democracy" whose population was the byproduct of centuries of racial and cultural mixing and therefore supposedly given to more amenable race relations than in countries like the United States.[43]

Black Americans like Booker Pittman, though, typically experienced Brazil's social fabric and racial politics through a distinct lens. Since early in the twentieth century, African American travelers to the country had reported a whole host of impressions of the South American nation. In 1920, one visitor reported to the Associated Negro Press that "Brazilians, without regard to race or color, are as one big family, standing together on grounds of absolute equality or opportunity. There are no distinctions whatsoever other than those imposed by wealth, culture, and position."[44] Such rose-colored views of Brazil echoed the opinions of many Brazilians themselves. By the 1940s, some African American intellectuals like E. Franklin Frazier questioned Freyrean notions of Brazil's race-blind society, signaling persistent instances of colorism in Brazil, even as he used what he saw as Brazil's rejection of a racial caste system to criticize Jim Crow policies in the United States.[45] By the 1960s, a new generation of travelers increasingly saw through the Brazilian veneer of racial harmony and cordiality. Sensitized by the struggle for civil rights in the United States, for instance, history professor Leslie B. Rout Jr. recounted several instances of racial profiling during his travels to Porto Alegre, São Paulo, and Rio de Janeiro in 1965, though he also learned that "[y]anking out my passport and shouting 'Americano, Americano' was the equivalent of Ali Baba's 'Open Sesame'" in terms of his treatment by police and lighter-skinned Brazilians.[46]

Amidst this ambiguous backdrop of outward racial harmony and less overt though persistent segregation and prejudice, the growing visibility of Black entertainers in Rio de Janeiro threatened the white elite status quo of middle-class cultural circuits in Copacabana and inevitably fomented confrontation. Such changes to the racial landscape sometimes made Booker Pittman feel more rather than less vulnerable in the face of conflicts such as the Manhattan Club incident or the dust-up at TV-Excelsior. Now that he had settled down and embraced Brazil as his national identity, moreover, he could no longer count on full immunity from many of the problems that native-born Afro Brazilians (like his wife and stepdaughter) faced on a regular basis. Invoking national privilege was not as simple as it used to be.

## *THE JACK PAAR PROGRAM*

Just as Brazil was beginning to feel at once more comfortable and also more complicated, Eliana and Booker were invited to perform on the US weekly entertainment show *The Jack Paar Program* after the host himself caught a performance of theirs in Rio while visiting Brazil with his family. Though it is difficult to ascertain, the Pittmans' compelling backstory probably seduced Paar as much as their musicianship and onstage charisma. It is also likely that the famous host identified with Booker in some essential ways, and the feeling may well have been mutual. Paar was already a veteran broadcast journalist and a legend in the business when, in 1960, upset over a dispute about censorship with his show's producers, he stormed off the set of NBC's *Tonight Show*. "There must be a better way of making a living than this," he said before leaving. Paar's blowup revealed to the nation that he was not just testy and impetuous but also principled and no-nonsense. When he returned to the network two years later with the weekly *Jack Paar Program*, he famously opened his monologue with the line: "As I was saying before I was interrupted . . ."[47]

The national talk show as a genre bore the mark of Jack Paar's influence for decades to come. Even so, he was an entertainer who could barely bring himself to stomach the US entertainment industry. On a regular basis, his legions of nightly viewers, even before his infamous walkout, witnessed the host's knack for doling out brutal honesty but also brilliant ad-libs and sudden shows of emotion. He was just as likely to shed a tear as he was to raise his voice on the set. Paar's affectionate, even sentimental, predisposition, his unpredictable edginess, and his instinctive showmanship no doubt appealed to the Pittmans. Like Booker, Paar knew how to woo his audience, to gather them into his coils, and then just as quickly cast them out if they misbehaved. Jack Paar also knew that his main means of seduction were his power and influence. Between the late 1950s through his early, definitive retirement in 1965, he was a talent scout extraordinaire, a media kingmaker. There was perhaps no one better in the world by whom to be discovered and promoted. Eliana and Booker also knew well how to beguile strangers and with considerably scarcer means at their disposal. Jack Paar and his family were likely not prepared for just how seductive the Pittmans could be, or for that matter, for how compelling *Brazilians* could be when they put their minds to it. Booker himself had succumbed to the country's spell decades before, first in Paris (through Bibi Miranda) and then in Rio. But now he was on the other side, and what he once thought was magic he now knew to be artfulness, the inconspicuously direct machinations of flattery, mirth, and conquest.

*Tribuna da Imprensa* first reported in late August 1964 that Eliana and Booker had signed a contract to play on Jack Paar's show. When columnist Maria de Lourdes Pinhel announced that "it seems they're really going to steal away Eliana from us," she had reason to be worried. But the focus on Eliana was new. "Of all the female singers of the new generation," Pinhel wrote, "Eliana is one who is soaring the highest, and without having to depend on cheap gimmickry, without connections in high places, and without having to rely on her good looks."[48] Then, there were the optimistic, nationalist commentaries. "Uncle Sam will samba with them," went the headline in *Última Hora*. As proof, the newspaper listed all the Brazilian compositions that "nossa Eliana brasileiríssima" ("our exceedingly Brazilian Eliana") would take with her, as if the songs were rare objects stashed away in her suitcase.[49]

In his opening remarks on the night of their appearance on the *Jack Paar Program*, on October 2, 1964, the host foregrounded the obligatory set pieces of talent and discovery. He also turned the backstory into a family affair of the Paars as well as the Pittmans. He humble-bragged about his own reputation and track record for "having a special touch with people" and a nose for young talent who had gone on to become stars in the world of music and entertainment. Then, after crediting his teenage daughter Randy with discovering and befriending Eliana at a party in Rio thrown in their honor, Paar skillfully set the stage for the Pittmans' arrival on stage. Eliana was, he said, a girl who actually *lived* in Ipanema. *She isn't tall, but she is tan and lovely.*

That Eliana opened the biggest televised performance of her young life with the massively popular eponymous song was neither surprising nor coincidental. By October 1964, bossa nova was riding high in the United States. Stan Getz, João Gilberto, and Astrud Gilberto's hit version of Tom Jobim and Vinícius de Moraes's masterpiece "A garota de Ipanema" ("The Girl from Ipanema"), which had topped the charts in March of that same year, was the peak of bossa nova's ascendance. But it was not the first rendition of the song. In truth, bossa nova's conquest of the United States dates back at least to a Carnegie Hall omnibus concert in November 1962, a show and ensuing record that introduced many US listeners to Brazilian musicians like João Gilberto, Roberto Menescal, Carlos Lyra, and Sérgio Mendes, even if jazz stalwarts like Dizzy Gillespie, Charlie Byrd, and Herbie Mann had already made hay with the new idiom.[50] The US talk show circuit was key to the spread of bossa nova. Before the Pittmans' appearance on *The Jack Paar Program*, CBS's *Ed Sullivan Show* had featured the likes of the Brazilian instrumental group *Bossa Três* and Xavier Cugat and Eydie Gormé performing "Blame it on the Bossa Nova."[51] Even fresher in everyone's televisual memory were Astrud Gilberto and Stan Getz, who had just, weeks before, performed "The Girl from Ipanema" together on ABC's variety show *The Hollywood Palace*.

The main irony of Eliana's rendition of the song on *The Jack Paar Program* is that it was not done in the style that made the number famous to begin with. In fact, it did not even come close to exuding the cool approach of *Getz/Gilberto*, but this did not stop Eliana from putting over the number with her usual exuberance. Another part of the young siren's seduction package was just how well she knew how to sell whatever song she was singing, regardless of style or genre. Wearing a girlish puffy skirt and beehive haircut, Eliana cut a brash and gamine figure as she sang and danced, backed by Paar's punchy big band. She belted out the number in a way that could not have been much different from Astrud Gilberto's demure performance just a few weeks earlier. Technically solid, bouncy, and coquettish, Eliana gave "The Girl from Ipanema" a swinging, show-tune treatment in English and Portuguese.[52]

After a climactic "por causa do amor!" Eliana burst into stage tears, met by the famously emotional host's embrace. "Randy's crying, everybody's crying. You were great!" he said. "*Eu estava tão nervosa* [I was so nervous]," Eliana babbled in Portuguese. "I'm crying; that means you were a smash," Paar replied, in what had now become a comic schtick, possibly a rehearsed one. Milking the moment, Eliana played up her ignorance of the host's comebacks and inside jokes. "Anyway, she has no agent," Paar responded. "And if you negotiate, you have to talk to her mother." When Eliana demanded an explanation, the host struck a pose of irritation, his face quickly stiffening. "You'd better get humble quick, kid, I'll tell you that."

Was Jack Paar actually annoyed with Eliana's attempt to upstage him with her assertiveness and mock naïveté? Did he expect her to be more submissive, more polite, more *innocent*? Or was this just his way of milking the scene for laughs, drawing attention to linguistic confusion at the expense of his doe-eyed, dark-skinned guests? It was unclear. When Paar pivoted into seriousness again to tell the story of Booker Pittman, it seemed a carefully tailored tale and also an inaccurate one, peppered with misinformation. Not only was *Time* magazine credited with having found Booker after he had "disappeared in the jungles of Brazil," but Eliana was now cast as the Americans' savior: "He went out of retirement when a daughter came along." No mention was made of Booker's drug and alcohol abuse—the Pittmans would never have spoken candidly with Paar about their family secrets, and anyway, FCC rules and normative practices of US national television in the mid-1960s would likely not have allowed it. But it is remarkable that Paar, who was usually so sensitive to issues of censorship, would gloss over something as central as Eliana's true parentage, spinning Booker's reemergence as nothing more than an instinctive reaction to a pregnancy that never happened.

Once the aftermath of "The Girl from Ipanema" subsided, the new number began, "Hello Dolly." For three long seconds, the house band hovered in a sonic holding pattern. Finally, Booker emerged out of the shadows stage right, his gait a tad accelerated, as if arriving overdressed and slightly late for the bus uptown. The entrance must have been somewhat disconcerting for the audience, though all was quickly forgotten once the melody began. "Hello, Dolly" was another recent hit, the titular tune from the 1964 Broadway musical. Louis Armstrong quickly cannibalized the song, turning it into one of his greatest successes of all time. For his star turn on *The Jack Paar Program*, not only did Booker mimic Louis Armstrong's vocal style, but he seemed to impersonate his visual tics as well: the too-broad smile, the languid squinting eyes, his outstretched arms holding the trumpet-like soprano sax. They were fresh reminders of the early Swing Era and faint remnants of the vocabulary of minstrelsy permeating jazz performance of the 1920s. Was Booker an impersonator or a novelty act? Behind the surface incoherence was a half-hidden strategy: with his glossy tuxedo and Prohibition Era mannerisms, Booker was announcing himself to the world as something at once dated and durable, unique and derivative—the vivid progenitor of his stepdaughter's youthful talent, modern dress, and fresh dance moves. At the same time, behind the studied artifice, there was a deep connection with Jerry Herman's lyrics:

> Hello, Dolly
> This is Booker, Dolly
> I'm so glad to be back home where I belong

After Eliana joined him for the second refrain, singing in Portuguese, Booker peeled off a solo that drew mild applause with its elegance, swing, and polish: an immaculate recreation of a bygone era. The solo lacked the fresh ideas, the sudden, brilliant swerves into the unpredictability of his recorded work from previous years. But this was surely lost on the studio audience. They were there to witness the Story: the return of a man fully intact from the abyss of musical obscurity. Paar had made sure of that. Such a tale would only work—the host seemed to understand intuitively—if Booker played the part correctly, a happy embodiment of himself before his epic fall. His success on *The Jack Paar Program*, in other words, hinged on a fabricated sense of continuity, a morally clean fable of disappearance and reappearance, of unmarked burial and unscathed resurrection: *As I was saying before I was interrupted.*

It also would work only if Booker allowed Eliana to upstage him, something he did willingly, even eagerly. By the second number, Eliana, always the quick study, had already mastered NBC's cameras; she knew when to hold still for a close-up and when to engage the studio audience, boate-style. Her handle on "Hello Dolly" was deft, powerful, her singing more impressive than his. At the end of the number, Paar summoned Ofélia to the stage along with his own daughter, Randy. And so, in the very year Lyndon B. Johnson's signature civil rights legislation was signed into law, a mini-tableau of 1960s racial harmony materialized. Eliana and Randy embraced tenderly, whispering niceties to each other with teen complicity. Jack Paar, meanwhile, seemed not to want to be touched by Ofélia, but she hugged and kissed him anyway. *Estou tão contente*, she gushed. *Obrigada* ("I'm so happy. Thank you.").

How often had Brazilian Portuguese been heard on prime-time US television in spoken form? Probably quite rarely up to that point, or at least since Carmen Miranda's untimely death in 1955. A decade later, live television was still the norm, and for a moment, no one was there on the NBC soundstage to translate or to direct traffic. It was a sloppy spectacle, almost amateurish. No one knew quite where to stand. Booker especially was on unsure footing, so he did the only thing he knew how: he improvised, drifting in front of people, between them, behind them. Although he smiled incessantly, it would be wrong to conclude that his joy was disingenuous. The musical numbers had gone off well, after all. Not without a couple of timing problems, but the Pittmans had made up for any stumbles with pluck and preparation, charm and showmanship.

Not once, however, had Paar asked Booker to tell his own story. Why hadn't it occurred to him to do so? Perhaps the host was too focused on

Eliana, blinded by her youthful beauty and magnetism. Or perhaps, more disturbingly, he wanted to control the Booker T. Pittman backstory, strip it of its accidental revelations, its unsavory details and unusual genealogies, its *errancy*, to return to Glissant's term. Surprisingly, the televised appearance was devoid even of the historical hook of Booker T. Washington, an angle repeatedly played up in middle-class African American publications of the period like *Jet* and *Ebony*. Instead of messy eccentricity, instead of the epic circuitousness of Booker's return, there was only wholesomeness and rootedness, manufactured racial harmony and feel-good simplicity. The long-lost hero had come full circle, and the circle was symmetrical, shiny, immaculate.

When Paar finally got around to shaking Booker's hand, it was to get rid of him. *Goodbye, Booker.* The celebrated talk show host hardly seemed to grasp what he had just delivered to US audiences. The binational stepfamily affair rang out with symbolic potential. It almost demanded to be read as an informal, rag-tag staging of American cultural conquest in Latin America, of grassroots, musical Pan-Americanism. The live spectacle was a far cry from the scripted kind of exchange officially pursued by the State Department in the 1950s and 1960s by the likes of Duke Ellington, Dizzy Gillespie, Woody Herman, Dave Brubeck, and, of course, Louis Armstrong himself. The underlying goal of the jazz offensive was Cold War propaganda, to present jazz as an emblem of US talent, racial harmony, and global democracy against Soviet claims to the contrary. As Penny Von Eschen has written, "[US] government officials and supporters of the arts hoped to offset what they perceived as European and Soviet superiority in classical music and ballet, while at the same time shielding America's Achilles' heel by demonstrating racial equality in action."[53]

Yet another kind of cultural work, less spectacular and more granular, had long been undertaken by jazz's unofficial representatives in the region, one that had little to do with the larger theater of Cold War geopolitics. Typically, these were not shallow, fleeting forays into Latin American cultural landscapes, funded and coordinated by government entities, but rather long-term immersions and lone wanderings. In this sense, Booker Pittman and others like him did not fit squarely within the more conventional categories of cultural diplomats or expat musicians, much less "lifestyle migrants" or "residential tourists."[54] As I mentioned in this book's introduction, Booker and his ilk were better described as global migrants who comprised an off-grid branch of Black Internationalism: errant aural artists who nourished and helped to define shifting transnational musical scenes in the middle decades of the twentieth century.[55] On *The Jack Paar*

Booker and Eliana on *The Jack Paar Program*, October 2, 1964. Photo courtesy of Eliana Pittman.

*Program*, instead of Armstrong and Herman, audiences beheld an eerily familiar yet mostly forgotten musician who, for three decades, had been laying the groundwork for his moment in the spotlight; someone who night after night had been doing the invisible labor of hemispheric encounters, the dirty work at the far-southern crossroads. Booker now came back to his homeland, having sown the seeds of jazz in South America for half a lifetime. And with him now, as proof of his travails as US Secret Ambassador, emerged his musical progeny, his jazz offspring.

## RIDING THE WAVE

The US press corps seemed to like what they saw on *The Jack Paar Program*. *Variety* called Eliana and Booker's routine and the ensuing Pittman–Paar lovefest an "emotional blowout" full of laughter and tears. "The whole bit went over winningly."[56] The appearance led to a series of new offers—NBC's "Nightlife," WOR-TV's "The Joe Franklin Show." In November 1964, *Jornal of Brasil* reported that Eliana and Booker were staying at the Great Northern Hotel in New York City. Also reported was that Eliana had sent a letter to samba icon Zé Keti expressing Leeds Music Corporation and

Musidisc's interest in making a record with him.[57] These long-range missives suggest that Eliana had begun to eclipse her stepfather in the public eye. They also show how the young singer, encouraged by her mother, had started to assert herself on stage, where she increasingly played master of ceremonies and occasionally *raconteuse* and not just *chanteuse*. Offstage, her vision and experience began to match her chutzpah.

Booker Pittman wished to think of his appearance on *The Jack Paar Program* as the inauguration of his international fame. But it really turned out to be the climactic event of his comeback. Though journalists were careful to mention Booker's supporting role in subsequent US performances, for his guidance in rehearsals and musical savoir-faire, the message was clear enough: Eliana, not Booker, was now the star-ascendant. Based on her nightclub appearances alone, Eliana drew glowing reviews from the major New York City publications: the *Post*, the *Daily News*, the *World Telegram*, *Backstage*. The *New York Times* reported that the Pittmans appeared at a new music-and-variety venue called The Phone Booth on East 55th Street in Manhattan. While Eliana showed "so much vitality and sparkle that she manage[d] to cut through the superficiality of her surroundings," her stepfather "quietly [played] in the shadows at the side of the stage whenever his daughter [sang]."[58]

Not all the reviews were uniformly positive. *Variety* said of the Pittmans' stint at the Living Room that the "pretty café au lait chanteuse" was "personable, lively, but too gimmicked to really showcase herself effectively." While the reviewer commended Booker for adding musical heft to the show with his "touching display of paternal devotion," he suggested that Eliana should tone down her act and get serious, preferably without the aural clutter and showmanship of her stepfather.[59] The Pittmans took such comments to heart. Just two months later, Eliana had taken her talents downtown to headline at the Greenwich Village venue Bon Soir, this time without Booker. The change was immediately apparent. *Variety*'s reviewer "José," who had penned the earlier review as well, approved the way Eliana had "dropped many of the mannerisms that militated against her in the uptown environs." He praised her new, stripped-down act as "tremendously improved."[60]

## MANHATTANITES

Homelife in New York for the Pittmans was a mix of luxury and unpretentious informality. Booker did not want to rent a normal house or apartment in New York. His home was now Brazil, not the United States. The kind of lodging that suited him was not some apartment in the Upper West Side, or in the Village, or in Harlem. It was the spacious suite they found and rented in the Hotel Great Northern. Located at 118 West 57th Street in Midtown Manhattan, the hotel was surrounded on all sides by the glamour, noise, and verticality of New York City in the mid-1960s. Steps from a variety of restaurants, bars, theaters, and live music venues, two blocks from Central Park, a five-minute stroll to the fashion heart of Fifth Avenue, and practically next door to Carnegie Hall, the Great Northern possessed every amenity imaginable and even housed four sound recording studios.[61] Once settled in, the Pittmans made it their home as only they knew how, and with their elegant apartment and the hotel's opulent foyer, they felt as though they had *arrived* in a way that none of them could have imagined even two years prior. They entertained and made feijoada for their American and Brazilian friends.[62] They landed a gig at the swanky Park Sheraton Hotel to do a Brazilian carnival show.[63] The Great Northern's proximity to a burgeoning Brazilian district on 45th and 46th Streets only added to the Pittmans' uncanny sensation of home away from home. "Little Brazil" (as it would come to be known) contained more than just the Brazilian Trade Bureau; it also featured restaurants, stores, and even barbershops where tourists, foreign residents, and naturalized citizens could talk politics, listen to samba, feast on feijoada, and find Portuguese-language goods and services in the heart of Midtown.[64]

It must have been a surreal experience for Booker. With his Brazilian family, friends, and haunts, he now felt something like a reverse expat in the United States. But he was too focused on work, and in particular on Eliana's career, to give his sense of double alienation much thought. Although Booker was loathe to evoke his grandfather's name to gain advantage for himself, when it came to Eliana's career, he pulled out all the stops. It turned out that being Booker T. Washington's grandson could still open doors in the 1960s. With the two Bookers' help, Eliana studied in the Actor's Studio with Fred Steel, who counted among his pupils Sammy Davis Jr. and Eydie Gormé, among others.[65]

Unlike their first tour of New York and Washington, DC, in 1962, this time, fortune seemed to shine on Booker and Eliana. Still, not everything fell magically into place. Where, for instance, was the record deal that all the exposure on television and the nightclub circuit seemed to promise? Brazilian critics and fans wanted to know. Early in 1965, the Pittmans wrote to *Última Hora* saying a long play was in the works that would include versions of "Girl from Ipanema," "Estrelinha," and a few sambas by composer Elton Meneses. The record evolved into two shorter records, the first an extended play of Eliana's with Musidisc, the second an EP of Booker's. Eliana's extended play did not end up including either "Girl from Ipanema" or sambas by Elton Meneses, but it was still very much a samba and bossa nova record and is notable for its dearth of material in English and complete absence of saxophone.[66] The EP did include a composition of Eliana's ardent admirer Luis Bittencourt, "O amor do amor," as well as Zé Keti and Paulinho da Viola's "Samba de você," and Eliana's technique reveals the evolving benefits of voice lessons as she shows off a huskier lower register than she had in her previous records with Booker.

Meanwhile, Musidisc capitalized on Booker's Jack Paar performance of "Hello, Dolly" to release an EP of the same name. The songs included on the record would form the basis of a long play *Booker Pittman + Sax Soprano = Sucesso*, which would turn out to be Booker's last studio-recorded album.[67] "Nobody Knows the Trouble I've Seen" is a highlight of the sessions, an upbeat, swinging version of the slave spiritual. Compared to his earlier Satchmo knockoffs, Booker sings almost without affectation, matching the minimalism of the arrangement with a spritely vocalization suspended between pained and playful. With more room to improvise than in previous recordings, his instrumental virtuosity takes center stage, though his playing is more controlled and disciplined than ever, reflecting the spit and shine of his nightclub work in Manhattan.

In December 1965, *Ebony* did a cover story on Eliana, announcing her as the second coming of Carmen Miranda. The piece featured glossy photos of Eliana and her small entourage in a few Manhattan settings: cavorting in Central Park, shopping with her family, singing at a nightclub, relaxing at the Great Northern. They were sunny images of 1960s bourgeois consumerism, with the spotlight trained firmly on Eliana: "Now poised on the brink of a brilliant career, Eliana is faced with the question of whether she can achieve stardom in a foreign land." Booker was relegated to the sidelines of the magazine's glossy celebration of fresh-cut celebrity, typecast as the loyal stepfather "determined to shepherd [the] gifted girl to success he thinks she deserves." But his credentials as the US-born grandson of Booker T. Washington were not merely incidental. The difference between the Afro Brazilian Eliana and the white Carmen Miranda, *Ebony* suggested, went beyond race: it had more to do with pedigree, mentorship, and national provenance. Unlike the original Brazilian bombshell, Eliana had "absorbed the lessons of jazz through the teachings of her stepfather."[68] The emphasis on national origin echoed the magazine's longstanding project of adapting the American Dream to the needs and wants of middle-class Black American consumers. It also helped to sell Eliana as a crossover talent with intimate ties to the English material that she was increasingly including in her songbook.

## TROUBLE ON THE HORIZON

In the *Ebony* photo captions, Eliana also revealed her profound homesickness for Rio de Janeiro, in stark contrast to the joyful ebullience she projected in her photos. Pining for the homeland was a staple and a trope of displaced celebrities dating back to the early days of Hollywood. It played well in the US press as well as journalists back home. But Eliana's laments went beyond the standard nostalgia and stock responses of a young foreign-born star. Candid as always, she did not pass up the chance to criticize the US entertainment industry. "She is excited by [the] prospect of success in America," wrote the *Ebony* reporter, "but has become somewhat embittered by [the] sordid show business maneuverings [and] broken promises she has met."[69] That same month, *Manchete* reported that Eliana's triumph was so resounding that she could not walk a few feet at a time on the streets without someone asking her for an autograph. Not only was Eliana the hit of Manhattan nightclubs, the magazine pointed out, but she had just signed a new contract with the William Morris agency, which suggested she was about to break out in a big way. The sky was the limit for Eliana but not for Booker. The *Manchete* story featured a glamorous color photograph of Eliana *sans* Booker on the streets of New York City with the caption, "Eliana has adapted so well to the North American world of entertainment that many people refuse to believe that she is Brazilian."[70]

Looks could be deceiving. The Pittmans were not settling in anywhere. *Backstage* noted that Booker had formed his own combo, but his quest for jam-session autonomy did not appear to get very far.[71] The duo had too many club engagements in Manhattan, a wealth of riches that began to feel stifling. Eager to break free from the New York nightclub circuit, Booker and Eliana hit the road. In November 1965, the "Brazilian thrush" took her talents and diverse repertoire of songs to Georgia, Mississippi, and, significantly, Missouri.[72] In Kansas City, the duo played the Playboy Club at the Hotel Continental, a far cry, as the *Kansas City Star* noted, from the underground gambling speakeasy that Booker and Count Basie had haunted some thirty-six years prior.[73]

The father-stepdaughter duo also toured Booker's home state of Texas. As they had done in 1962 during their first trip to Washington, DC, and New York City, Eliana and especially Ofélia asked Booker if he wanted to show them ground zero of his formative years. He did not. He and Eliana played clubs in Houston and Ciudad Juárez, right across the Rio Grande from El Paso, but when they made it up to Dallas, Booker refused to show his new family the hallowed ground of his old one: not Booker T. Washington High School, or the pawn shop where he bought his first clarinet, or the Tip-Top Club, or his childhood home on Liberty Street, and certainly not the Grand Lodge of the Colored Knights of Pythias, whose very name reminded him of his late father. Booker also made a point of avoiding the state of Alabama entirely, where the Tuskegee Institute loomed as a visible reminder of the legacy he still mostly preferred to forget.

The West Coast, however, carried no such dangerous connotations and so was not off-limits for Booker. California was new to all three of them. The Pittmans jetted to Hollywood after Eliana was hired for a guest role in the NBC drama series *Run for Your Life*; Booker even briefly appeared, playing his soprano in a carnival scene.[74] The role led to more interest in Eliana's acting talents. In San Francisco, she read for the lead role in the hit stage show *The Owl and the Pussycat*.[75] By Spring, Eliana had recorded a single on the Decca label, "Lonesome Old Town," with "You Are My First Love" as the B-side.[76]

The last months of the Pittmans' stay in the United States, notwithstanding the hyperbolic press coverage in Brazil, corresponded with an almost imperceptible ebbing of expectations for the father-stepdaughter duo, if not of Eliana's international ambitions. First came news that Booker and Eliana had signed a contract to record with Warner Brothers Records.[77] A few months later, this had been amended to say they had signed a two-year contract with Musidisc.[78] The trip also witnessed the slow effacement of Booker as the duo's headliner. *Revista do Rádio* published a short article featuring a photo of Eliana posing vixen-like in a bikini. The magazine announced that Eliana had now joined the ranks of Carmen Miranda and, more recently, Astrud Gilberto as one of the few Brazilian women to have conquered the US entertainment industry. It reported that a trip that was supposed to last only a few months had lasted well over a year, "and if they finally made it back here it was only to satisfy their nostalgia for carnival." Booker was scarcely mentioned. Similar to what had happened in the United States, he had, almost embarrassingly, become an afterthought to the Brazilian press: a benevolent auxiliary figure and a feel-good subheading to Eliana's rapid ascent rather than her artistic partner and celebrity equal.

When *Tribuna da Imprensa* announced in late February 1966 that the Pittmans had returned to Rio de Janeiro, the newspaper predicted that "they will probably not stay here for long." However, in a short interview, readers of *Intervalo* magazine learned that Booker had tired of the hustle and bustle of New York. Eliana, meanwhile, gossiped with some derision about stars she encountered there: Bette Davis, Glenn Ford, Frank Sinatra.[79] She expressed disillusionment with life on the road in the United States, especially with promoters and managers. So much chaos and confusion, she said. But now there was the sense that she was trying too hard to convince herself not to go back. Maybe it was a way to clear their palette of the rushed atmosphere of the United States and their vague disappointment with their life there. Or perhaps it was a way to get back to the basics, to mark their new settledness, their proud resignation to being Brazilian after their quixotic rite of passage abroad.

Either way, Eliana and Booker quickly signed a two-week contract with a promising new nightclub called Porão 73. Despite all the commercial work, the stream of radio and television appearances, the society parties and public events, Eliana and Booker were usually most at home in their freewheeling live performances, especially in Rio de Janeiro's dynamic boates. *Manchete* commented that Eliana's performances in Porão 73 revealed "the true Eliana. On television, there are certain restrictions, but there at the Porão, she is something else. She has art in her blood."[80] Another writer said that before their stay in New York, Eliana was "a little, talented girl who sang well." She came back as a Brazilian Lena Horne.[81] Booker, meanwhile, besides showing off his usual virtuosity on the saxophone, as a singer now supposedly had "all the verve of an American Negro complemented by the *malícia* [slyness] of the Brazilian he has transformed himself into."[82]

Several of the sessions were recorded with the intention of cutting an album with the Musidisc label. *O Jornal do Brasil* reported in late March 1966 that "the release of the LP will be slightly delayed" due to technical problems. However, there had already been bad blood between Ofélia and the label's representative, Nilo Sérgio, that threatened to spill over into a lawsuit.[83] The tapes were shelved and abandoned and were only released five years later as *Eliana Pittman & Booker Pittman, Ao vivo na boate Porão 73*. The recordings provide a sonic snapshot of Eliana and Booker in the environment that best played to their separate strengths (Eliana's precocious command, Booker's versatility and soul) as well as their common ones (their technical precision, their stage presence, their showmanship). The first track of the show and the album is the iconic "St. Louis Blues" and begins with an extended solo on the soprano sax. Booker's tone is airy, agile, his approach to the melody aggressively syncopated. One of the tune's advantages is its wide-open space for instrumental and vocal improvisation, as evidenced by the countless versions of the song performed and recorded over the previous decades: Bessie Smith, Cab Calloway, and Louis Armstrong, just to name three. The song had been with Booker as long as he had known how to play jazz, since his first days in his father's garage on Liberty Street. More than a trusty blues number, "St. Louis Blues" was a sonic talisman, a summation of Booker's musical influences and knowledge. He freely molded the song to fit his own history, ad-libbing most of the lyrics and making sure to sing about three other places besides St. Louis where he had found and foiled the blues:

> Every morning
> In Kansas City, ooo
> In Copacabana, and Paraná too
> I got the St. Louis blues

The Porão 73 sessions poignantly marked a final transition in the *dupla* format developed by Booker and Eliana since their first public performance together four years earlier. Compared to his effortless claret-clear playing throughout the record, Booker's singing on "St. Louis Blues" and "Joshua Fought the Battle of Jericho" lacked the force it had had only a couple of years earlier. His voice was not just hoarse; it was frail and tentative, and his memory failed him on the lyrics of more than one song. Booker seemed more comfortable sharing the stage with Eliana, starting with the third number, "Hello Dolly," the song the two of them had debuted on *The Jack Paar Program*. It became clear as the night progressed that Booker's blues material was leading up to the final crescendo of the medley "Summertime / Stormy Weather / You're Nobody till Somebody Loves You," by which point in the performance, the American had morphed into a backup singer and prestige sideman, limiting himself to adding accents and subdued runs.

There was an odd ambivalence to Eliana's performance. "Desculpe pai" ("Forgive Me, Father"), she said more than once, as if to apologize for nudging her stepfather to the sidelines for the final numbers. At the same time, her apologies showed Eliana's abiding tenderness for Booker, her gratitude, as well as her deep *carinho*. If the stage was hers now, the show would have been impossible without him. Whereas in earlier years together, *he* had promoted *her*, now Eliana became the booster, the gracious cheerleader, even if she assumed the role of master of ceremonies throughout. By now, it was readily apparent that Eliana's last two years of experience in New York, all the vocal lessons and nightclub gigs and television appearances, had turned her into an accomplished, polished singer of jazz standards and show tunes. So thorough was her transformation—her diction in English had improved greatly as well—that the show's final number, Haroldo Lobo and Niltinho's "Tristeza," seemed to serve as a consecration of Eliana's *brasilidade*. With the help of Dom Salvador on piano, Edson Lobo on bass, and Victor Manga on the drums, Booker helped her get there, riffing his heart out on the soprano over the final bars of the hit samba from that year's carnival. After a night of jazz and blues, he seemed happy to get back to Brazil. Back home where he *really* belonged.

## AMERICANIZED

A year and a half after her breakthrough performance on *The Jack Paar Program*, Eliana was still negotiating the transition from family jazz singer to solo pop performer. The transition was not a simple one for several reasons. One was political. A coup d'état that led to the overthrow of the country's democratically elected president João Goulart happened in early April 1964, just months before the Pittmans' second departure to the United States. By the time they returned, the military regime had begun to tighten its noose around the nation's institutions. At least until the passage of the so-called Fifth Decree (Ato Institucional num. 5) in 1968, musicians and performers enjoyed a certain degree of creative latitude or at least the semblance of creative latitude. In part, this was because their increasing visibility on the expanding medium of television lent them a modern aura that the regime was eager to promote. Still, insidious pressures on entertainers, as well as the cultural media, began to mount with each passing year.[84] Within a short period of time, state censorship led to the prohibition of dozens of songs, films, plays, and art exhibitions, not to mention tighter control of television content and the confiscation of books by such celebrated authors as Carlos Drummond de Andrade and Jorge Amado.[85]

Eliana often displayed a prickly relationship with the press and the recording industry during this period. Though Rio newspapers were generally kind to her and universally praised her stepfather, occasionally, there was sniping. One critic accused the post-New York Eliana of megalomania and "talking [on stage] more than she sings."[86] While it is true that Eliana had long ago shed any adolescent deference, clearly, there were other motives behind the resentment. Dona Ofélia's assertiveness, coupled with her up-front *afro brasilidade*, appeared at times to be too much for many white male journalists, producers, and promoters to bear. Particularly after 1965, Eliana had begun to adopt a similar personality in her dealings with the entertainment industry. Part of the issue, Eliana admitted in a 2018 interview, was that she had inherited from her stepfather a certain aversion to studio recordings. Even after his return in the late 1950s, Booker cut fewer records than perhaps he could have, and Eliana said much the same of herself about the early stages of her career in the 1960s. The music industry at the time demanded a steady stream of singles and long plays, punctuated by live concerts and particularly tours. The Pittmans worked the other way around and, therefore, against the grain of market mandates, giving a multitude of performances in a wide array of venues, from tiny boats to large theater shows, punctuated occasionally by a record. Booker was, at heart, a live performer who thrived off the energy of the crowd, a predisposition that adapted well to radio and television of the period. His protégé followed suit.

Then there was the question of Eliana's Americanization. In this sense at least, she really did bear comparisons to Carmen Miranda two decades prior. Miranda had famously crumpled beneath the unique, intense pressures of Hollywood, but things were just as bad whenever she flew home to Rio de Janeiro, where she routinely suffered the recriminations of carioca elites. She was so insulted by hysterical accusations of selling out, in fact, that she recorded a samba, "Disseram que voltei americanizada" ("They Said I Came Back Americanized"), whose lyrics explicitly addressed and contested the envious snobs and gossip-peddlers who tormented her. If Eliana's foreign celebrity never reached Carmen Miranda proportions, she too resented the whispers of cultural influence usually attributed to her association with Booker and the perception that her time abroad had further corrupted her Brazilian-ness. In a 1967 interview, Eliana admitted that being Booker's quasi-kin and protégé had begun to play to her disadvantage. At the same time, her defiantly ecumenical approach to music made it difficult for her to be marketed at home as a Brazilian singer. If she planned to stay in Rio de Janeiro and make a go of it on her native soil, she would continue to sing a wide range of material. This was another Booker inheritance: their home resembled "a laboratory of composers and singers" from different countries, speaking different tongues.[87] Still, Eliana could be defensive about questions of Americanization. "You sing very well . . . in English," she would hear often. Her mother, too, grew tired of the insinuations. To the notions that Eliana was the Brazilian version of Lena Horne or "our very own great" Eartha Kitt, Dona Ofélia had a quick retort: "Nonsense. We have our very own great Eliana."[88]

At once proud and jealous of her precocious globetrotting, fearful of a permanent return to Booker's homeland, and puzzled by her multilingual repertoire, the local press corps looked for ways to keep Eliana tethered to Brazil. With her newfound celebrity, her fetching looks, and her "advancing age" (in 1966, she was all of twenty-one), pressure increased for Eliana to marry and settle down with a Brazilian man. Even before she had begun performing, she had steady boyfriends, and with rising fame came speculation about impending engagements and weddings. Many of the rumors were false. One of the first serious names that appeared in the press was the writer and composer Sérgio Bittencourt. Their supposed relationship had begun in 1963. But two years later, they were still not married, even if the match was said to have the approval of Booker, as well as Bittencourt's father, Jacó do Bandolim.[89] While in the United States, Eliana had recorded a song by Bittencourt, "Estrelinha," for an EP on Musidisc that also included Edu Lobo's "Vamos amar." Though the two may have been friends, most of the engagement story was fake news: Bittencourt was interested romantically in Eliana, but the feeling was not mutual.[90]

As she received more work offers, including one to make television movies, Eliana became the subject of even more intense speculation and insinuations about her love life. An older Brazilian magnate based in the US asked for her hand in marriage.[91] And then there was the case of the earnest and talented if hard-drinking journalist Fernando Lopes, with whom she had been rumored to be engaged as early as 1964 and who had long covered, praised, and defended the Pittmans in his *Tribuna da Imprensa* column A Noite é Nossa.[92] Unlike the case of Bittencourt, Eliana and Lopes's involvement had some basis in truth to the extent that an alcohol-wary Booker warned his stepdaughter about the journalist's love of whiskey. Upon her return to Brazil in 1966, *Intervalo* reported that Eliana was once again involved with Lopes, now director of public relations at TV-Globo in São Paulo, where Booker and Eliana did a series of four programs after their stint at the Porão. Lopes must have noticed how Eliana was beginning to get the star treatment. TV-Globo even installed a dressing room next to the stage so that she could more easily slip in and out of her different wardrobes.[93]

When the wedding with Lopes never materialized, gossip columnists only increased their keen interest in Eliana's love life, seemingly always beset by whispers and ambiguities. The cover of *Intervalo* said it all: "What exactly is there between Brasa [Roberto Carlos] and Eliana Pittman?"[94] What follows is a flirtatious interview interspersed with kisses, though toward the end, Roberto Carlos says he has a brotherly love for Eliana since Booker had been one of his biggest boosters when he was younger. As the decade advanced, Eliana had to refute rumors that she had adopted a child—it was her domestic servant's daughter, she said; incidentally, it was Fernando Lopes who reported the clarification.[95] The young singer told one reporter that she received, on average, three marriage offers per week, offers that inevitably fell into the discerning hands of Dona Ofélia.[96]

Booker found the frenzy of the match-making amusing. He knew that most of Eliana's pretenders were just that—pretenders—if not pure figments of the media's imagination. Far from being protective or jealous, the American wrote off the rumor mill as a frivolous part of young celebrity and, as such, a sign that he had succeeded in making a star of his stepdaughter. And that much was true.

*Chapter Eight*

# THE LONG ADEUS

BOOKER BREATHED IN THE STEAM FROM A PLATE OF *PEIXE AO MOLHO DE camarão* at the Bar Castelinho. It was one of his last nights in Rio de Janeiro before the Pittmans had to leave again, returning who knew when.[1] If it were up to him, it would be very soon, but it was no longer up to him. Ofélia and Eliana would have their say, and he would follow them willingly. Meanwhile, his body seemed to demand that he remain here in this exact spot, at this sumptuous restaurant overlooking the beach. Food had taken on special importance to Booker ever since beer and cachaça could not. As he nibbled the soft white flesh of the fish bathed in butter and wine, he reflected that wine sauce was now the extent of his alcoholism. It was a plate and a moment he did not ever want to end, and it was not just because of the flavors and textures, the garlic fried into the *farofa* (toasted manioc flour). It was the whole experience that the meal kept time to. There was the sheer visual splendor of the spot, of course, and it had changed little since he had first stumbled onto the dawn rising over a primeval Ipanema in 1935. Arpoador, located where Ipanema meets Copacabana, was a more crowded corner of Rio now, whereas it had once defined the city's outer limits. But the beach and the *morro* (hill) were much the same, the same red-orange and blue hues, the smell of brine and piss, shrimp and beer. The sound of O Castelinho was what really made it for Booker: the voices of street vendors, the flip-flop of sandals, a cavaquinho on the *azulejos* (patterned tiles) of the sidewalk, the roar and stench of big-motored cars, the thrum of voices ebbing and flowing like the waves themselves, and sometimes, when the Atlantic was rough enough, drowned out by them. In the foreground were Eliana and Ofélia, his inseparable beauties bantering rapid-fire in the lovely language Booker still could not get quite right, singing and giggling and then suddenly laughing loudly, almost shouting at each other. It was an ensemble of sights and sounds that seemed as though it had been on this beach forever, even though he knew it had not been. The warm cocoon of the senses made him feel protected, whole.

## ABROAD

The Pittmans reached the height of their fame just as Booker began to tire appreciably and in ways he initially did not understand. He knew that he had lived a hard life, and when he added up all the beds he had slept in, all the boats and trains and buses he had boarded, all the different bills and coins he had stuffed into his pockets, all the cocaine he had sniffed and cachaça he had quaffed, it occurred to him that he had lived enough for ten men. But he looked in the mirror and still did not see an old man, not quite yet. He was in his mid-fifties, and he still *resembled* himself, if that was possible. His playing also resembled itself; his fingers and his lungs could still hit notes and make runs that he heard first in his head a split second before he rendered them audible. But if he still looked and sounded like the person he had always been, he did not exactly feel like himself. He tired too quickly. He slept too little or too much and at the wrong times. It was the onset of what would surely be a long and happy old age, he told himself.

And so, he soldiered on, for Eliana mostly, and also for her mother, whom it was difficult to imagine without Eliana and vice versa. Certainly, the money did not hurt, although at least publicly Booker liked to say that money did not move him. "I'll take poverty in Paraná any day over Broadway with its millions of dollars," he once told a reporter.[2] What mattered to him more than a wad of bills were the large, ecstatic crowds that had eluded him for so many years. He had not felt this *wanted* since his halcyon days in Buenos Aires in the late 1930s, when anything seemed possible, before his nosedive into addiction made everything dull and hollow. Except now, the audiences did not exactly want him. They wanted Eliana, in ways that were musical and ways that were not. They wanted her voice, and they wanted her body and her energy and her newness, her spirit. But they *revered* Booker. This reverence rubbed off on Eliana and elevated her just as their desire for Eliana made Booker feel young and cutting-edge even when he well knew he was no longer either. It was second-hand desire, second-hand celebrity, and that was good enough for Booker. He was not simply proud of his stepdaughter. Her success carried with it the imprint of his own.

Eliana's career had begun to take on a life of its own, and as it did, not even Ofélia could keep Eliana from expanding into places she could not fully control. Her celebrity became unwieldy, centrifugal, a foreign object always pushing them outward. Eliana's career became too far-flung for the family to manage properly, but they stayed with her anyway. They had to.

The plane trips abroad were happening more regularly. In April 1966, the Pittmans somewhat reluctantly returned to the United States to fulfill their contractual obligations, including a stint in California and a two-week engagement at the Playboy Club in Chicago.[3] While in New York, they performed on the nationally broadcast *Merv Griffin Show* in what would be their last appearance together on American television.[4]

To Booker, the third return to his native country seemed almost like overkill. He already revisited the haunts he had wanted to revisit and saw the people he had wanted to see. Prior to their trip back to the United States in the spring, Booker expressed his worry that Brazilian music ran the risk of being diluted, vulgarized; he complained that the US recording industry was dominated by a "gang."[5] Even before leaving Brazil again, he appeared road weary, worn down by the bland food on airplanes, the checking in and out of hotels, not to mention the vagaries of international show business, each year a little harder for him to take. He vowed to local journalists that this would be his last trip abroad. After all, there was so much to Brazil, especially in the northern states, that he still had not gotten a chance to see. "What I really want to do is stay home," he said.[6]

But what did that word mean—home? Booker thought of that often around this time, when words like *becoming* and *arrival* and *future* stopped meaning as much to him as they once had. Even in the depths of his dreadful stupor in hospitals in Uruguay and São Paulo or when he was living off frog legs and fumes in Paraná, he always had the sense that there was a return to something just over the horizon, to becoming someone he had not yet become. The question of home did not interest him then because he knew he had not stopped traveling, not yet. Others may have declared him dead, but he never had, just as his mother had not either.

But now, back in Rio de Janeiro, Booker no longer needed to think of himself as a working musician forever in motion, of being on the road to recognition. That had finally left him like an unwanted ghost in the second trip to the United States: the notion that a return was an inevitable part of his story. But a return to what exactly? To Harlem? It had changed. Kansas City? Too far from the ocean and no longer what it once was. Dallas? Also too far from the ocean and *hell no* to Texas, anyway. The same went for Alabama: the mere sound of the name "Tuskegee" smarted, maybe because it reminded him not so much of his famous grandfather as his father and his mother, the hallowed origin story that had sown the seeds of his mother's unhappy marriage and his own less-than-happy childhood.

Booker did not really know what a return meant, and that was the long and the short of it. He had to remind himself why he had left the United

States to begin with, or rather, why he had not gone back right away, why he kept on not going back. *That* part of America—the mute and sometimes brute hostility of racism, the obstacle course of unspoken judgments and gestures, the dark litany of daily harassments and exclusions—had not gone away with the Civil Rights Act, signed into law shortly before their arrival. Jim Crow still lingered in the shadows, waiting, skulking. Perhaps on some level, Booker hoped and even half expected things would have changed overnight, miraculously. He was stubbornly optimistic that way. But he had already seen in 1962 that three decades had not made a real difference in terms of how he felt about the place or in how the place felt about him as a Black man of no special privilege or great renown whose grandfather was no longer revered the way he had been in the 1930s. In the end, the only return that made sense to him was the walk or taxi back to his apartment in Rio de Janeiro at the end of a show, the return to his bed, to Ofélia's shape and softness beside him, the familiar sound of her voice and the brown of her shoulders and the rhythm of her breathing as she fell asleep.[7]

## CENTRIPETAL

Deep down, Booker did not want to be anywhere else. Yet he had one problem: the demand for his services only increased as Eliana's star rose. After their time in the United States and a short trip to Aruba, the Pittmans returned to Brazil in August.[8] At the airport, they were met by Fernando Lopes. All three of them looked happy, but Booker's joy was so unbridled it struck Lopes as touching in its sheer puerility. "It's impressive the love this American has for all things and manners Brazilian," he remarked.[9]

For the rest of the year, the work did not stop, and neither did the travel. But the Pittmans remained within the country, at least, ping-ponging between Rio de Janeiro and São Paulo. They immediately signed a contract to headline at the Bar Cangaceiro, then sped off to São Paulo for television work.[10] By October 1966, they were back in Rio, headlining at the Café Concerto Casa Grande.[11] They traveled to São Paulo again later in the year to sign copies of Eliana's Decca single "It's a Lonesome Old Town," released in Brazil with Chantecler.[12] At year's end, the Pittmans would return to São Paulo yet again to perform at a jazz festival held at the Teatro Cultura Artística, where Eliana headlined and Booker provided his "fire" as usual.[13] Ofélia was also rumored to be taking part in the program. "And if they let Dona Ofélia speak, watch out," quipped one reporter.[14]

The novelty of Ofélia's participation in the Booker-and-Eliana routine was an ominous sign in disguise. It had become obvious to people closest to him, especially off-stage, that Booker had not been himself since returning from his last trip abroad. Outwardly, not much had changed. The Pittmans played at a much-ballyhooed opening set of shows at a new boate in Porto Alegre at the end of the year, a performance sponsored and filmed by TV Globo.[15] The recording of one of the shows, along with a brief interview of Booker, is a rare document that sheds light on his public persona beyond the schtick of his live musical performances. Nimbly threading the needle between bravado and candor, Booker regaled the interviewer and the club audience with his nostalgia for the *gaúcho* culture he had first experienced in his time in Santana do Livramento. When asked about his most emotional memory of Brazil in all his time living there, the musician responded that it was difficult to answer. "Brasil é uma emoção" he said. *Brazil itself is an emotion.* When pressed lightly about his lost years in Paraná, he waxed evasive ("I can talk about this when we have more time") and made light of his alcoholism by saying that he belonged to the *velha guarda* of cachaça connoisseurs.

Yet there were revelations as well. Speaking of his childhood in Dallas, Booker justified his aversion to his mother's wish for him to study classical music and his father's imperatives for him to follow his footsteps in architecture by declaring that "my style was a favela style because [in the United States] there are favelas as well, you know." About his time in New York in the early 1930s, Booker claimed to have recorded not just with Blanche Calloway but also Cab Calloway and Louis Armstrong.[16] (The latter boast was dubious. He had certainly played with Louis in Paris, but there is no evidence that he had cut a record with him.) Booker seemed at pains to cement his legacy at this recorded moment in Porto Alegre, as if he could sense this would be one of his last opportunities to set the record straight. But it is what he said between the lines that made the interview so riveting. His Portuguese was rapid-fire to the point of unintelligibility, heavily accented, rife with borrowings from Spanish and English, and propped up, often comically, with Brazilian colloquialisms. It was a sort of argot all his own, a linguistic palimpsest revealing different layers of his lived experience in South America while never quite managing to extract himself from the defining, traumatic matrix of the United States. He also seemed to be struggling to overcome something beyond the morass of language or the fog of memory; a physical limitation, an obstacle of some kind that was not age or drugs or alcohol.

The first public acknowledgment of Booker Pittman's serious health problems came to light in early January 1967 after Míster Eco reported that the American was under observation at the Casa de Saúde Santa Lúcia, where he had been admitted for a surgical procedure. At first, it did not seem that serious. By the end of the month, it was announced, Booker would return to the stage alongside Eliana. Still, ominously, there was confusion and obfuscation in the press reports. Fernando Lopes wrote that Booker was "completely recovered," while Míster Eco would only say that Booker had had his tonsils removed.[17] By February, Booker felt well enough to attend carnival. And how could he miss it, even if revelry likely went against the doctor's orders? The Pittmans always took carnival very seriously. For Booker, the festivities were not just a symbol of Brazilian culture or a gaudy tourist attraction. They were where, immersed in the *farra* (intense partying), soaking in the benevolent frenzy of the carnival troupes following the *batucada* rhythms with his body, and mouthing the words to the popular sambas he now knew by heart, Booker did not have to talk; he got to *be* Brazilian. It was not all about immersion and anonymity. After all the press coverage, live shows, and television appearances, people in the streets and balls recognized him by now. They called out his name. *Buca. E ai, Buca? Tudo beleza, Buca?* Booker usually chose not to wear a mask to carnival, not because he craved the adoration or the veneration that he increasingly received from the crowds of revelers. Rather, he wanted something smaller and simpler: recognition, acknowledgment.

Reinvigorated by the festivities, Booker joined Eliana and Ofélia on their trip to West Germany, where they would represent Varig at an international airlines symposium. The closing concert was broadcast widely across the continent as part of Eurovision, then a decade old.[18] The rest of his last European trip was an especially poignant experience for Booker. In a rush of emotion, he remembered his years there in the early 1930s. The Pittmans traveled to Lisbon to play in a festival of Lusophone music.[19] But it was Paris that delighted them the most. In Paris, Eliana and Booker played at the nightclub Tête de l'Art for a two-week stint of Brazilian music. "The warmth of the applause and the affection of the French really moved me," Eliana told Míster Eco. "Never before, in Brazil or in the United States, had I found such a reception, such human warmth." As for Booker, he naturally relished meeting old friends and jazz fans after three decades of absence even if he resented no longer being recognized in the City of Light. "In Brazil, I'm important," he told whoever would listen. "Over there, I have a name." Still, if his memories of the United States were deeply conflicted, his feelings for Paris were another story. Proof of this was how he showed Eliana and Ofélia the cafés and cabarets where he had played during his brief time there, a nostalgia tour he steadfastly avoided while in the United States.

Booker and Eliana outside the Café do Brasil. Paris, 1967. Photograph by Ofélia Pittman. Photo courtesy of Eliana Pittman.

"I think I may have spied a few tears in his eyes," Eliana said, "behind an immense glass of Beaujolais."

Míster Eco seemed concerned. "*Too much* Beaujolais?"

"I got permission from Mama Ofélia first," Eliana replied. "After all, he was dealing with a thirty-year backlog of *saudades!*"[20]

A photo from the trip captures Booker's elation in Paris. Strolling along the Champs Élyseés on the way to a show, the Pittmans spy the Café do Brasil food stand in the Arcade du Lido. Ofélia sees the perfect opportunity for a snapshot. Booker spontaneously strikes a pose in profile with his soprano sax as if saluting his adopted home. It is a pose he has struck so many times before on stage, on television, for magazine shoots, that it is almost a reflex by now. Eliana assumes her own stance, her hips swung out slightly in chic defiance, perhaps belting out a line from Vinícius de Moraes or Chico Buarque. Passers-by look on with shy curiosity, even amusement. One man looks up from his newspaper with a light scowl, but even he cannot ignore the joyfulness of the scene. It is high street theater, jazz performance art, a show that no one prepared for and no one *is* prepared for, the kind of environment that Booker most relished and imagined as unique to Paris: purely spontaneous music with no cover charge, no booking agent, only a non-captive, unselfconscious audience whose rapt attention and insouciant elegance could mean nothing but true bewitchment.

## É PRECISO CANTAR

Upon their return to Brazil later in April, Booker's throat and voice continued to bother him. The news that Érlon Chaves would be taking Booker's place in the Geraldo Casé show "É preciso cantar" at Teatro de Bolso was the first public acknowledgment that Booker's health issues were not expected to go away anytime soon. Míster Eco reported that Booker had been under doctor's orders not to play for a while due to an "affliction of the larynx." Eliana admitted to Fernando Lopes that she was worried about *papai*, though the only indication she revealed publicly at the time was that he suffered from "an excess of calcium."[21] In fact, Booker had been diagnosed with cancer of the larynx upon his return from Europe. As was to be expected, the news devastated him. "The doctor told me I should have stopped working three years ago," he told Ofélia.[22] It would not be until early July that Booker would perform again, this time joining Eliana on her short-lived TV show *Fahrenheit 2000* on TV Tupi in São Paulo.[23] At first, Eliana too had a great deal of trouble accepting her stepfather's illness. Her first reaction was to want to stop performing entirely, to put her career on pause so that she could help her mother nurse Booker back to health. But her stepfather would have none of it. "I didn't train you so that you would suddenly stop performing," he told her. "You've got to go out there and sing."

In an interview from 2018, Eliana remarked that she saw the nearly three years between the outset of Booker's illness and his death as deeply challenging on a personal level, of course, but also as a crucial period of professional trial-and-error. Even as a young woman, Eliana was a realist. She knew that her stepfather had cancer and this meant his health could go into steep decline without warning, so she did not want to be left unprepared. His mentorship had been so comprehensive and profound that she felt something beyond mere stage fright when he was no longer performing by her side: she felt artistically bereft. If his death had come too soon after his diagnosis, before Eliana was ready, she simply would not have kept singing. "I would have died artistically when he died," she said years later.[24]

But Booker did not perish right away, and for a time, Eliana could still count on her *papai* to coach her when she needed it. She soon learned that forming another duo with other musicians was not the way forward. It simply did not work: the level of trust in herself and familiarity with her repertoire were just not there. Worse, it was next to impossible to find a partner with the level of technique and knowledge that Booker possessed who also exhibited his selflessness as a performer. So she worked alone and found a way forward.

Eliana's performance in "É preciso cantar" was, among other things, a statement of her survival as an artist. The show wowed crowds as well as critics. The title came from a samba by the young composer Marcos Valle but was inspired by Booker, who had uttered the words é preciso cantar to help Eliana overcome her stage fright that fateful day at TV Rio seven years prior. Singing now seemed more essential than ever. No longer in the least bit afraid of the spotlight, Eliana seemed to have found her sweet spot with modern, revue-style musical theater. In this sense, too, she bore the stamp of Booker's mentorship. Her stepfather continued to shape Eliana's repertoire behind the scenes. Booker had come of age at a time when popular musical performance was imbued with theatricality. For large stretches of his career, he had competed on the cultural circuit not just with other jazz musicians but also with samba-canção and bolero singers, comedy acts and tap dancers, showgirls and magicians. As a result, showmanship was so woven into Booker's musical performance that, at times, it seemed like his only natural means of expression.

Even when *papai* could no longer join her on the stage, Eliana had much the same inclination, though naturally her tastes reflected the musical trends of the new era. The Rio press corps now lauded her as a complete singer, creative and personal in her interpretations of diverse material from blues, spirituals, and Broadway show tunes to Chico Buarque's "Carolina" and Caetano Veloso's "Alegria, alegria." At times, critical gushing veered unexpectedly into insouciant racism and sexism that seemed to belong to another era. When a reporter for *Diário de Notícias* praised Eliana's ability to combine the "mulatta sex appeal" with that of "naive child that marvels at her own success," he sounded uncannily like any number of Jazz Age critics describing Josephine Baker four decades earlier.[25] Míster Eco, as usual, was more sanguine and discerning in his comments than most of his contemporaries. Pointing out that few had thought Eliana could thrive as she had in *É preciso cantar*, he declared that she had "cut the umbilical cord that tied her to Booker."[26] That the audience still saw Eliana's success as connected to her stepfather became clear when Booker finally felt well enough to attend one of her performances. He was enthusiastically applauded as he set foot in the Bar Rui Bar Bossa.[27]

## IMAGINARY RIFFS

Booker was rarely good about listening to doctors, but all the trips to the clinics and hospitals got him to think more about his body and its limits—what it told and did not tell him, what it was asking of him. What his body told him was to lay low, move slow, and stick to his beloved routines: his coffee and his cassava cake, his strolls to the corner market, to the beach promenade, the little rituals and small talk with butchers and doormen that were as meaningful as anything else, maybe more so, when all was said and done. He had never realized how much pleasure was to be had flipping through gossip magazines at a *quiosque*, sitting on a bench with a newspaper and a *pamonha doce*, watching the pigeons and the toddlers and the janitors shuffle along the dirt paths around the fountain. Sometimes, he could barely make himself understood in any language and was shorter of breath than usual, but if he walked and talked slowly, it could be managed. He took pride in not appearing to be ill, even if he knew he was. Since he stuck to the familiar routes, there were always people on the streets and in the shops who recognized him. *Como vai, seu Buca?* they would say; *Como vai, o senhor?* And he would smile and whisper *bem*, sometimes *muito bem* if he was having one of his good days. *Estou melhor*, he would answer. *I'm better.*

Booker was not yet dying, but he was dying to play, and this the doctor would not allow. Neither would his family. Sometimes, back at the apartment, he held his alto gingerly, almost fondled it, admiring the gleaming brass of his new Selmer. Then he worked out scales and runs in his head as he silently pressed the keys. He spent hours like this on the sofa, playing imaginary riffs, make-believe songs, and sets. He might blow softly through the mouthpiece, but he rarely dared to produce amplified notes, mostly out of fear that someone—the maid, the upstairs neighbor—might hear and report him to Ofélia.[28]

While Booker lay low, Eliana was hitting her stride. The long play *É Preciso Cantar* that appeared later that year on the Copacabana label underscored, even more than the club show on which it was based, Eliana's professional separation from Booker. Led by two Marcos Valle compositions and the Mangueira samba school's award-winning "O Mundo Encantado de Monteiro Lobato" from the 1967 Rio Carnival, Eliana went almost entirely Brazilian. A sophisticated and stylistically diverse offering, *É Preciso Cantar* was not so much a declaration of independence as it was an exorcism. Gone were the spirituals, the blues and jazz numbers. In their place was a potpourri of sambas, frevos, bossa nova, and slower numbers with orchestral accompaniment. For all those who had whispered about Eliana's Americanization, this was her answer.[29]

Her own reaction to professional life without Booker was telling. On one hand, as she commented to a reporter, she felt liberated, finally free to develop her own artistic voice without a kindly chaperone. For the past three years, Eliana's critics, and sometimes Eliana herself, had mused openly about the need for her to escape Booker's shadow. Now that it had happened, she felt a kind of guilty gratitude for the opportunity. She relished her newfound freedom, yet she could not wait to be reunited with her *papai*. "When I'm with my parents, I feel much more relaxed; I feel protected," she told a reporter. "They are my best friends and my motivators, and for this reason I don't mind them being with me all day long." In the same interview, Eliana alluded to her stepfather's illness without addressing it directly. Asked what she had learned from her experience in the United States and her travels abroad, Eliana said that she now knew to put her all into every performance, whatever personal problems she was facing.[30] Problems be damned.

## IN HONORARIUM

As word of Booker's illness spread into wider circles, the honors began to trickle in. In late 1966, the *deputado* Silbert Sobrinho proposed that Booker be designated "Cidadão Carioca," an honorary citizen of Rio de Janeiro.[31] Shortly after Booker's illness first surfaced publicly, Roberto Eça organized a tribute to the saxophonist.[32] In April 1967, Booker received the title of Comendador da Ordem da Bossa at the Clube de Jazz e Bossa. "It should have been the Ordem do Jazz," complained Míster Eco.[33] Either way, musicians and fans clamored to pay homage to Booker Pittman. Perhaps they sensed his frailty even before his illness was publicly confirmed. Or maybe it was because the musician's newfound immobility defused fears that he would leave Brazil for good, a serious possibility just a year earlier. Until his illness grew debilitating, Booker could and would bolt in a heartbeat. *Leaving* was practically his trademark, his pattern for so many years that some of his friends and admirers had come to expect it from him. Now, suddenly housebound, Booker was no longer seen as a flight risk. Friends, fans, and boosters began to realize that, by default, he might not ever stop being Brazilian; he was *terminally* Brazilian, and as a Brazilian, he was a legitimate national treasure; everyone agreed about that. The painter Emiliano Di Cavalcanti, when Eliana told him she was working on a new record and that Booker, too, would be making one soon, remarked: "After creating you, your father doesn't need to create anything else."[34] It was a *cantada*, of course—a piece of flirtatious praise—but Booker might have agreed himself.

In late August, Fernando Lopes announced that Booker was taking advantage of his time off from performing to write his memoirs. The book was bound to be a bestseller, Lopes wrote, because "Buca knows a lot and has paid his dues."[35] By May 1968, Booker was said to be completing the final chapters of the manuscript. What the book was called depended on what day of the week it was and who was doing the talking. *O Jornal* reported that the autobiography was provisionally titled *Assim caminha o sax* (Thus Walks the Sax).[36] *Jornal do Brasil*, meanwhile, claimed the manuscript was titled *Booker's Book* and that it would be published in English and Portuguese. Unlike the other papers, *Jornal do Brasil* published a full-blown retrospective of Booker that doubled as a book preview. The piece was plagued by the usual fanciful dates and misspellings of important figures in the musician's life. But it held the distinct advantage of including one of the very last interviews of Booker Pittman at a time when he had begun to fall out of the public eye.

Maybe Booker sensed it was one of his last opportunities to set the record straight about his life and legacy. He certainly knew that his signature hoarse voice was quickly giving out on him, so he figured he might as well share his views with the public while he could. "With jazz, and more specifically with the blues," he told the interviewer, Diane Lisbona, "I have the possibility of telling a different story in each phrase that I play or sing. If you can't put your soul, your feelings into it, [if you can't] transmit a personal message when you play, you might as well forget about jazz." Ostensibly answering the criticism that he rarely diverged from jazz and blues standards, at least in his recordings, Booker ended up shedding light on the mutable essence of his personality: "I might repeat a song, but never an interpretation. A feeling can never be the same as one already felt before, just as the state of the spirit is ever-changing." Booker also used the interview with Lisbona to articulate exactly how he thought about his grandfather, Booker T. Washington. Like so many others, Booker had been deeply moved by the words and accomplishments of the recently assassinated Martin Luther King, whom he had met in person in 1960. "My grandfather was also a supporter of nonviolence," he said. "A pacifist like King, but he differed fundamentally in his methods, maybe because of the era he lived in."[37]

It had taken decades for Booker Pittman to warm to his grandfather in this way. He had had very little contact with Washington as a small toddler. His memory of him—if he could call it that—was vague, almost spectral, and mostly secondhand, more of a moral presence than a physical one. Perhaps Booker had blamed the specter of his namesake for the severity of his father's actions toward him as a boy: the harsh words, the strict rules, the savage beatings. Nonetheless, he had always kept a copy of *Up from Slavery* with him as a reminder of who he had been in his other life, where he came from, and also what he had run away from. He read through it from time to time, and as he gained distance from his childhood, Booker began to realize that his own father had mostly misinterpreted Booker T. Washington's moral edicts and practical guidelines: he was a bad pupil. Big Pitt's treatment of young Booker and his siblings was not their grandfather's doing. It was his own, born of his own fears and frustrations, in spite of his father-in-law's mentorship rather than because of it.

The final interview also allowed Booker to gain clarity about where he stood on his national identity. In newspaper articles throughout the decade, reporters and columnists, sometimes Eliana, and occasionally Booker himself quipped that he was more Brazilian than American. These remarks sometimes came off as semi-facetious gestures intended to please the Brazilian public. But now, Booker was serious. Friends and acquaintances who visited from the United States sometimes offered to take him with them when they flew back home. They could forget about it, he said. He would never go back permanently to his native country. "I never found anywhere else the same worry-free mindset and *joie de vivre* so common here, from a poor woodcutter in the hinterlands of Paraná to a multimillionaire in São Paulo. The United States and Europe are great places. But Brazil is my homeland."[38]

The *Jornal do Brasil* profile appeared to energize Booker. In June 1968, he was feeling well enough to give a talk on American and Brazilian music at the Museu da Imagem e do Som in dialogue with his old friend Jorge Guinle, Lúcio Rangel, and several others.[39] Booker had plenty of things to say about music and the music industry. He had felt his thoughts gathering inside of him like thick clouds, especially since his trips to the United States, which had given him a crash course in the latest musical styles, as well as the latest vagaries of show business. In many ways, he felt he had finally come face-to-face with the gorgeous monster of commercial success that he had always feared and sometimes desired. So far, he had lived to tell about it, but just barely. Anyway, as he knew now more than ever, he was in a unique position to shed light on several central chapters in twentieth-century music history, from the early swing scene of Kansas City, Harlem, and Paris to the apogees of tango and samba in Buenos Aires and Rio, from Delta blues and hot jazz to the revivalist wave of the 1950s.

When Booker showed up at the museum, he looked the part, almost professorial in his dapper suit and bow tie. And he regaled his audience with a wealth of details about his life. A number of episodes he remembered vividly and with his usual flair and humor. But at times, when he opened his mouth, barely intelligible gusts of air and phlegm came out. He coughed savagely, over and over, and when he did, he could surely see the pity well up in the faces of his friends and family, the love and the worry. This is not what he wanted. Even when he stopped coughing, he struggled to make himself understood. In a last-ditch effort, as if to fool his vocal cords into efficacy and bypass speech altogether, he tried to sing. But he could not do that either.[40] It was a cruel fate for a lifelong musician: condemned to being a voiceless authority, a semi-mute scholar of the beloved craft he could no longer perform.

## ELIANA'S DILEMMA

By early 1969, Booker's health had declined further, and the press's narrative about the supposedly imminent book had changed as well. Now it was to be not the bilingual *Booker's Book* but rather Eliana's book about Booker in Portuguese. *O Jornal* reported that it would be called *Minha vida com papai*, was already under contract with an unnamed publisher, and would be narrated, not written, by Eliana on the basis of the "hundreds" of pages that Booker had written himself over the past "three or four years."[41] A few weeks later, Eliana told the *Tribuna da Imprensa* that before traveling to Mexico to perform at the Hotel Camino Real, she had submitted a draft of the book, now called *Booker Pittman, meu pai*.[42] *Correio da Manhã* revealed that the book would be published with Editora Saga. Eliana even told the paper she would be canceling her weekend engagements with Radio e TV Jornal do Comércio.[43] But *Correio* soon reported that Eliana never submitted the book to Saga before her trip as promised, nor did she communicate with the publisher.[44]

Eliana's evasiveness about the book was touching, if nothing else. She truly *wanted* to write her stepfather's autobiography. But her career would simply not let her; it had other ideas. Now a solo artist, Eliana had contracts to fulfill, and all three Pittmans knew they needed the money now more than ever. Eliana had to decide between spending quality time with her *papai*, writing the book she had promised, or earning enough money to give him the medical care he needed and deserved. She chose the latter because she had to.

As Booker grew sicker, his world grew smaller. The opposite was happening to Eliana. In March 1968, she debuted another musical spectacle,

*Positivamente Eliana*, at the Teatro Copacabana. Directed by Harold Costa, the show featured an assortment of songs from Caetano Veloso's "Soy loco por ti, América" to the "Ballad of Bonnie and Clyde." It was a further departure from the bossa and jazz staples the duo had stuck to a few years before. But even in Booker's absence, Eliana found a way to bring her stepfather on stage with her, to summon his presence: she dialogued with his recorded voice.[45]

Still, Booker's bodily absence took its toll on Eliana. She and her mother feuded more and more with record executives, promoters, and producers. After a contract dispute with the Copacabana label, they switched to the Mocambo label. Then there was television. Tensions between Eliana and director-producer Carlos Manga had simmered for years, ever since she and Booker were kicked off the set of TV-Excelsior. No longer a schoolgirl with a high-pitched voice, Eliana was now a public figure and an imposing young woman whose explosiveness belied her waif-like public persona. She clashed behind the scenes with Manga, who claimed that she had overcharged him for a series of concerts she gave throughout Brazil.[46] Sometimes, her mother joined her in her jousts. One television producer did not take kindly to Ofélia's tone and told her, "You, shut up. And you [*pointing to Eliana*], calm down."

Racism and sexism certainly played a role in such exchanges. Though she was reluctant to address the issue publicly at the time, Eliana later acknowledged that it was difficult indeed for her during the 1960s and 1970s, a time when white male elites still reigned with impunity and Black female artists were expected to smile and passively endure their insolence and abuse. The same could be said of being a Black Brazilian woman manager, promoter, and producer in this period, and Ofélia was all these things. Booker was, in many ways, the cool counterpoint to the mother-daughter tandem. His steadying hand and calm demeanor were sorely missed at such moments. It was ironic: Booker was one of the causes of the stress and anguish that he could have been the solution for.

Perhaps this same realization drove him to take work again despite everything. No longer physically able to play publicly, Booker accepted an invitation to perform the voice of King Louis in the Portuguese version of Disney's *The Jungle Book*. A comedic turn in an animated Hollywood children's film was all that was left for him professionally. His captivatingly hoarse voice now took on absurd dimensions, and it was painful for anyone familiar with his actual physical state. But absurd hoarseness was what the role called for, particularly the song "I Wanna Be Like You," where Booker's thick accent only added to the patina of authenticity that disguised a central irony: Disney's King Louie is an orangutan, a role in the original English version played by Louie Prima, the New Orleans–based Italian American singer who made a lucrative living in part by sounding very much like Louis Armstrong. Casting the white Prima as King Louie slyly helped the studio preempt any public accusations of racism. Booker's turn as the aspirational "ape like me [who] can learn to be human too" placed racial overtones front and center once again, albeit in a different linguistic and national context. It is difficult to listen to Booker's rendition without reading into it another kind of aspiration as well—that of the foreign-born Booker as a full-fledged Brazilian citizen. But in Brazil, now in the grips of a right-wing military dictatorship, the casting was uncontroversial if not ignored completely, while the Rio press remained characteristically mute on the subject. At the same time, *O Livro da Selva* positioned Booker Pittman, long Satchmo's admirer and emulator, as the imitator of his imitator: Louis Armstrong twice removed, both closer and more distant from the original. Ultimately, his final recording is cartoonish and also touching, the consummate translator of American mass culture reduced to a caricature of himself out of bare necessity.

## THE CONVALESCENT PAINTER

Around this time, Ofélia and Eliana agreed that they should move Booker back to São Paulo so that he could get the best medical care. But Eliana still had her career to worry about, and someone still had to manage Eliana's growing list of professional engagements. Booker did not mind the hospital at first. But he thought somehow it would be quieter, less eventful. When word spread in São Paulo that he was hospitalized, however, he began to receive visitors from his old circle of friends and acquaintances: Masao Ukon, Dudu, other musicians he had played with once or twice, journalists and bartenders. Even Orlando, Ofélia's estranged husband, felt moved by the news of Booker's illness and paid him a visit. On some level, Orlando regretted having acted like a spiteful brute not so many years before, especially when he learned that Booker had pawned his own instrument to keep Eliana in the school that Orlando tried to keep her out of. When he finally got to spend time with Booker, he realized how gracious and gentle his former rival could be and how forgiving. Because Booker did not hold Orlando's past indiscretions against him, Orlando also found it impossible to stay angry with his daughter's new *papai*. Quite the opposite: Orlando became one of Booker's most faithful visitors.[47]

Other patients wanted to meet him and wish him well, too. Booker could still move around quite a bit, so he quickly made new friends. When they visited him, he felt the need to reciprocate. This wore on the American quickly, though. Making new friends in the cancer ward was like making friends on the frontline: poignant and soul-enriching until they died on you. In the meantime, his doctors strongly advised him to remove his larynx; it was his best chance of survival, they said. But Booker would not have it. "I want to die in one piece," he told Eliana. "I know I won't live as long, but I want to be whole when I do go." He also wanted out of the hospital, that much was clear, so Eliana and Ofélia bought a sleek, modern apartment in central São Paulo on Rua Bela Cintra, just one block from Rua Consolação, where Booker had made his first comeback and met Ofélia barely a decade before. This corner of the city had sentimental importance to him; it seemed like the ideal place for repose, given that he could not remain in his beloved Copacabana.[48]

The person left to care for Booker in the new house was his mother-in-law, Dona Chiquinha. Booker had long been deprived of cachaça, and more recently, he had to give up cigarettes, another of his part-time vices. But the most difficult blow of all was having to relinquish his beloved saxophones. Solitude by itself was not so hard for him to endure. "His biggest connection was with his instrument," Eliana later commented. "He would play for hours without the need to eat or talk with others."[49] But now things had changed. When his throat burned cold each time he swallowed, when his lungs labored from walking to the bathroom or putting on his socks, he knew he could no longer count on his Selmer to give him the solace of sound. For music to be music, it had to be vigorous, it had to come from the body. And Booker's body was no longer fit for exercise.

So he took up painting.

The canvasses he filled are ingenuous yet dark, inoffensive yet ominous: churches, cemeteries, street scenes, landscapes. In some ways, they resemble the paintings of Heitor dos Prazeres (1898–1966), a Rio-based samba singer and composer-turned-artist who penned such famous songs as "Cantar para não chorar," further popularized in the 1970s by the renowned singer Cartola (a recording later to appear in the film *City of God*). Turning to painting later in his life, Prazeres, in his meticulous works, evocatively captures the daily life of Afro Brazilians in all its color and variety.[50] By comparison, Booker's works are moodier and less ethnographic in their content. Some are scenes Booker saw right outside his window on Rua Bela Cintra, the place where he feasted on *feijoada* at his favorite *restaurante a kilo* down the block. But most of them were images he likely saw in his

Booker Pittman, Untitled. Circa 1968–69. Courtesy of Eliana Pittman.

mind. Not isolated moments exactly, but general tableaus from his past. And not the well-documented recent past, either—the press clippings and snapshots from upscale dinners and television soundstages and birthday parties—but rather the more distant past, the mean primitive past without Rolleiflex cameras or loved ones to operate them. He wanted to give visual form to those blind spots in his memory to enlarge and enhance them. Several of Booker's paintings are set in Paris but not the Paris he had just seen again two years earlier with Eliana and Ofélia. The Paris he saw now in his mind's eye was the dirtier, poorer, rawer Paris of the interwar period when he was a young Black bohemian catching his first glimpse of endless possibility, of unscripted adventure. Still, there is a darkness to the work. In one piece, two men share a bottle of wine on a table bathed in red light. Behind them, the green spilling out of an opened door dances with the reflected crimson on their faces, annulling their natural features and hues, de-racing them. In the foreground, an engulfing darkness dappled with pinpoints of color. It is a nocturnal scene from a time and place where Booker lived for the night, where he could not wait until it enveloped him in its mantle of small favors and surprises.

Booker Pittman. Untitled. Circa 1968–69. Courtesy of Eliana Pittman.

A redheaded woman in the foreground dominates another Paris painting. We are standing at dusk or, more likely, dawn in the Place Pigalle, a built environment painstakingly rendered in the background. Is she a prostitute, a chorus girl, a drag queen? With her kimono and thick yellow makeup, she is an outrageous figure and an imperious one. Her dead-serious countenance belies her red-light attire, likely a woman who once held great power over Booker and still does. Perhaps it is Joyce, his wife at the time, reprimanding him for another of his peccadillos, his small betrayals: his failure to show up for a rendezvous or showing up stoned on reefer; his flirtation with another dancer, his dalliance with a streetwalker. Or simply his absence, his refusal to adhere to Joyce's rules and terms of commitment. She assumes the form of a lascivious schoolmarm, an overseer, a phantom of his American life pursuing him to the ends of the Earth.

Then there are Booker's landscape paintings. Two small rustic buildings with red tile roofs, the same red in the road appearing in the earthen gashes in the denuded hillside. Two large trees throwing shade over the farm. A small orchard of something, coffee trees, perhaps, a drainage ditch in the foreground. Curiously, the same color pattern of his first Paris painting slathered densely with lurid reds and greens. This is Booker Pittman's dream *chácara*.

Booker Pittman. Untitled. Circa 1968–69. Courtesy of Eliana Pittman.

In numerous interviews from the late 1950s till the late 1960s, Booker Pittman declared that his ultimate dream was to buy a farm in Paraná. The back-to-nature fantasy was one of the few common threads that held together Booker's narrative about himself. It seemed improbable, the notion of returning and retiring to the place that had held him in its clutches for several years, the place that had almost buried him several times and in several ways. Though, by now, Booker knew it was addiction itself that had nearly killed him, not an address or an abode. Through the fog of his delirium and his misery, the hinterlands of Paraná possessed something essential that he never wished to give up. Maybe this is why he refused for so long to leave the region. There was peace to be found in the thick-aired torpor of the green and red countryside, a tropical version of northeast Texas or eastern Oklahoma; a scene without the rednecks and constant reminders of Jim Crow nonsense, a version where violence and spite did not seem right around the corner. It was a place that reminded him vaguely of where he came from but where he imagined he would never run into people who would remind him of where he actually came from.

In the canvasses he filled in the last months of his life, there is one conspicuous absence: any explicit reference to the United States of America.

No nostalgic portrait of his sister or his mother or his childhood home. No Blind Lemon Jefferson at the Central Line in Dallas. No images of young Booker jamming with Count Basie in a Kansas City basement. Not even an evocation of street life in Harlem. Perhaps there were too many bitter memories attached to his native country. Perhaps he simply ran out of time. Or maybe Booker carried the music of his Stateside haunts in his mind, as he always had, and that was enough.

## BLOODLINE

Ofélia and Eliana visited Booker in his new apartment as often as they could. Sometimes, they found him sad, distant. Other times, he was upbeat, almost oddly so. One day, they arrived to find him alone in the service area at the back of the apartment.

"What are you doing here?" Eliana asked. "The front of the apartment is so much more beautiful."

"That's true," Booker responded. "But let me show you something."

He shakily opened the blinds to unveil the view from the living room: the apartment looked right into the Cemitério da Consolação.

"I know I'll be there soon enough," Booker said, "but I don't want to be reminded of that every day when I wake up." Without a second thought, the Pittmans immediately sold the apartment and bought a house in the Vila Olímpia neighborhood on Rua Professor Atílio Innocenti.[51]

Dona Chiquinha reported that Booker was placid in his final months. Nearly till the end, he was hopeful that his cancer would be reversed, that he would somehow receive an eleventh-hour reprieve. But Booker was also at peace with what he had left the world. At one point, he felt well enough to write his mother a letter, assuring her that he was feeling fine, that the doctor's strict regime seemed to be working, that he had put on so much weight that his old clothes did not fit him anymore. "Eliana has been working like mad," he added. "I am more than grateful."[52]

Each headline of Eliana's triumphs that Booker read about in *O Globo* only added to his conviction that she was his true daughter and his prime legacy. Yet she was not Booker T. Washington's descendant or his mother's, either: Eliana was *his* project, *his* spiritual progeny. Why should convention matter to him now? It had never ruled him before. Not that he did not feel some blind pull toward the plenitude of family that so many others had, the comforting solidity of children and grandchildren, the unthinking purpose of bloodlines. But he was grateful for Ofélia, the devoted companion who had come into his life in order to save it, and for the unquestioned love and respect of a young woman who proudly called herself his *filha*, who publicly chose to call him kin. Eliana was his daughter by choice; that meant something. The fact that she carried the Pittman name with her was a quiet acknowledgment that his love and mentorship were as indelible as biology. He would not trade places with Orlando even if he could, not for the world.

## THE CROSSING

Booker Pittman's death was not unexpected, but the end did come rather suddenly. He had seemed to rebound in September, eating more, gaining some weight. Even his voice returned somewhat: a miracle of sonority, perhaps, a fitting, final gift to a dying musician. Dona Ofélia did not trust the seeming improvement of Booker's health. She knew deep down that it was the calm before the storm. Meanwhile, Eliana was scheduled to travel to a shoot in Bahia for *The Sandpit Generals* (*The Defiant*), a Hall Bartlett–directed screen adaptation of the popular Jorge Amado novel *Capitães de Areia*. But as the date approached for the filming, Booker's health took a turn for the worse. Ofélia, who almost always traveled with her daughter, decided to stay home in São Paulo. Eliana spoke of doing the same, but Booker would not hear of it. On Friday, October 10, he insisted that Eliana and Ofélia travel to Salvador as planned, despite his delicate health.

"Go take care of the girl," he told his wife. "Or do you think I'm going to die on you?"[53]

According to Dona Chiquinha, Booker spent a calm day on October 12, receiving a yellow rose from a young neighbor of his in São Paulo, a rose that moved him deeply. Perhaps he thought of Gene Autry singing "Yellow Rose of Texas," a melody he had no doubt worked out on the alto saxophone and perhaps played for himself during homesick days. But he likely could not remember all the words and could not easily hum the tune either way.[54]

Booker Taliaferro Pittman died at his home in Vila Olímpia just after 2 a.m. on Monday, October 13, 1969. Since the telephones at Salvador's Hotel Plaza were down, Eliana and her mother did not receive the news until a few hours later the next morning. When the phone finally rang, it was Dona Ofélia's cousin Ivete on the line: "Booker morreu," she said. *Booker has died.* Among his last words, as reported by several media outlets, were: "Estou despreocupado, pois deixo Eliana muito bem [I'm not worried, because I leave Eliana in great shape]."[55] Perhaps it was fitting that Eliana and Ofélia received the news of Booker's death in Salvador. Along with Recife, the city had been Booker Pittman's introduction to Brazil thirty-four years earlier. Increasingly in his final years, "Buca de Pernambuco" identified with the Brazilian Northeast and took to embracing Northeastern music by the likes of Dorival Caymmi. In *The Sandpit Generals*, as though in tribute to her wayfaring *papai*, Eliana sings "Vou ver Juliana," a Caymmi song about death and separation. The composer himself accompanied Eliana on guitar:

> Eu não tenho mais dinheiro
> Pra pagar pra embarcá
> Como eu não tenho dinheiro
> O remedio é esperar
>
> I don't have the money
> to embark on the crossing
> And since I don't have money
> The only cure is to wait

With its lyrical backbone of forbearance and longing, the song fittingly translates the stark melancholy of the blues into the buoyant music of the Brazilian Northeast:

> Carangueijo so é peixe na vazante da maré
> É melhor esperá sentado
> Do que esperá em pé
> Pra vê, pra vê Juliana
>
> A crab is only a fish in low tide
> It's better to wait sitting
> Than to wait standing
> To see, to see Juliana

## A JAZZ FUNERAL

Booker Pittman's body may have traveled from São Paulo, but it would come to rest in Rio de Janeiro, the South American city that first captured his heart and fired his imagination. Last rites were to be given by Father João Linhares de Lima, the musical director at the Catedral São João Batista in neighboring Niteroi, whom Booker had met at a Brazilian restaurant in Manhattan during his first visit back to New York in 1962. Father Lima had been in Harlem lecturing on and performing Afro Brazilian music, one of a number of talks and recitals he gave as a "singing priest" and educator while living in New York and studying at Columbia University.[56] The two of them struck up a friendship that lasted the rest of Booker's lifetime. Father Lima and Booker shared not just musical affinities but a sense of spiritual restlessness that stayed with the American throughout his years in Brazil.[57]

There had to be music at the funeral, and so there was. The legendary sambista Zé Keti, the bossa nova artist Nara Leão, the singer Ângela Maria, and the television host Abelardo Barbosa (Chacrinha) were among the scores of renowned mourners. But there were many more whose names did not make the newspapers. Friends, friends of friends, writers and music critics, musicians, diehard jazz fans. And others who could not properly be called mourners. There were the curious children from the neighborhood and the surrounding favela tagging along the cortege; the generic celebrity seekers, who knew there would be famous people to gawk at; the rank-and-file journalists and the paparazzi. As much as Booker felt while alive that he had never really arrived, never become a demigod in the global pantheon of jazz, never mind a household name, his funeral had all the makings of a celebrity event.

At the procession between Capela da Real Grandeza and Cementério São João Batista, Booker's friend Aurino Ferreira gave Rio de Janeiro a taste of a New Orleans processional, moaning the melody of "St. Louis Blues" for several minutes. He was supposed to play with two trumpeters as well, but they were swept up in the crowd of over six hundred people, and when the moment to play arrived, Aurino was left to fend for himself. It was a short walk to the cemetery, and Eliana knew this as well as anyone: it was here in Botafogo that she had been born. But she had forgotten somehow that this was to be a *funeral* march, and people would be strolling in slow motion. The march felt like an eternity to Eliana, an eternity for which Aurino provided the soundtrack and Rio de Janeiro did the rest: sitting on top of a *morro*, São João Batista felt like it was halfway to the heavens. As they reached the final stretch of the march, Rua Gen. Polidoro looked directly toward Pão de Açucar in the distance.

Eliana Pittman's past pooled up inside her. Her earliest memories on these very streets perhaps made her think of Booker's experiences as a little boy in Dallas, as a teen phenom in Kansas City, as a hotshot in Harlem. All of those scenes now bereft of his living body, detached, and folded into hers. Eliana struggled with the unbearable poignancy of the moment, the displaced St. Louis blues. She looked one last time at her handsome *papai* covered with the flowers she had placed upon his body, petal by petal. It was all too much for her. "Stop already!" she yelled. For the past two days, she had been trying to hold it together while she helped her mother with the banal details of death and bereavement, the tickets issued, the calls made, the papers signed. Eliana broke down in tears, inconsolable. Only when she pulled herself together minutes later did Aurino pick up where he had left off.[58]

*Coda*

# HOW TO LAY A SAXOPHONE TO REST

ELIANA PITTMAN'S PENTHOUSE IS PERCHED ATOP A SEA AIR–MOTTLED mid-century apartment building in Posto 3 of Copacabana, the entrance to the elevator jealously guarded in the lobby by a discerning doorman. It is a clean apartment, spacious and well-preserved, with an ambiguous air of a frozen yet living past, at once unpretentious and austere. From the wraparound terrace, the expansive views of the Atlantic and, in the other direction, the pristine Morro de São João appear untouched by time, like the burnished urban landscapes of period films, with recent buildings, cars, and people erased. Inside the penthouse, the dark, heavy furniture carries the fragrance of thickly varnished old-growth lumber. The walls of the living and dining rooms are adorned with framed publicity photos and album covers, hairstyles, fashions, and artistic styles varying according to the period, although most are from the 1960s and 1970s during the pinnacle of Eliana's fame. In one painting, she sports blue hair and a white mink shawl, swarmed by mildly psychedelic butterflies. Only her stepfather's memorabilia compete with her, photos of Booker with Louis Armstrong, Booker with Dick Farney, Booker with Jack Paar, Booker with Eliana. And then there are the paintings, the scenes and memories that haunted the convalescent musician in the last months of his life: Paris, Buenos Aires, Paraná.

The centerpiece of the living room, though, is Booker Pittman's tenor saxophone, encased in mirrored glass, the only instrument of his that Eliana and Ofélia held onto following his death. The saxophone has become a shrine, complete with faux flower bouquets and jewel cases of recent CD reissues. In the mouth of the well-polished instrument lies the thin gauze of a light orange scarf. It was Booker's scarf, Eliana says, the one he was wearing when she last saw him alive. The scarf now doubles as a muzzle, a reminder that the saxophone will never be played again for the simple reason that Booker T. Pittman is not here to play it.

Eliana and Booker posing with two saxophones, circa 1966. Courtesy of Eliana Pittman.

Amidst the pomp and chaos of Booker's 1969 jazz funeral, a minor controversy emerged, and it had to do with this very saxophone. Minutes before the procession to the catacomb, the Museu da Imagem e do Som's young director Ricardo Cravo Albin, who had forged a friendship with the American after his interview at the Museu the previous year, showed up using a walking cane, having gotten into a minor car accident on his way to the chapel. When he saw that Eliana and Ofélia were planning to bury Booker with several of his musical instruments, Albin pleaded for them to reconsider. "Everyone knows that tomorrow, someone will break into the catacomb and steal the instruments. That just can't be allowed to happen."[1] Several family friends agreed with Albin that the museum was a better home for Booker Pittman's instruments. Ofélia had her doubts, but in some ways, they were the opposite of Albin's. She feared not that the donated instruments would fall into the hands of graverobbers but rather those of other musicians.² And so, even before his body had been buried, Booker Pittman's legacy was in dispute. At the heart of the matter was a question of symbolism. For Booker, the saxophones and clarinets of his life had been more than mere instruments: they were oversized amulets, throughlines for his long and disjointed story, soothing companions for him during the many years when he had little else. But as the amulets of a dead man, where exactly did they belong? For Ofélia, the instruments were extensions of Booker's power that would give him protection and solace in the afterlife, retaining their talismanic virtues six feet under. For Albin as well, the instruments should never be played again—that much he and Ofélia could agree on—but they should be *seen* by the living under the aegis of the Brazilian government. The initial uncertainty of the fate of Booker's instruments only added to their aura. *O Jornal*, for its part, wrote that his instruments had not been buried with him "as had been predetermined."³ Two days later, Fernando Lopes reported that the family had decided to donate a saxophone, a clarinet, and a flute of Booker's to the Museu da Imagem e do Som; Albin had reserved a spot for them.⁴ But, in fact, only one instrument was buried with the musician. A compromise had been worked out whereby the soprano sax would accompany Booker's remains at the mausoleum, the alto would go to the museum, and his tenor (probably his least used instrument) would remain at the Pittmans' house.⁵

Booker Pittman and his horns might finally have been temporarily laid to rest, but Eliana and Ofélia Pittman never stopped moving. Their next foray abroad was underway before the year ended. It was supposed to be a two-week trip to "lift the spirits and to administer a self-examination, to see if I wanted to continue singing," Eliana said at the time. Initially, mother and daughter jetted to Caracas for a series of television and nightclub appearances, but once there, Eliana was invited to Munich for a television gig in November. After they arrived in Europe, more invitations poured in for club contracts and televised performances: the Casino Espinho in Porto, the popular German television show *Der Goldene Schub*, the Hotel Biblos in Saint Tropez, a month-long engagement at the Grand Hotel in Stockholm, a show in Spain later broadcast on Eurovision, and a one-week engagement at the Teatro de la Pergola in Venice. And then there was Paris, where Eliana headlined for three weeks at the luxurious Cabaret Don Camilo; months later, she performed with Sacha Distel on his highly successful music variety show Guitares et Copains.⁶ In the wake of her stepfather's passing, Eliana was taking the world by storm, just as Booker would have wanted and just as he had expected.

Eliana made sure to touch base in Brazil every few months—*pra matar saudades*, she said, to satisfy her nostalgia for home. But she kept up her transatlantic exploits for much of the first half of the decade. It was as though she sought to honor Booker not just by her success but also through her restlessness, flitting from engagement to engagement, delivering immaculate performances for polyglot audiences, night after night, in ways that were both accommodating and uncompromising, with no clear idea of when or where the tour might end or whether it would end. The road became a salve for her in ways perhaps only her stepfather could have understood. But it was a high road. Rather than the compulsive work of desperation, Eliana's exploits were the glamorous travels of conquest: what Booker had always imagined for her, and earlier in life, for himself.

Eliana's apex of popularity in Europe in the early 1970s coincided with two well-received albums on the Odeon label. Increasingly, though, her repertoire veered away from jazz and toward Brazilian idioms like samba, bossa nova, and forró. Much as Booker had sought to represent the music of the United States, sticking to a jazz diet whenever he could, Eliana now became an ambassador of Brazil abroad. Throughout the decade, she also frequently toured in Venezuela, especially after the meteoric success of her recording of "Carimbó," fashioned after a traditional musical idiom and dance style from Pará in the north of Brazil. The song first appeared on the LP *Tô chegando, Já cheguei* (1974) and signaled Eliana's return to the RCA Victor label, where she would remain until the end of the decade.⁷

Even as her recorded work, responding to Brazilian demand, tended more toward the different iterations of the national idioms, Eliana's export-friendly live performances still featured ample international material, especially jazz. In one large-budget super show called *Brazilian Follies*, the versatile Eliana toggled between *samba de gafieira* and MPB (*música popular brasileira*), carnival tunes, and jazz. The highlights included a rendition of Pixinguinha's classic tune "Carinhoso" alongside the Booker favorite, "St. Louis Blues." The spectacle also featured Eliana in the role of Carmen Miranda, a gesture that at once mocked and reinforced the buzz surrounding Eliana's career since the late 1960s. Brazilian publications still routinely declared her the second coming of the Brazilian Bombshell.⁸ Universally applauded for her vocal technique and her showmanship, widely if nebulously associated with a certain *americanidade* fit for export, perceptions abounded that Eliana was similarly taking the world by storm. Her global success in the 1970s, especially in Europe, had reached such heights that coming home felt like something of a letdown. "Without trying to compare myself to Carmen in terms of prestige," she told *Manchete*, "I suffer from the same resentment she suffered when she returned to her native country."[9]

Other critics compared Eliana Pittman to Josephine Baker and even to Liza Minnelli. But Eliana's career arc since her stepfather's death also mirrored Booker's, with the same centrifugal impulses at the expense of a conventional family life; the same technical perfectionism, showmanship, and professionalism on stage; and the same urge to disseminate abroad the sounds of her homeland while often neglecting her base, or seeming to, and being neglected by it in turn. While Eliana was a fixture of national media and had brought renown to the Pittman name both in Brazil and abroad, at times, her fame threatened to eclipse Booker's memory rather than promote it. Partly for this reason—though also, of course, out of a sense of love, duty, and devotion—Eliana and Ofélia, months after his death, relocated Booker Pittman's remains, along with his sax, to a more distinguished resting place inside the Cemitério São João Batista in a gravesite not far from those of Carmen Miranda and Francisco Alves.[10]

Booker Pittman's memorialization did not end with his relocation. In 1971, Eliana wrote and performed a new show at the Teatro Glória called *Eliana, cravo e canela*, with songs accompanied by slides and spoken reminiscences about her stepfather. It was, as she said at the time, a chance to finally express her grief and abiding disbelief about his death and to speak publicly about Booker's life for the first time in a format she was comfortable with.[11] While the show brought Eliana some closure, it only temporarily kept her stepfather in the public light. Three years after his death, *Tribuna da Imprensa*'s Ernani Duarte da Silva bemoaned Booker's fast track to oblivion. All that remained of him, wrote Duarte da Silva, were a handful of news clippings in Brazil and the very occasional reference in American and European jazz histories.[12] This was not quite true. Just months after Booker's death, the Brazilian soul pioneer Tim Maia closed his first long-playing record with "Tributo à Booker Pittman." Penned by rising jazz trumpeter Cláudio Roditi, the song championed Booker as a still-living force and a role model for younger Brazilian musicians, including Black artists like Maia.

> Stay, we've got you always dawg, I know.
> I hope in heaven you can play and hear
> What we are trying to do
> Because you're blessing [*sic*].

It was a touching tribute, sung in precarious English as if to match Booker's broken Portuguese. Thanks to Tim Maia's unique talent and magnetism, the album itself was also a smash hit in Brazil, remaining atop the charts for weeks. It launched a promising career that, like Booker's, was marred by drug and alcohol abuse and ultimately ended prematurely.

Meanwhile, Eliana rode her own steadier path to fame. Besides her international travels, Eliana also frequently went on tour in Brazil. And here, too, she performed in the footsteps and name of her stepfather. Nowhere was this more apparent than in her travels through inland Paraná and São Paulo in 1973. In a tour of fifteen towns, she played most, if not all, of Booker's old haunts, beginning with Santo Antônio da Platina. Everywhere she went, she was regaled with high honors, festivities, and warm applause. In the town of Assis, Eliana received from the mayor a plaque dedicated to her accomplishments and Booker's memory; in Cornélio Procópio, she paraded through the confetti-strewn streets in a convertible; and in Presidente Prudente, in São Paulo, she was invited to give talks on theater and music.[13]

Even so, Eliana and Ofélia felt they were not doing enough for Booker. The creeping sense of her stepfather's fading legacy drove Ofélia to take over from Eliana the long-discussed project of his biography.[14] And that was not all. As if booking her daughter's shows and juggling her many commitments were not enough, Ofélia hatched the idea to hold an annual competition in Booker Pittman's name to recognize the top Brazilian recording artists of the year.[15] That same year, in what had become an annual tradition advertised in local newspapers, Eliana and Ofélia held a mass at the Igreja de Santo Antônio commemorating the fifth anniversary of Booker's passing.[16] Finally, Ofélia announced that she was in possession of pristine recordings of one of Booker's final live performances. Since the tapes included his storytelling, Ofélia pitched them as "biographical" in nature.[17]

It was as though Ofélia and Eliana were doing double duty, determined to seize Eliana's moment in the sun, all while casting about with what little extra time they had in search of the ideal venue through which to hallow Booker Pittman's name. At times, their urge to consecrate his memory led to actions that verged on desperation. In 1973, when the television program *Globo em 2 minutos* was about to interview visiting jazz stalwart Horace Silver, Eliana sent word from backstage to announce that *she* and not the Globo host would be interviewing Silver since, she said, her father had known him personally. The announcement came as a shock to the show's host, who postponed the interview rather than yielding to Eliana's demand. One reporter accused the singer of "vedetismo" (diva behavior).[18]

Criticism of Eliana Pittman's assertiveness could be partly written off as the lingering race anxiety of the white middle-class media confronting the newfound upward mobility of Afro Brazilian artists at every turn. Still, despite her young age, Eliana was whip-smart and a sober realist and knew the negative press coverage contained a grain of truth. She admitted to her irascibility in a brief interview for a Father's Day article. Of all the people in her life, she remarked, it was Booker who knew best how to calm her down. "He knew how to stay silent during one of my explosions, and then when the moment was right, he would convey a message of peace and tenderness."[19]

Most Stateside recollections of Booker Pittman died with the passing of his childhood friends and fellow musicians in the latter decades of the twentieth century. Few of these men and women published autobiographies or were the subjects of biographies. This was the case even of prominent players and bandleaders like Budd Johnson and Sammy Price, Blanche Calloway, and Freddy Johnson, all of whom seemed as improbable as candidates for neglect as Booker himself, given how brightly their stars shone in early and mid-century New York and Paris. Those who did manage to have their stories told—Louis Armstrong, Count Basie, Coleman Hawkins, Bill Coleman—scarcely mentioned Booker when they did at all. One problem, no doubt, was that Booker lay buried too far back in their minds, one of a faraway chorus of musical voices rather than a major protagonist close at hand. The other factor was Booker's long disappearance from the northern spotlight. The late 1920s and early 1930s were fading memories by the time Armstrong began plumbing his roots in the 1950s and distant ones when Count Basie recounted his life and career to Albert Murray in the 1970s. Their brief encounters with Booker later in life hardly stood out as central to their stories.

In the United States, at least, the struggle to maintain Booker's legacy lay in the hands of his mother and her biographers. That they relegated the prodigal son to something of a bit player was likely due to sheer lack of information. Booker also had stiff competition, namely his grandfather, whose legacy Portia took upon herself to preserve in earnest once she returned to Tuskegee with Fannie after leaving her husband in the 1930s. After World War II, she led a drive to establish a Booker T. Washington memorial at her father's birthplace in Virginia, an effort funded by a commemorative coin signed into law by President Truman in 1946. Eleven years later, Portia cut the ribbon at the opening of the Booker T. Washington National Monument; a commemorative stamp soon appeared to mark the occasion.[20]

In the 1960s, however, Portia struggled against indifference to, and even hostility toward, her father's legacy during the heady days of the US Civil Rights Era and the stridency of the Black Power movement. After Booker Pittman's death and two years after her other son Sidney's unexpected passing, the family matriarch went into a tailspin. In 1970, *Jet* magazine ran an article revealing that Booker T. Washington's daughter now lived in a run-down Washington, DC, tenement apartment, where she survived on a few hundred dollars a month. Now in her late eighties, Portia Washington Pittman was repeatedly victimized by burglars and petty criminals, some of whom introduced themselves as guardians of her father's legacy, only to steal what belongings and memorabilia they could find.[21] By the time her daughter Fannie died in 1973, the primary source for information on Booker Pittman in the United States was Portia herself, based mostly on memories of conversations she had with him during his two stays in the 1960s. Though Portia was lucid almost until her death in 1978, her son's musical legacy was hardly her first focus or, in all probability, her last thought.

Portia's final fade-out came after a bitter last few years as she found herself cast into obscurity amidst the poverty and turmoil of the period. Her demise mirrored the erasure of Booker's memory in the United States. The pilfering of whatever letters and family memorabilia she had in her possession added insult to injury. With Portia and most of her belongings gone, along with the last remaining chroniclers of the golden age of Kansas City and Chicago, New York and Paris, there were precious few people in the Northern Hemisphere to keep the memory of Booker Pittman alive.[22]

In the early 1980s, the frenzy and fog of Eliana's fame began to lift. With a lull in recording sessions, theatrical rehearsals, travel, and live engagements, Eliana had more free time on her hands for the first time in nearly two decades. She had room to breathe, to think. It was only then that the *Booker Book* began to take definitive shape, except it would not be Eliana who would write it. Instead, it would be Ofélia, and Booker himself, albeit posthumously. Booker's incomplete, sometimes delirious memoirs were long assumed to be the backbone of the book, but their skeletal final form meant that they would have to be filled out somehow. Eliana began to encourage her mother to put down her own recollections from childhood onward, her resilience in the face of poverty and abuse, her building of a successful business in São Paulo. In many ways, her life made for as colorful and moving a story as Booker's. In the end, the decision was made to place Ofélia's recollections alongside her husband's, chapter by chapter, until their two worlds converged on that fateful night at the Paramount.[23]

Ofélia Pittman's *Por você por mim por nós (For You, for Me, for Us)* was published in 1984 by Editora Récord. If the book consecrated Booker as a major figure in Brazilian popular music of the twentieth century, it also (through no fault of its own) consigned his memory to a rather small Portuguese-speaking readership. The problem was not just the public's fading memory of Booker but also flagging interest in jazz itself. Booker Pittman had returned to the spotlight just as the genre was about to go into gradual decline. By the late 1960s, interest in jazz and the various musical hybrids with which it was associated had clearly and permanently waned. Eliana's own shift to Brazilian popular genres was as sure a sign as any that record companies no longer favored styles that they had embraced in the 1950s and early 1960s. This is not to say that the Brazilian jazz scene that Booker Pittman had helped to found simply disappeared overnight. Far from it: in the 1960s and 1970s, new figures emerged on the international stage. Besides Roditi and Paulo Moura, there was the *sui generis* composer Moacir Santos, the multi-instrumentalist Hermeto Pascoal, the guitarist Egberto Gismonti, the vocalist Flora Purim, the percussionists Airto Moreira and Naná Vasconcelos. The 1980s brought the rise of the saxophonist Léo Gandelman and pianist and vocalist Eliane Elias, and somewhat later, the vocalist Luciana Souza, just to name a few artists.

Still, by the end of the twentieth century, jazz in Brazil, as elsewhere, had been reduced to a mostly minority pursuit and niche audience, a mode of interpretation that flavored recordings but was no longer the main course. Eliana Pittman herself only occasionally revisited jazz later in her career. The music had become, for her, a point of reference rather than the sound of the unfolding present: an indexing of the age that defined her ascent and the man that shaped it. Booker's voice was the Black American accent that, perhaps more than any other, marked not just Eliana's early career but also the sonic map of urban Brazil in the 1950s and 1960s, just as it had in Argentina and Uruguay in the decades prior.

Copacabana, the neighborhood that Booker Pittman kept coming back to over the course of his decades-long residence in South America, today still holds a tentative grasp on his memory. Over the last ten years of Booker's life, the Pittmans moved frequently, their lives upended by travel, success, and finally, illness. Before decamping to São Paulo, Booker rarely strayed far from the spaces where he had made and remade his musical career: the Cassino Atlântico, the Hotel Vogue, the Copacabana Palace. Today, the lodestones of the mid-century jazz scene in Brazil are either gone or shells of their former selves. The Atlântico was torn down to make room for a high-end indoor shopping center that today goes by the same name. No trace remains of the ill-fated Vogue or the building it occupied. The Palace still brings in the same well-heeled crowds as ever, yet the hotel is not the vital musical destination it once was. One block north of the Palace, Beco das Garrafas, Bottles Bar, and the Little Club have gone through cycles of neglect and revival. More than two decades into the twenty-first century, they still host disarmingly intimate performances of Brazilian jazz and bossa nova. If the storied cul-de-sac still manages to retain its patina of bohemian history, minutes away by foot, on Rua Carvalho de Mendonça—the site of earlier iterations of Rio's own private Jazz Age—one finds laundromats and glassmakers, small furniture stores and mom-and-pop repair shops. Nothing that remains resembles the Mei Ling, where Booker's blue alto once cried and bellowed "The Walls of Jericho" into the early hours of the morning.

Just beyond the luxuriant green precipice of Morro de São João, less than a mile away from Beco das Garrafas as the crow flies, Booker Pittman still holds his saxophone close to his chest. The Cemitério São João Batista is a majestic space, befitting of the city whose dead and bereaved it serves. Perched on a sloping hill between the Morro and the middle-class neighborhood of Botafogo, the cemetery is encircled immediately by the discreet though not quite inconspicuous favela of Tabajaras. The confluence of wealth and poverty, silence and commotion, light and darkness would make São João Batista a microcosm of Rio de Janeiro if only there were anything micro about it. As the vast, nearly shadeless eastern and northern stretches descend into the older center, the common gravestones give way to ever more vertical statues and mausoleums, divided by a central avenue lined with trees.

Just above this paean to the nation's imperial and modern-day elites lies a less imposing grouping of Brazil's twentieth-century artists, musicians, and entertainment figures. The tombs of this section strike a balance between the opulence below and the humbler abodes up the hill. It is here where Booker Taliaferro Pittman's remains lie alongside those of his beloved Ofélia, who passed away in 2000.

The view from the Pittman gravesite. Cemitério São João Batista, Rio de Janeiro. Photo by Jason Borge, 2022.

>   Booker Pittman
>   Famoso músico americano
>   Jazz aquí

Eliana and Ofélia could not resist the pun: "jazz aqui" means "(there is) jazz here," even as it hints at *jaz aqui* or "he lies here." It was a fitting testament, not just to Booker's lifelong vocation but also his sense of humor—which, as Eliana tells it, outlasted even his career despite his illness. Yet other than this unexpected comic flourish, there is little about the Pittmans' tombs to distinguish them from those of their neighbors. Their *jazigos* (tombstones) are elegant but hardly ostentatious; they seem at home in their surroundings, in their final neighborhood. It is as though only in death did Booker put his restlessness to rest, declaring himself not as a long-lost American or a wandering citizen of the world but finally as a Brazilian, and specifically, as a carioca, his unblinking gaze directed not seaward but shoreward, toward the city he loved, and upward, at the cloud-draped *Cristo Redentor*.

# NOTES

## PRELUDE: TEATRO PARAMOUNT

1. Derek Walcott, "The Antilles: Fragments of Epic Memory," Nobel Lecture, December 7, 1992. https://www.nobelprize.org/prizes/literature/1992/walcott/lecture/.

2. Penny Von Eschen, *Satchmo Blows Up the World: Jazz Ambassadors Play the Cold War* (Cambridge: Harvard University Press, 2004), 19.

3. "Latin Blowout for Louis," *Life*, November 25, 1957, 169–70.

4. *O Cruzeiro*, December 7, 1957, 128.

5. *O Cruzeiro*, December 7, 1957, 128.

6. Ofélia Pittman, *Por você por mim por nos* (Rio de Janeiro: Editor Record, 1984), 131.

7. Tyler Stovall, *Paris Noir: African Americans in the City of Light* (Boston: Houghton Mifflin, 1996), xvi.

8. Brent Hayes Edwards, *The Practice of Diaspora: Literature, Translation, and the Rise of Black Internationalism* (Cambridge: Harvard University Press, 2003), 205.

9. The language used here combines two strands of cultural theory. I use "aurality" in this context after Ana María Ochoa, in the sense of "ontologies and epistemologies of the acoustic . . . produced by and enmeshed in different audile techniques, in which sound appears simultaneously as a force that constitutes the world and a medium for constructing knowledge about it." Ana María Ochoa Gautier, *Aurality: Listening and Knowledge in Nineteenth-Century Colombia* (Durham: Duke University Press, 2014), Kindle, loc. 383. At the same time, the concepts of errancy and "root" are drawn from Glissant's seminal insights into exile and mobility. Errancy for Glissant expresses movement driven not by sheer economic necessity (what he calls "circular nomadism") or the thirst for discovery or conquest ("arrowlike nomadism") but rather embodies a kind of wanderlust that "silently emerges from the destructuring of compact national entities that yesterday were still triumphant and, at the same time, from difficult, uncertain births of new forms of identity that call to us." Édouard Glissant, *Poetics of Relation*, trans. Betsy Wing (Ann Arbor: University of Michigan Press, 1997), 18–20.

10. "[O]ne can never be an expatriate, really," James Baldwin once remarked. "One cannot possibly leave where he came from. You always carry home with you." Cited in Nancy L. Green, "Expatriation, Expatriates, and Expats: The American Transformation of a Concept," *American Historical Review* (April 2009), 309.

11. Edoardo Vidossich, *Jazz na garoa* (São Paulo: Associação dos Amadores de Jazz Tradicional, 1966), 40.

12. Saidiya Hartman, "Venus in Two Acts," *small axe* (June 2008), 11–12.

13. Hartman, "Venus in Two Acts," 4.

## CHAPTER ONE: THE ESCAPE ARTIST

1. Here and over the next four paragraphs, I attempt to capture Booker Pittman's mindset at the time, basing my speculative impressions on fragments of his memoirs and later interviews.

2. Chalú, "Booker Pittman esteve à beira do fracasso: tóxicos," in Pittman, *Por você por mim por nos*, 169.

3. The same could be said of Black Americans. In the decades after Washington's death, countless schools, parks, libraries, and streets would bear his name. As historian Robert J. Norrell points out, "[T]he Tuskegee legacy may have been viewed as acceptable to powerful whites in the Jim Crow South when other blacks of note might not have been, but blacks independently embraced these names as symbols of their own success." Robert J. Norrell, *Up from History: The Life of Booker T. Washington* (Cambridge: Harvard University Press, 2009), 423.

4. Michael Rudolph West, *The Education of Booker T. Washington: American Democracy and the Idea of Race Relations* (New York: Columbia University Press, 2006), 19.

5. W. E. B. Du Bois, *The Souls of Black Folk* (Digireads, 2001), Kindle, 32.

6. Robert J. Norrell, *Up from History*, 407–12.

7. Louis R. Harlan, *Booker T. Washington: The Wizard of Tuskegee 1901–1915* ((New York: Oxford University Press, 1983), 448–54.

8. Andrew Zimmerman, *Alabama in Africa: Booker T. Washington, the German Empire, and the Globalization of the New South* (Princeton University Press, 2010), 6–10.

9. Harlan, *Booker T. Washington*, 450–54.

10. Harlan, *Booker T. Washington*, 199–200.

11. Harlan, *Booker T. Washington*, 451–52.

12. Ruth Ann Stewart, *Portia: The Life of Portia Washington Pittman, the Daughter of Booker T. Washington* (Doubleday, 1977), 26–28.

13. Stewart, *Portia*, 45, 54.

14. Stewart, *Portia*, 55–72; Roy L. Hill, *Booker T's Child: The Life and Times of Portia Marshall Washington Pittman* (2nd ed., Three Continents Press, 1993 [1974]), 50–51.

15. Stewart, *Portia*, 72–75.

16. Stewart, *Portia*, 77–78.

17. "Negro Architect's Skill: Government Accepts W. S. Pittman's Plans for Exposition Building," *New York Times*, November 24, 1906: 2.

18. Stewart, *Portia*, 79–81.

19. The Brownsville Affair was a national controversy that ensued when Black "Buffalo Soldiers" of the 25th Infantry Regiment stationed in Fort Brown were scapegoated for the murder of a white resident in nearby Brownsville. Ultimately, President Roosevelt dishonorably discharged several dozen of the Black soldiers. In a 1908 letter to Booker T.

Washington, who pressured the White House to reverse the decision, President Roosevelt sidestepped the issue of racial justice at the heart of the affair while offering to support Sidney Pittman's involvement in the building project. *Letter from Theodore Roosevelt to Booker T. Washington*, Theodore Roosevelt Papers. Library of Congress Manuscript Division, Theodore Roosevelt Digital Library, Dickinson State University. https://www.theodorerooseveltcenter.org/Research/Digital-Library/Record?libID=o204963.

20. Karl Hagstrom Miller. *Segregating Sound: Inventing Folk and Pop Music in the Age of Jim Crow* (Durham: Duke University Press, 2010), Kindle, 55–56.

21. Alan Govenar and Jay Brakefield, *Deep Ellum: The Other Side of Dallas* (Texas A&M University Press, 2013), 14–15, 47.

22. Govenar and Brakefield, *Deep Ellum*, 38–39.

23. As Du Bois puts it, double-consciousness was a "peculiar sensation" that came from "always looking at one's self through the eyes of others, of measuring one's soul by the tape of a world that looks on in amused contempt and pity" (Du Bois, *The Souls of Black Folk*, 2).

24. Ruth Ann Stewart, "William Sidney Pittman," *African American Architects: A Biographical Dictionary, 1865–1945* (Routledge, 2004), 449–51.

25. Stewart, *Portia*, 86.

26. Booker Pittman, Unpublished memoirs, c. 1968, 2.

27. B. Pittman, Memoirs, 2–3.

28. B. Pittman, Memoirs, 6–8.

29. Booker Pittman's name appears in the 1921 Dallas City Directory as a "boot black," common parlance at the time for African Americans who shined shoes. According to the directory, Booker's employer was named V. T. Tubbs (*Dallas City Directory*, 1921, 1,226).

30. B. Pittman, Memoirs, 9–10.

31. B. Pittman, Memoirs, 10.

32. Miller, *Segregating Sound*, 78.

33. Nicholas Gilmore, "Herbert Hoover's Meatless Wheatless World War I Diet," *Saturday Evening Post*, February 25, 2018, n.p. https://www.saturdayeveningpost.com/2018/02/herbert-hoovers-meatless-wheatless-diet/. Accessed on April 17, 2024.

34. Roy L. Hill, *Light for the Blind: A Biographical Sketch of the Life and Times of Booker T. Pittman* (McDaniel Press, 1975).

35. B. Pittman, Memoirs, 5.

36. B. Pittman, Memoirs, 5.

37. B. Pittman, Memoirs, 9–13.

38. From an interview in Porto Alegre, Brazil, first recorded December 1966. Rebroadcast on the show *Mémoria Popular Brasileira*, Rádio Cultura FM 103.3, Dec. 27, 2015. http://culturafm.cmais.com.br/memoria/mestre-do-saxofone.

39. B. Pittman, Memoirs, 12, 14

40. B. Pittman, Memoirs, 13.

41. B. Pittman, Memoirs, 14.

42. B. Pittman, Memoirs, 14–17.

43. B. Pittman, Memoirs, 16–17.

44. B. Pittman, Memoirs, 4.

45. B. Pittman, Memoirs, 20–21.

46. Carl Woideck, *Charlie Parker: His Music and Life* (Ann Arbor: University of Michigan Press, 1998), 82.

47. B. Pittman, Memoirs, 23.

48. B. Pittman, Memoirs, 24–25; 29–30.

49. B. Pittman, Memoirs, 31–33.

50. B. Pittman, Memoirs, 36–37.

51. B. Pittman, Memoirs, 37–39.

52. Sidney Jr. apparently internalized his father's moral lessons so deeply that, once he was at Howard, he concealed his identity as Booker T. Washington's grandson so as not to win any special favors or attention and worked in Washington restaurants on the side to spare his parents any undue financial burden. ("Howard 'U' Student Concealed Identity: Turns Out to Be Grandson of Booker T. Washington," *New York Amsterdam News*, Dec 4, 1929, 19.

53. Stewart, *Portia*, 101.

54. *Dallas Morning News*, January 22, 1924, 5; May 27, 1944, 4; September 11, 1924, 12; November 16, 1924, 7; June 7, 1925, 11.

55. Stewart, *Portia*, 96–97.

56. Stewart, *Portia*, n.p.

57. B. Pittman, Memoirs, 41.

58. Frank Driggs and Chuck Haddix, *Kansas City Jazz: From Ragtime to Bebop, a History* (Oxford: Oxford University Press, 2005), 62–65.

59. Nathan W. Pearson Jr., *Goin' to Kansas City* (University of Illinois Press, 1994), 64–71.

60. B. Pittman, Memoirs, n.p. (loose pages).

61. B. Pittman, Memoirs, 40.

62. B. Pittman, Memoirs, 42.

63. B. Pittman, Memoirs, 42.

64. Amber R. Clifford-Napoleone, *Queering Kansas City Jazz: Gender, Performance, and the History of a Scene* (Lincoln: University of Nebraska Press, 2018), 22–24.

65. Driggs and Haddix, *Kansas City Jazz*, 6–7.

66. B. Pittman, Memoirs, 43–44.

67. B. Pittman, Memoirs, n.p.

68. Pearson, *Goin' to Kansas City*, 103.

69. B. Pittman, Memoirs, 56–7.

70. Driggs and Haddix, *Kansas City Jazz*, 204

71. Stanley Dance, *The World of Count Basie* (Scribner, 1980), 116.

72. B. Pittman, Memoirs, 60.

73. Frank Buchmann-Moller, *Someone to Watch over Me: The Life and Music of Ben Webster* (University of Michigan Press, 2008), n.p. https://www.press.umich.edu/pdf/0472114700-appendix.htm.

74. B. Pittman, Memoirs, 61.

75. B. Pittman, Memoirs, 47.

76. Jos Willems, *All of Me: The Complete Discography of Louis Armstrong* (Lanham, Maryland: Scarecrow Press, 2006), 369

77. Frank Driggs, *Jazz* (October 1963). Portuguese translation in O. Pittman, *Por você, por mim, por nós*, 160.

78. Diane Lisbona, "Booker faz sax-alto biografia," *Jornal do Brasil*, May 6, 1968, 41.

79. Recorded interview. "Depoimento para posteridade de Booker Pittman." A discussion between Booker Pittman and Lúcio Rangel, Sérgio Cabral, Jorge Guinle, Ricardo Cravo Albin, Eliana Pittman, and Ofélia Pittman. Museu de Imagem e do Som (MIS), Rio de Janeiro. June 25, 1968. Transcription by Laura Souza.

80. B. Pittman, Memoirs, 58–59.

81. Recalled by Budd Johnson in Ira Gitler, *Swing to Bop: An Oral History to the Transition in Jazz in the 1940s* (Oxford University Press, 1985), 107.

82. Alyn Shipton, *Hi-De-Ho: The Life of Cab Calloway* (Oxford University Press, 2010), 64; Driggs and Haddix, *Kansas City Jazz*, n.p.

83. Blanche Calloway and Her Joy Boys, "Just a Crazy Song/Sugar Blues" (Shellac, 10" 78RPM; Victor-22661), June 1931.

84. Gareth Murphy, *Cowboys and Indies: The Epic History of the Records Industry* (Thomas Dunne Books, 2014), 57.

85. B. Pittman, Memoirs, 50.

86. B. Pittman, Memoirs, 53.

87. Briggs, *Jazz*, 159.

88. Perhaps the most influential of these histories was the pioneering work of Nathan Irvin Huggins; see Huggins, *Harlem Renaissance*, updated edition (Oxford: Oxford University Press, 2007 [1971]). More recent studies include George Hutchinson, *The Harlem Renaissance in Black and White* (Cambridge: Belknap Press of Harvard University Press, 1996) and Caroline Goeser, *Picturing the New Negro: Harlem Renaissance Print Culture and Modern Black Identity* (Lawrence: University of Kansas Press, 2022).

89. Andrew Warnes, "The Pulse of Harlem: African American Music and the New Negro Revival," 307–8. From *A History of the Harlem Renaissance*, ed. Rachel Farebrother and Miriam Thaggert (Cambridge: Cambridge University Press, 2021), 307–24.

90. Constance Valis Hill, *Tap Dancing America: A Cultural History* (Oxford University Press, 2010), 97–104.

91. Maurice Waller and Anthony Calabrese, *Fats Waller* (Minneapolis: University of Minnesota Press, 2017 [1977]); retrieved on Google Books, April 20, 2024, n.p.

92. Dustan Prial, *The Producer: John Hammond and the Soul of American Music* (New York: Picador, 2006), 47–48.

93. B. Pittman, Memoirs, 70–72.

94. B. Pittman, Memoirs, 71–72. The bare bones of the story, including the musicians involved, the tune, and the setting, remain mostly as they are written in Booker's memoirs. To add more weight and emphasis to this pivotal moment, however, I have imagined or rephrased some of Booker's subjective experiences.

95. Maria de Simone, "Sophie Tucker, Racial Hybridity and Interracial Relations in American Vaudeville," 155–56. *Theatre Research International* 44, no. 2 (2019), 153–70.

96. Reneé C. Romano, *Race Mixing: Black-White Marriage in Postwar America* (Cambridge: Harvard University Press, 2003), 45.

97. Romano, *Race Mixing*, 49.

98. B. Pittman, Memoirs, 75–76.

99. Peggy Pascoe, *What Comes Naturally: Miscegenation Law and the Making of Race in America* (Oxford: Oxford University Press, 2009), 115–19. For statistics and attitudes about intermarriage in New York City in the first two decades of the twentieth century, see James W. Oberly, "Julius Drachsler's *Intermarriage in New York City*: A Study in Historical Replication." *Historical Methods* 47, no. 2 (April–June 2014), 95–111.

100. B. Pittman, Memoirs, 75–76.

## CHAPTER TWO: LE JAZZISTE

1. Driggs, *Jazz*, 162.
2. Chappy Gardner, "'Lucky' Millinder Plays Monte Carlo," *Chicago Defender*, July 1, 1933, 5.
3. B. Pittman, Memoirs, 54.
4. Bill Coleman, *Trumpet Story* (Palgrave Macmillan, 1981), 83–84.
5. B. Pittman, Memoirs, 54.
6. Coleman, *Trumpet Story*, 83–84.
7. B. Pittman, Memoirs, 54.
8. Stovall, *Paris Noir*, 84–89.
9. Coleman, *Trumpet Story*, 85.
10. Stovall, *Paris Noir*, 97–99.
11. Coleman, *Trumpet Story*, 84–86.
12. Coleman, *Trumpet Story*, 85.
13. Coleman, 86.
14. Coleman, *Trumpet Story*, 87.
15. Lawrence McClellan Jr., *The Later Swing Era, 1942–1955* (Greenwood Press, 2004), 68–70.
16. B. Pittman, Memoirs, 73.
17. Some of Booker Pittman's general perceptions of Paris in this chapter are based on information gathered from interviews conducted with Eliana Pittman in Rio de Janeiro in 2019 and 2022.
18. Rachel Anne Gillett, *At Home in Our Sounds: Music, Race, and Cultural Politics in Interwar Paris* (New York: Oxford University Press, 2021), 42.
19. See Eugene Marlow, *Jazz in China: From Dance Hall Music to Individual Freedom of Expression* (Jackson: University Press of Mississippi, 2019).
20. William A. Shack, *Harlem in Montmartre: A Paris Jazz Story Between the Great Wars* (University of California Press, 2001), 77–81.
21. "Depoimento para posteridade de Booker Pittman," Museu de Imagem e do Som (MIS), Rio de Janeiro. June 25, 1968. Transcription by Laura Souza.
22. Jeffrey H. Jackson, *Making Jazz French: Music and Modern Life in Interwar Paris* (Duke University Press, 2003), 161–62.
23. Travis Atria, *Better Days Will Come: The Life of Arthur Briggs* (Chicago Review Press, 2020), 124–25.
24. H. H. Niesen Jr., "Freddy Johnson, The Piano-Playing Postman," *Melody Maker*, June 6, 1936, cited in Paul Vernon, *Jean "Django" Reinhardt: A Contextual Bio-Discography* (Taylor & Francis, 2017), 72–73.

25. Freddy Johnson and His Harlemites, featuring Arthur Briggs, "I Got Rhythm/Tiger Rag" (Shellac, 10", 78 RPM; Decca UK-F.5110), 1934.

26. For a discussion of the complex racial and ethnic politics of jazz manouche, see Siv B. Lie's *Django Generations: Hearing Ethnorace, Citizenship, and Jazz Manouche in France* (Chicago: University of Chicago Press, 2022).

27. Paul Vernon, *Jean "Django" Reinhardt: A Contextual Bio-Discography, 1910–1953* (New York: Routledge, 2016), 16–17.

28. Shack, *Harlem in Montmartre*, 94.

29. Michael Dregni, with Alain Antonietto and Anne Legrand, *Django Reinhardt and the Illustrated History of Gypsy Jazz* (Speck Press, 2006), 199.

30. Hill, *Light for the Blind*, 8.

31. "Depoimento para posteridade de Booker Pittman," Museu de Imagem e do Som (MIS), Rio de Janeiro. June 25, 1968. Transcription by Laura Souza.

32. Jos Willems, *All of Me: The Complete Discography of Louis Armstrong* (Scarecrow Press, 2006), 92.

33. "A Chops Session": The Slivovice Interview, That's My Home: Louis Armstrong House Museum Virtual Exhibits. https://virtualexhibits.louisarmstronghouse.org/2020/04/13/a-chops-session-the-slivovice-interview.

34. Hugues Panassié, *Hot Jazz: A Guide to Swing Music*, trans. Lyle and Eleanor Dowling (New York: M. Witmark & Sons, 1936), 100.

35. Frank Driggs, "Tommy Douglas," *Jazz Monthly* 5–6 (1959), 4.

36. Anne Anlin Cheng, *Second Skin: Josephine Baker and the Modern Surface* (Oxford: Oxford University Press, 2020), 12.

37. See Jason Borge, "The Portable Jazz Age: Josephine Baker's Tour of South American Cities (1929)," in Bianca Freire-Medeiros and Julia O'Donnell, eds., *Urban Latin America: Images, Words, Flows, and the Built Environment* (New York: Routledge, 2018), 127–41; and Jason Borge, *Tropical Riffs: Latin America and the Politics of Jazz* (Durham: Duke University Press, 2018), 33–45.

38. Daniella Thompson, "The Globetrotting Romeu Silva: The Saxophonist and His Band in France," November 7, 2003. daniellathompson.com/Texts/Investigations/Romeu_Silva.htm,

39. Thompson, "The Globetrotting Romeu Silva," n.p.

40. Lie, *Django Generations*, 5–8.

41. Matthew B. Karush, *Musicians in Transit: Argentina and the Globalization of Popular Music* (Durham: Duke University Press, 2017), 27.

42. Sérgio Cabral, *Pixinguinha: Vida e obra* (Rio de Janeiro: Lumiar, 1997), 74.

43. Rafael José de Menezes Bastos, "Les Batutas, 1922: Uma antropologia da noite parisiense (*Concinnitas* [Rio de Janeiro] 23, no. 44, May 2022: 100–31), 106. https://www.e-publicacoes.uerj.br/concinnitas/article/view/71521/46512.

44. Cabral, *Pixinguinha*, 110.

45. José Ramos Tinhorão, *O samba agora vai . . . A farsa da música popular no exterior* (JCM Editores, 1969), 36–39.

46. Sergio Pujol, *Oscar Alemán: La guitarra embrujada* (Buenos Aires: Planeta, 2015), Kindle, loc. 1237. https://americanhistory.si.edu/collections/search/object/nmah_1200797.

47. Clyde E. B. Bernhardt, *I Remember: Eighty Years of Black Entertainment, Big Bands, and the Blues* (Philadelphia: University of Pennsylvania Press, 1986), 86–87, 94.

48. "Silhuetas... Bibi Miranda," *Correio da Manhã*, August 17, 1952: (V)1; Sábato Magaldi, "Bibi voltou para sempre; foi morar num sitio, em Jacarepaguá," *Diário Carioca*, August 14, 1952, 6.

49. B. Pittman, Memoirs, 89.

50. B. Pittman, Memoirs, 90–91.

51. B. Pittman, Memoirs, 86.

52. Although Booker Pittman hints at the ambivalence he felt toward committing to Joyce at various points in his memoirs, some of the "darker calculus" I am attributing to him in this paragraph is speculative.

53. Shack, *Harlem in Montmarte*, 83.

## CHAPTER THREE: BECOMING CARIOCA

1. "Curvello SS (1917~1925) Siqueira Campos SS (+1943)," Wreck Site. https://wrecksite.eu/wreck.aspx?152883. Accessed May 27, 2024.

2. Although the anecdote that follows was recounted by Booker in a later interview, other details from the voyage are speculative.

3. Interviewed by Globo in December 1966, rebroadcast on the show *Mémoria Popular Brasileira*, Rádio Cultura FM 103.3, December. 27, 2015. http://culturafm.cmais.com.br/memoria/mestre-do-saxofone.

4. Elpídio, who was from Recife, would not have been part of the transatlantic leg of the trip. However, his name appears in the daily newspaper *O Jornal do Comércio* (Rio de Janeiro) on May 3, 1935, along with other members of Silva's orchestra (including Booker's) upon their arrival in Rio de Janeiro.

5. B. Pittman, Memoirs, 85. The specifics of the paragraph and the one that follows are partially speculative.

6. "Depoimento para posteridade de Booker Pittman," Museu de Imagem e do Som (MIS), Rio de Janeiro. June 25, 1968. Transcription by Laura Souza.

7. *O Jornal do Comércio*, May 3, 1935.

8. B. Pittman, Memoirs, 87.

9. Although some of the details here are conjectural, the main facts of Booker's arrival in Rio de Janeiro are found in his memoirs.

10. B. Pittman, Memoirs, 86.

11. B. Pittman, Memoirs, 87, 91.

12. B. Pittman, Memoirs, 91.

13. Luís Martins, *Noturno da Lapa* (Rio de Janeiro: José Olympio, 2004 [1964]), 173. For a sense of Lapa's place in Rio de Janeiro's history prior to the 1960s, see also Gasparino Damata, ed., *Antologia da Lapa; vida boêmia no Rio de ontem* (Rio de Janeiro: Editora Leitura, 1965).

14. B. Pittman, Memoirs, 92–94.

15. B. Pittman, Memoirs, 94; "Depoimento para posteridade de Booker Pittman," Museu de Imagem e do Som (MIS), Rio de Janeiro. June 25, 1968. Transcription by Laura Souza.

16. B. Pittman, Memoirs, 75.

17. B. Pittman, Memoirs, 94.

18. Booker's beach epiphany is included in his memoirs, though I have taken the liberty of changing and expanding on some of his ruminations for greater effect.

19. B. Pittman, Memoirs, 94–95.

20. B. Pittman, Memoirs, 95.

21. Marc A. Hertzman, *Making Samba: A New History of Race and Music in Brazil* (Durham: Duke University Press, 2013), 11.

22. Cabral, *Pixinguinha*, 97–99.

23. Cabral, *Pixinguinha*, 100.

24. Hertzman, *Making Samba*, 11.

25. Marília Giller, "Breve panorama histórico del jazz en Brasil," *Revista Musical Chilena* 72 (2018), 42–43.

26. Jorge Guinle, *Jazz Panorama* (José Olympio, 2002 [1953]), 93.

27. Paulo Fernando, "Josephine Baker, Banana Slide, and other rhythms," *Crítica*, November 22, 1929, 2.

28. Marília Giller, "Breve panorama histórico del jazz en Brasil," 45; Jonathan Wipplinger, *The Jazz Republic: Music, Race, and American Culture in Weimar Germany* (Ann Arbor: University of Michigan Press, 2020), 51.

29. Bryan McCann, *Hello, Hello Brazil: Popular Music in the Making of Modern Brazil* (Durham: Duke University Press, 2004), 11.

30. Hertzman, *Making Samba*, 211–24.

31. Zuza Homem de Mello, *Copacabana: A trajetória do samba-canção (1929–1958)* (São Paulo: Editora 34: 2017), 109.

32. B. Pittman, Memoirs, 86.

33. B. Pittman, Memoirs, 87.

34. B. Pittman, Memoirs, n.p.

35. B. Pittman, Memoirs, 87.

36. For an account of the bohemian ambience and clientele of the Café Nice, see Nestor de Holanda, *Memórias do Café Nice: Subterrâneos da música popular e da vida boêmia do Rio de Janeiro*, 2nd ed. (Rio de Janeiro: Conquista, 1970).

37. Zuza Homem de Mello, *Copacabana*, 106–7.

38. *Jornal do Comércio*, May 18, 1935, 7.

39. *Jornal do Comércio*, June 13, 1938, 8.

40. Rafael do Nascimento Cesar, "Cariocas de New Orleans: Brazilian Interpretations of North American Jazz," *Latin American Music Review* 42, no. 2 (Fall/Winter 2021), 226–52; 241.

41. *Jornal do Comércio*, July 31, 1935, 6; August 3, 5; August 4, 14; and August 5, 7.

42. *A Noite*, August 8, 1935, 4.

43. *Jornal do Comércio*, December 19, 1935, 5.

44. "O jovem tataravô," *Cinearte*, June 1, 1936, 13.

45. "Cinema Brasileiro," *Cinearte*, May 1, 1936, 13.

46. B. Pittman, Memoirs, 87.

47. Sérgio Cabral, *Grande Otelo: Uma biografia* (São Paulo: Editora 34, 2007), 69.

48. Elio Delgado Legón, "Isidro Benítez, un músico cubano en América del Sur." *Havana Times*, September 26, 2013, n.p. https://havanatimesenespanol.org/cultura-cubana/isidro-benitez-un-musico-cubano-en-america-del-sur/.

49. Álvaro Menanteau, *Historia del jazz en Chile*, 2nd ed. (Santiago, Chile: Ocho Libros Editores, 2006), 47–48.

50. *A Nação*, June 14, 1935, 5.

51. *A Noite*, October 4, 1935, 38.

52. B. Pittman, Memoirs, 97–98.

53. Thompson, "The Globetrotting Romeu Silva: The Saxophonist and His Band in France."

54. *Jornal do Comércio* (RJ), May 14, 1936, 9.

CHAPTER FOUR: SOUTHERN STAR

1. B. Pittman, Memoirs, 97.
2. B. Pittman, Memoirs, 97–98.
3. B. Pittman, Memoirs, 98–99.
4. Borge, *Tropical Riffs*, 55.
5. Borge, *Tropical Riffs*, 65–70.
6. Victor Tapia, "Éramos felices, pero no lo sabiamos," *Revista Tramas* (October 2017), n.p. https://revistatramas.com/2017/10/30/eramos-felices-pero-no-lo-sabiamos/.
7. Sergio Pujol, *Jazz al sur: La música negra en la Argentina* (Buenos Aires: Emecé, 1992), 111–13.
8. Gene Poole, *Enciclopedia de swing* (Buenos Aires: Academia Americana, 1938), 43.
9. Edgardo Carrizo, *La Argentina en banda de jazz* (Buenos Aires: Autores de Argentina, 2019), Kindle, loc. 2885–9.
10. Fernando Iriberri, "Panorama del jazz argentino: Las orquestas," *Síncopa y Ritmo* 2, no. 26 (September 1936), 4–5. Also see Pujol, *Jazz al sur*, 111. One example of boogie-woogie was Mickey's "Pedido doble" ("Double Order"), recorded on Odeon (Argentina) in 1944. https://www.youtube.com/watch?v=vYgU73zYsI4. Later, a more stripped-down version of his orchestra covered Bill Haley's hit "Rock Around the Clock" as "Al compás del reloj," included in the 1958 LP *44 Melodías Favoritas Para Bailar* (Vik-LZ-1005). https://www.discogs.com/master/1801209-Harold-Mickey-44-Melod%C3%ADas-Favoritas-Para-Bailar.
11. Ricardo Risetti, *Memórias del jazz argentino* (Buenos Aires: Corregidor, 1994), 139–41.
12. https://www.youtube.com/watch?v=gNZDhp2Q4ws (page no longer available). Accessed May 13, 2025.
13. Paulina L. Alberto and Eduardo Elena, "Introduction: The Shades of a Nation." *Rethinking Race in Modern Argentina*, eds. Paulina L. Alberto and Eduardo Elena (Cambridge University Press, 2016), 6–7.
14. Alberto and Elena, "Introduction: The Shades of a Nation," 2–3.
15. Paulina L. Alberto, *Black Legend: The Many Lives of Raúl Grigera and the Power of Racial Storytelling in Argentina* (Cambridge: Cambridge University Press, 2022), 39–40.
16. Lea Geler, "African Descent and Whiteness in Buenos Aires: Impossible *Mestizajes* in the White Capital City," *Rethinking Race in Modern Argentina*, 218–19.

17. Rafael José de Menezes Bastos, "Les Batutas, 1922," 106.

18. Michael Brocken and Jeff Daniels, *Gordon Stretton, Black British Transoceanic Jazz Pioneer: A New Jazz Chronicle* (Lanham, Maryland: Lexington Books, 2018), 190–91.

19. Chip Deffaa, *Profiles of Eight Vintage Jazzmen* (Urbana: University of Illinois Press, 1992), 1–27; Pujol, *Jazz al sur*, 30–36.

20. See Borge, *Tropical Riffs*, 35–45.

21. Elliott S. Hurwitt, "Introduction," *W. C. Handy's Blues: An Anthology* (Mineola, NY: Dover Publications, 2012), x.

22. "Depoimento para posteridade de Booker Pittman," Museu de Imagem e do Som (MIS), Rio de Janeiro. June 25, 1968. Transcription by Laura Souza.

23. Pujol, *Jazz al sur*, 148.

24. *Síncopa y Ritmo*, January–February 1937, 10.

25. Juan Rafael Grezzi, "Una ráfaga de jazz negra pasa por los estudos de CX 28 Edison Broadcasting," *Cine-Radio-Actualidad*, January 15, 1937, 41.

26. Ruy Castro, *Carmen: Uma biografia* (São Paulo: Companhia das Letras, 2005), 145; "Depoimento para posteridade de Booker Pittman," Museu de Imagem e do Som (MIS), Rio de Janeiro. June 25, 1968. Transcription by Laura Souza.

27. Juan Rafael Grezzi, "The Swing Stars," *Cine-Radio-Actualidad*, April 30, 1937, 31.

28. Hugues Panassié, "Saxofonistas 'altos,'" trans. Fernando Iriberri, *Síncopa y Ritmo* 3, no. 32 (March 1937), 3–4.

29. Acede, "Booker Pittman," *Síncopa y Ritmo*, January–February 1938, 10, 23.

30. Booker Pittman's recordings as part of Booker Pittman's Boys were later included in a UK compilation LP called *The Rhythmakers of Buenos Aires* (Harlequin-HQ 2064), 1988. In 2000, these same recordings appeared on a CD titled *Argentine Swing 1936–1948* (Harlequin CD 142).

31. Liner notes, *The Rhythmakers of Buenos Aires* (Harlequin-HQ 2064), 1988.

32. Pee Wee, "Booker Pittman en el Odeon Bar," *Síncopa y Ritmo*, February 1941, 4–7.

33. Juan Duprat, liner notes, *The Rhythmakers of Buenos Aires* (Harlequin-HQ 2064, 1988).

34. "Nuestros ases: Booker Pittman," *Síncopa y Ritmo*, April 1941, 8.

35. With the exception of one letter sent by his mother weeks before his death and included in his memoirs, I have found no other correspondence between Booker and his family.

36. "Booker Washington's Daughter Interviewed in California," *The People's Voice* (New York), October 17, 1942, 17.

37. Pujol, *Oscar Alemán*, 168–79.

38. B. Pittman, Memoirs, 96.

39. Henry Calu, "Booker Pittman esteve à beira do fracasso: Tóxicos," *Radiolândia*, July 7, 1960, n.p., cited in O. Pittman, *Por você, por mim, por nós*, 167–69.

40. Juan Duprat, liner notes, *The Rhythmakers of Buenos Aires* (Harlequin-HQ 2064, 1988).

41. Mauro Federico e Ignacio Ramírez, *Historia de la droga en la Argentina: De la cocaína legal y los fumaderos a los narcos y las metanfetaminas* (Buenos Aires: Aguilar, 2015), 103–6.

42. Calu, "Booker Pittman esteve à beira do fracasso: Tóxicos," 168.

43. Calu, "Booker Pittman esteve à beira do fracasso: Tóxicos," 167–68.

44. Saxo Tenor, "Ritmo Rápido," *Sintonía*, January 31, 1940, 16; Saxo Tenor, "Ritmo Rápido," *Sintonía*, February 14, 1940, 18.

45. Juan Rafael Grezzi, "En escasos momentos estuvo presente el 'jazz' en el espectáculo del martes 2 en el 'Trocadero.'" *Cine Radio Actualidad*, September 12, 1941, n.p.

46. Grezzi, "En escasos momentos," n.p.

47. George Reid Andrews, *Blackness in the White Nation: A History of Afro-Uruguay* (Chapel Hill: University of North Carolina Press, 2010), 9–19, 92–95.

48. For the most part, Booker's thoughts on and activities in Montevideo are left to conjecture, as his memoirs and periodical sources reveal precious little on his whereabouts in 1942.

49. B. Pittman, Memoirs, 114.

50. Though precise dates on his departure are unclear, Booker likely would have spent around a year in Montevideo, leaving for Rivera in late 1942.

51. B. Pittman, Memoirs, 116.

52. B. Pittman, Memoirs, 116; recorded interview. "Coleção de depoimento para posteridade de Booker Pittman." Museu de Imagem e do Som (MIS), Rio de Janeiro. Transcription by Laura Souza.

53. "Depoimento para posteridade de Booker Pittman," Museu de Imagem e do Som (MIS), Rio de Janeiro. June 25, 1968. Transcription by Laura Souza.

54. B. Pittman, Memoirs, 116, 133–34; author's interviews with Eliana Pittman.

55. It is unclear if Maria was Uruguayan or Brazilian. Her name appears in an article in a Brazilian newspaper some years later as "Maria Fernandes Pittman, esposa de Sr. Booker Pittman," though I was not able to ascertain if the two were ever legally married. *A Tribuna* (Santos, Brazil), January 9, 1947, 2.

56. B. Pittman, Memoirs, 116.

57. As elsewhere in this section of the chapter, I have used some creative license based on fragments of information from Booker's memoirs, as well as conversations with Eliana Pittman.

58. B. Pittman, Memoirs, 116.

59. B. Pittman, Memoirs, 116, 183–84. Now sometimes used interchangeably with "polyneuropathy," "polyneuritis" refers to an inflammation of motor neurons that, in acute cases, can lead to paralysis. See, for example, https://www.britannica.com/science/neuritis#ref754799.

Until the 1930s, alcoholism was frequently viewed as the chief cause of polyneuritis, though other causes, such as B vitamin deficiency, were later also seen to play a role as well; see, for example, Robert Goodhart and Norman Jolliffe, "Effects of Vitamin B (B1) Therapy on the Polyneuritis of Alcohol Addicts," *Journal of the American Medical Association* 110, no. 6 (February 1938), 414–19.

60. B. Pittman, Memoirs, 183b.

61. B. Pittman, Memoirs, 128; recorded interview. "Depoimento para posteridade de Booker Pittman." Museu de Imagem e do Som (MIS), Rio de Janeiro. Transcription by Laura Souza.

62. Fats Elpídio, "O jazz pelo mundo," *Vida Doméstica* (Rio de Janeiro), January 1945, 115.

63. Pee Wee, "El jazz en los locales," *Síncopa y Ritmo*, August 1944, 49–50.

## CHAPTER FIVE: SOME NEGLECTED SPOT

1. Matthew Karush, *Culture of Class: Radio and Cinema in the Making of a Divided Argentina, 1920–1946* (Durham: Duke University Press, 2012), 185.
2. *Diario da noite*, April 6, 1946, 7.
3. Borge, *Tropical Riffs*, 99–101.
4. Zuza Homem de Mello, *Copacabana: A trajetória do samba-canção, 1929–1958* (São Paulo: Editora 34, 2017), 125.
5. *A Tribuna* (Santos), June 2, 1946, 3; June 7, 1946, 14; August 10, 1946, 14.
6. B. Pittman, Memoirs, 139.
7. Alvares da Silva, "Sax no. 1," *O Cruzeiro*, May 14, 1960, 82–87.
8. *A Tribuna*, January 9, 1947, 2.
9. This information also comes from the MIS interview. Even though he specifies 1946 and 1947, it is possible that Booker's recollection of both the Oasis and the Teatro Municipal has been confused with his stay in São Paulo in the late 1950s. Recorded interview. "Coleção de depoimento para posteridade de Booker Pittman." Museu de Imagem e do Som (MIS), Rio de Janeiro. Transcription by Laura Souza.
10. B. Pittman, Memoirs, 139.
11. *Diário Carioca*, February 16, 1938, 10.
12. *Jornal dos Sports*, October 31, 1940, 3.
13. *A Manhã*, July 19, 1944, 5.
14. *O Triângulo* (Minas Gerais), March 26, 1941, 4.
15. *A Manhã*, February 13, 1942, 5.
16. Robert W. Harwood, *I Went Down to St. James Infirmary* (Harland Press, 2006), 134–35.
17. *O Jornal*, January 8, 1944, 6.
18. Bud Freeman, *Crazeology* (University of Illinois Press, 1989), 66–67.
19. Homem de Mello, *Copacabana*, 218.
20. Castro, *A noite de meu bem*, 51–52.
21. Sylvio Cardoso, "Swing-Fan: A jam-session do 'Mei Ling.'" *A Cena Muda* 32 (August 10, 1948), 23.
22. Castro, *A noite de meu bem*, 51–52.
23. B. Pittman, Memoirs, 176, 192.
24. https://humbertoamorim.blogspot.com/2009/10/booker-pitman-talento-desconhecido.html.
25. B. Pittman, Memoirs, 192.
26. B. Pittman, Memoirs, 192–93.
27. B. Pittman, Memoirs, 193–95.
28. Nice Lecocq Müller, "Contribuição ao Estudo do Norte do Paraná," *Geografia* (Londrina) 10, no. 1, 89–118, January/June 2001 (1956), 111.
29. Müller, "Contribuição ao estudo do Norte do Paraná," 100, 106.
30. B. Pittman, Memoirs, 195.
31. B. Pittman, Memoirs, 194–97.
32. In his memoirs, Booker is not expansive about his off-the-grid years in Paraná, and much of what he does say is fragmentary. Consequently, the following pages are partially

speculative, based loosely on later interviews of his and my own interviews with Eliana Pittman, as well as additional sources where noted.

33. Richard F. Nyrop, ed., *Brazil: A Country Study*, 4th ed. (Washington, DC: American University, 1983), 125–27.

34. *Correio da Manhã*, October 14, 1969, 7.

35. B. Pittman, Memoirs, 190.

36. B. Pittman, Memoirs, 190, 194.

37. B. Pittman, Memoirs, 190, 216.

38. Nyrop, *Brazil: A Country Study*, 127.

39. "No Paraná Ganhou o Batismo de 'Baiano' e agora Voltará para a Glória: é o famoso Booker Pittman," *O Correio do Paraná*, December 13, 1960, 9.

40. "No Paraná Ganhou o Batismo de 'Baiano,'" 9.

41. B. Pittman, Memoirs, 190.

42. B. Pittman, Memoirs, 235.

43. The following paragraphs, though based on pieces of information found in Booker's memoirs and a small number of articles and interviews, are mostly conjectural accounts.

44. "No Paraná Ganhou o Batismo de 'Baiano' e agora Voltará para a Glória," 9.

45. Alvares da Silva, "Sax no. 1," *O Cruzeiro*, May 14, 1960, 82–87.

46. *Correio da Manhã*, October 14, 1969, 7.

47. B. Pittman, Memoirs, 235.

48. Sérgio Porto, *Manchete*, February 14, 1953, 24.

49. *O Globo*, April 30, 1953, 4.

50. Fernando Lobo, "Morre um nome," *Manchete*, February 14, 1953, 36.

51. B. Pittman, Memoirs, 235.

52. "Ele toca o samba," *Realidade*, November 1966, 57.

53. Sérgio Porto, "O morto," *Tribuna da Imprensa*, December 12–13, 1953, 7.

54. "Booker vivo e pintando paredes," *Manchete*, December 12, 1953, 4.

55. Lúcio Rangel, "Booker Pittman, um músico de jazz," *Samba Jazz & Outras Notas*, (Rio de Janeiro: Agir, 2007), 204. First published in the magazine *Senhor* in July 1959.

56. Allan Morrison, "Booker T's Grandson Exports Jazz to Brazil: Crack Pittman returns to Gotham after 29-Year Exile," *Jet*, June 28, 1962, 58–61.

57. O. Pittman, *Por você, por mim, por nós*, 140–41. In his 1968 MIS interview, Booker tells a slightly different version of this episode, according to which the owner of the cabaret in Londrina was also the owner of the "abandoned" farm. Booker says he adopted Tex only once he had arrived at the farm to serve as a caretaker. The meat from the chicken in question, the musician quipped, must have gone bad, since it made him sick.

58. "No Paraná Ganhou o Batismo de 'Baiano' e Agora voltará Para a Glória," 9.

59. Vidossich, *Jazz na garoa*, 39.

60. *O Globo*, December 20, 1955, 6.

61. Vidossich, *Sincretismos na música afro-americana* (São Paulo: Edições Quíron, 1975), ix.

62. Vidossich, *Jazz na garoa*, 44; Govenar and Brakefield, *Deep Ellum*, 28.

63. Vidossich, *Jazz na garoa*, 42.

64. *Correio Paulistano*, May 26, 1956, 5 (II). Vidossich, *Jazz na garoa*, 40.

65. Vidossich, *Jazz na garoa*, 48.

66. Sílvio Tulio Cardoso, "O globo nos discos populares," *O Globo* (morning edition), December 6, 1956, 7.
67. Sílvio Tullio Cardoso, "O globo nos discos populares: Booker Pittman and the São Paulo Dixielanders," *O Globo* (morning edition), December 26, 1956, 3.
68. *Correio Paulistano*, July 27, 1956, 5 (II).
69. Vidossich, *Jazz na garoa*, 45.
70. *O Jornal*, November 23, 1957, 2 (II).
71. Vidossich, *Jazz na garoa*, 52.
72. Vidossich, *Jazz na garoa*, 46.
73. Vidossich, *Jazz na garoa*, 52–53.
74. Borge, *Tropical Riffs*, 108–9.
75. Vidossich, *Jazz na garoa*, 58.
76. "No Paraná Ganhou o Batismo de 'Baiano' e Agora voltará Para a Glória," 9.
77. *O Correio do Paraná*, December 13, 1960, 9.
78. *O Correio do Paraná*, December 13, 1960, 9.

## CHAPTER SIX: THE REVIVALIST

1. Mattos Pacheco, "Ronda social," *Diário da Noite*, September 9, 1957, 6.
2. Von Eschen, *Satchmo Blows Up the World*, 3–4.
3. *Diário da Noite*, October 29, 1957, 2.
4. *Diário da Noite*, November 22, 1957, 8; *Mundo Ilustrado*, December 4, 1957, 44.
5. "Latin Blowout for Louis," *Life*, November 25, 1957, 169–70.
6. See, for example, Thomas Ewbank's eyewitness account in *Life in Brazil* (1856). https://archive.org/details/lifeinbrazilorjoooewba.
7. *Revista da Semana*, November 30, 1957, 32.
8. "Companheiros de rua e de provaçoes volta a abraçar-se 23 anos depois," *Diário da Noite*, November 25, 1957, 11.
9. *O Cruzeiro*, December 7, 1957, 128.
10. O. Pittman, *Por você, por mim, por nós*, 131.
11. O. Pittman, *Por você, por mim, por nós*, 131–32.
12. *Revista do Globo*, January 1967, n.p.
13. O. Pittman, *Por você, por mim, por nós*, 130–32.
14. A subjective profile based loosely on Booker's memoirs and various passages of O. Pittman, *Por você, por mim, por nós*, in addition to the author's conversations with Eliana Pittman.
15. O. Pittman, *Por você, por mim, por nós*, 132.
16. Based in part on conversations with Eliana Pittman.
17. O. Pittman, *Por você, por mim, por nós*, 132–33.
18. *Diário da Noite*, September 19, 1957, 25; April 25, 1958, 15.
19. *Por você, por mim, por nós*, 145. http://dicionariompb.com.br/maysa/dados-artisticos.
20. Morgana Cintra and Booker Pittman, "Serenata do adeus/Let's Fall in Love," Copacabana (5919), 1958.

21. Booker Pittman, *Booker Pittman Plays Again*, RCA Victor (BBL 1028), 1959.
22. *Diário da Noite*, November 25, 1957, 5.
23. O. Pittman, *Por você, por mim, por nós*, 133, with added details based on conversations with Eliana Pittman.
24. The terms *casal* and even *casados* had long been used informally in couples where legal matrimony was not granted. See subsequent footnote.
25. Legal divorce was prohibited in Brazil until 1977. Though "judicial separation," which "allowed the separation of the spouses and ended the matrimonial regime," had been on the books since 1916, even this status precluded a formal dissolution of the marital bond, and therefore, remarriage. See Antônio J. Maristrello Porto and Pedro H. Butelli, "Impacts of Divorce Law Changes in Brazil and the 'Extinction' of Judicial Separation," *Revista de Estudos Empiricos em Direito (Brazilian Journal of Empirical Legal Studies)* 3, no. 2 (July 2016), 149–61.
26. *Por você, por mim, por nós*, 134–35, 152.
27. *Por você, por mim, por nós*, 135.
28. *Por você, por mim, por nós*, 146; the author's conversations with Eliana Pittman.
29. *Por você, por mim, por nós*, 146–47.
30. "Desperta invulgar interesse o concerto de jazz no Municipal," *O Globo* (morning edition, June 18, 1959, 15.
31. "Desperta invulgar interesse o concerto de jazz no Municipal," 15.
32. "Siluetas . . . Bibi Miranda," *Correio da Manhã*, August 17, 1952, 1 (iv).
33. Ciro Rímac's Rumba Orchester, "Cubanacan/E Bom Parar" (Berlin: Telefunken, A 2375), 1938. https://www.youtube.com/watch?v=AsaGEKGANws.
34. Sábato Magaldi (Sérgio Porto), "Bibi voltou para sempre; foi morar num sitio, em Jacarepaguá," *Diario Carioca*, August 14, 1952, 6.
35. "Josephine Baker na Frente Occidental," *Diario da Noite*, October 5, 1939, 1; *O Globo* (afternoon edition), September 12, 1942, 6.
36. "Siluetas . . . Bibi Miranda," *Correio da Manhã*, August 17, 1952, 1 (iv).
37. *Jornal dos Sports*, August 8, 1940, 5; June 13, 1941, 5.
38. *Diário Carioca*, September 23, 1951, 4.
39. Sábato Magaldi (Sérgio Porto), "Bibi voltou para sempre; foi morar num sitio, em Jacarepaguá," *Diario Carioca*, August 14, 1952, 6; *Diário Carioca*, September 14, 1952, 5.
40. *Correio da Manhã*, July 20, 1952, (V)1.
41. Luis Sodré, "Jam Session," *Revista da Semana*, June 19, 1954, 20; *O Jornal*, May 15, 1954, 7.
42. *Manchete*, August 18, 1956, 47.
43. *Diário Carioca*, April 12, 1957, 6; *Diário Carioca*, April 13, 6; Míster Eco, "Louis Cole Não Poderá Mais Cantar," *Diário Carioca*, May 3, 1957, 6.
44. *Diário Carioca*, June 27, 1957, 6.
45. *Revista da Semana*, May 29, 1954, 50.
46. *Jornal do Brasil*, May 18, 1958, A7.
47. *Jornal do Brasil*, June 8, 1958, (A)16; Benjamim Costallat, "Claude Austin," *Jornal do Brasil*, June 13, 1958, A3.
48. Lúcio Rangel, *Samba Jazz & Outras Notas* (Rio de Janeiro: Agir, 2007), 203.
49. Carolyn Perritt, "The Dissident Voice of William Sidney Pittman," *Legacies: A History Journal for Dallas and North Central Texas* 16, no. 1 (Spring 2004), 45–46.

50. Perritt, "The Dissident Voice of William Sidney Pittman," 45.

51. Perritt, "The Dissident Voice of William Sidney Pittman," 47–49; Ruth Ann Stewart, "William Sidney Pittman (1875–1958)," in *African American Architects: A Biographical Dictionary, 1865–1945* (New York: Routledge, 2004), 446–51. It is unclear when exactly Booker became aware of his father's death, though it very possibly did not happen until he reunited with his mother in 1962.

52. *Por você, por mim, por nós*, 148–49.

53. *Por você, por mim, por nós*, 149.

54. While Booker indeed eventually moved back to the Posto 2 neighborhood and almost certainly frequented Praça do Lido, this particular walking tour of his, and his ruminations on the past, are conjectural.

55. Ary Vasconcelos, "O Jornal de bolso," *O Jornal*, January 22, 1960, 3.

56. *O Jornal*, February 28, 1960, 2.

57. *Radiolândia*, February 16, 1960, 18.

58. Ary Vasconcelos, "Jornal de Bolso," *O Jornal*, March 22, 1960, (II) 2.

59. *O Jornal*, April 23, 1960, 10.

60. Jean Pouchard, "Sociedade," *Diário Carioca*, May 3, 1960, 6.

61. Vasconcelos, "Jornal de Bolso," *O Jornal*, November 12, 1960, 6.

62. Booker Pittman, *The No 1 Soprano Sax in the World, The Fabulous Booker Pittman*, Musidisc (M-16006), 1960.

63. *Billboard*, January 25, 1960, 21.

64. Sidney Bechet, *Treat it Gentle: An Autobiography* (New York: Da Capo Press, 2002 [1960]), Kindle, loc. 1757–1822.

65. "Abdias promete levar negros à boate que barrou Booker Pittman," *Jornal do Brasil*, November 25, 1960, 9.

66. Última Hora, November 25, 1960, 2; December 9, 1960, 10.

67. "Abdias promete levar negros à boate que barrou Booker Pittman." *Jornal do Brasil*, November 25, 1960, 9.

68. Flávio E. Macedo Soares, "A geração esquecida," *Diário Carioca*, June 10, 1960, 17.

69. *Jornal do Brasil*, March 18, 1961, 4.

70. Diane Lisbona, "Booker faz sax-alto biografia," *Jornal do Brasil*, May 6, 1968, 41.

71. *O Cruzeiro*, November 16, 1963, 33.

72. Sônia Góes, "Bob's é precursor do fast food no Brasil," *Tribuna da Imprensa*, September 17, 1998, 18.

73. *Tribuna da Imprensa*, March 6, 1961, 2 (II).

74. Última Hora, March 7, 1961, 12.

75. Flávio E. Macedo Soares, "Jazz: A geração esquecida," *O Diário Carioca*, October 9, 1960, 17.

76. *Diário Carioca*, June 3, 1961, 7; *Diario Caricoa*, June 18, 1961, 6.

77. *Diario Carioca*, July 2, 1961, 6.

78. *O Jornal*, June 28, 1961, 6.

79. Borge, *Tropical Riffs*, 110–11.

80. *Jam Session: Dick Farney e Booker Pittman*. Discos RGE (XRLP-5.105), 1961.

## CHAPTER SEVEN: SAXOPHONE, MICROPHONE, TELEPHONE

1. To gain perspective on Booker's early interactions with Eliana and Ofélia, my conversations with Eliana Pittman proved invaluable.
2. *Por você, por mim, por nós*, 150.
3. Ronaldo Bôscoli, "Eliana Pittman: Só não sou estrela no Brasil." *Manchete*, June 2, 1979, 121.
4. O. Pittman, *Por você, por mim, por nós*, 150–51.
5. Author's conversations with Eliana Pittman; B. Pittman, Memoirs, 274–75.
6. *O Cruzeiro*, May 14, 1960, 90.
7. Odillo Licetti, "Eliana Pittman: É preciso cantar," *Intervalo* 260 (1968), 10.
8. *Por você, por mim, por nós*, 154.
9. *Diário Carioca*, June 4, 1961, 6.
10. *Radiolândia*, July 1961, 49.
11. *O Jornal*, August 16, 1961, 6.
12. *Diário Carioca*, May 30, 1962, 6.
13. *Eliana e Booker Pittman*, Mocambo (LP 40083), 1962.
14. *O Jornal* March 9, 1962, 2 ii; *Diário Carioca*, April 8, 1962, 6; *Última Hora*, January 23, 1962, 8.
15. "Booker Pittman in Buenos Aires," *Lyra* (1962), 186–88, 232.
16. As recalled by Eliana Pittman in a 2022 interview with the author.
17. "People-to-People Program," Dwight D. Eisenhower Presidential Library, Museum & Boyhood Home, National Archives. https://www.eisenhowerlibrary.gov/research/online-documents/people-people-program.
18. *Jornal do Brasil*, July 24, 1962, 5.
19. Frank Driggs, *Jazz* (October 1963), 158–59.
20. *Jet*, July 26, 1962, 64.
21. Allan Morrison, "Booker T.'s Grandson Exports Jazz to Brazil," *Jet*, June 28, 1962, 60.
22. *Jet*, June 28, 1962, 59.
23. Stewart, *Portia*, 132.
24. *Jornal do Brasil*, July 24, 1962, 5.
25. *Revista do Radio* 711 (1963), 14; 737 (1963), 20; 740 (1963), 45.
26. *Diário Carioca*, November 8, 1962, 8.
27. *Diário Carioca*, April 15, 1963, 8.
28. Míster Eco, "Sonho em BG," *Diário Carioca*, September 26, 1963, 8.
29. Míster Eco, "Vocação sanguínea," *Diário Carioca*, July 30, 1964, 6.
30. Based on the author's conversations with Eliana Pittman in 2019 and 2022.
31. For a more in-depth discussion of the Tinhorão-Bossa Nova controversy, see Borge, *Tropical Riffs*, 114–18.
32. Eliana & Booker Pittman, *News from Brazil—Bossa Nova* (Polydor, LPNG-4.069), 1963.
33. Interview from *O Som do Vinil*, Canal Brasil, May 24, 2010. https://www.youtube.com/watch?v=aHN0UKk-hAo (video no longer available).
34. K. E. Goldschmitt, *Bossa Mundo: Brazilian Music in Transnational Media Industries* (New York: Oxford University Press, 2020), 30.

35. *Diário Carioca*, December 15, 1963, 8.
36. *Tribuna da Imprensa*, January 22, 1964, 13.
37. *Tribuna da Imprensa*, February 7, 1964, 13; February 13, 1964, 11.
38. *Jornal dos Sports*, April 29, 1964, 10.
39. *Tribuna da Imprensa*, July 28, 1964, 3 (II); *Tribuna da Imprensa*, July 17, 1964, 11.
40. *Tribuna da Imprensa*, July 17, 1964, 11.
41. Paulo Rehder, "A noite é negra," *Jornal do Brasil*, May 17, 1964, B6.
42. Jasmine Mitchell, *Imagining the Mulatta: Blackness in U.S. and Brazilian Media* (Urbana: University of Illinois Press, 2021), 49–50. Significantly, in the *Jornal do Brasil*'s coverage of Booker's funeral at the end of the decade, the late musician was referred to as a *mulatto* (*Jornal do Brasil*, October 15, 1969, 16).
43. Gilberto Freyre, *The Masters and the Slaves*. Trans. Samuel Putnam. New York: Alfred A. Knopf (1946).
44. Associated Negro Press, "Wonderful Opportunities Offered in Brazil for Thrifty People of All Races," *Tulsa Star*, December 11, 1920, cited in David J. Hellwig (ed.), *African-American Reflections on Brazil's Racial Paradise* (Philadelphia: Temple University Press, 1991), 40–41.
45. E. Franklin Frazier, "Brazil Has No Race Problem," *Common Sense* 11 (November 1942), 363–65, in Hellwig (ed.), 122–30; E. Franklin Frazier, "A Comparison of Negro-White Relations in Brazil and the United States," in Hellwig (ed.), 131–36.
46. Leslie B. Rout Jr., "Brazil: Study in Black, Brown and Beige," *Negro Digest* 19 (February 1970), in Hellwig (ed.), 192–93. Ironically, as Patrícia de Santana Pinho has recently suggested, a more clear-eyed and nuanced assessment of racism in Brazil by Rout and others did not prevent an uptick in what she calls "roots tourism" by Black Americans to Brazil in the 1960s and 1970s. See Patricia de Santana Pinho, *Mapping Diaspora: African American Roots Tourism in Brazil* (Chapel Hill: University of North Carolina Press, 2018), 28–29.
47. John. J. O'Connor, "A Master of the Small Chuckle," *New York Times*, February 2, 1997, 42 (II).
48. *Tribuna da Imprensa*, August 31, 1964, 3 (II).
49. "Booker e Eliana de costa a costa nos EUA: Tio Sam vai sambar com eles," *Última Hora* (Rio de Janeiro), September 24, 1964, 11.
50. Borge, *Tropical Riffs*, 118–19.
51. Borge, *Tropical Riffs*, 121.
52. *The Jack Paar Program*, NBC, October 2, 1964. To watch a fragment of the episode, see https://www.youtube.com/watch?v=IBtr-_v1-p8.
53. Penny Von Eschen, *Satchmo Blows Up the World*, 6.
54. Although critical bibliography on the subject of expatriatism is still relatively thin, two revealing studies have sought to understand the meanings of twenty-first-century expatriate populations in Latin America. In his study of an expatriate community in Cuenca, Ecuador, Matthew Hayes describes "lifestyle migrants" as mostly white, middle-class people whose voluntary translocation to mostly poor, non-white Cuenca reveals the complexities of the coloniality of power (*Gringolandia: Lifestyle Migration under Late Capitalism* [Minneapolis: University of Minnesota Press, 2018], 8–10). From a different perspective, Mason R. McWatters uses the term "residential tourists" to describe a population of expats in Boquete, Panama. These "landscape nomads," he writes, "predominantly experience Boquete as a *landscape* from

which they are, in many ways, distanced and alienated." Mason R. McWatters, *Residential Tourism: (De)Constructing Paradise* (Channel View Publications, 2008); 2, 157.

55. See Ochoa, *Aurality*, loc. 383; and Glissant, *Poetics of Relation*, 18–20.

56. "Tele Followup Comment: *The Jack Paar Show*," *Variety*, October 7, 1964, 35.

57. *Jornal do Brasil*, November 18, 1964, B6.

58. John S. Wilson, "Clubs Refreshed with New Twists: 3 Vacated Nightspots Come Alive with Gimmicks," *New York Times*, June 1, 1965, 44.

59. *Variety*, July 21, 1965, 60.

60. *Variety*, September 15, 1965, 74.

61. "Fine Recording Inc.: Pioneers in High-Fidelity Studio Recording: UPDATED—5," *Preservation Sound: Information and Ideas About Audio History* (February 7, 2010), n.p. http://www.preservationsound.com/2012/02/fine-recording-inc-pioneers-in-high-fidelity-studio-recording/.

62. *Diário de Notícias* January 30, 1965, 13.

63. *Tribuna da Imprensa*, March 11, 1965, 11.

64. Richard F. Shepard, "City's Brazilians Cluster Colorfully in West 40s," *New York Times*, April 30, 1968, 41, 95.

65. According to Eliana Pittman in conversations with the author.

66. Eliana Pittman—*Sim, Deve Ser Amor / O Amor do Amor / Samba do Amor / Vamos Amar* (Musidisc EP, LPM-12.061), 1965.

67. Booker Pittman, *Booker Pittman + Sax Soprano = Sucesso* (Musidisc, EP, HI-FI-2118), 1965.

68. "Eliana Pittman: Newest Bombshell from Brazil," *Ebony*, December 1965, cover, 60–68.

69. "Eliana Pittman: Newest Bombshell from Brazil," *Ebony*, December 1965, cover, 60–68.

70. *Manchete*, December 18, 1965, 105.

71. Ted Green, "Main Street," *Backstage*, November 12, 1965, 1; *Backstage*, December 3, 1965, 2.

72. *Tribuna da Imprensa*, November 13–14, 1965, 9; November 24, 1965, 9.

73. Tom Stites, "A Night on the Town: Sax Player Takes a 36-Year Trip," *Kansas City Star*, November 12, 1965, n.p.

74. In an interesting coincidence—or perhaps it was not—one of *Run for your Life*'s recurring actors and directors was Fernando Lamas, an Argentine-born actor who was in Buenos Aires at the same time as Booker in the mid- to late 1930s, working for some time as a crooner in Harold Mickey's orchestra (Carrizo, *La Argentina en banda de jazz*, loc. 4636n). Lamas went on to make his mark in Hollywood, playing the "Latin lover" in a number of films and television series in the 1950s and 1960s. Although I have found no mention of Lamas in Booker-related archival sources, it is likely that he and Booker had become acquainted during their days together in the Buenos Aires jazz scene.

75. "Eliana Pittman: Songbird with a Past," *Chicago Daily Defender*, May 16, 1966, 11.

76. Eliana Pittman, "It's a Lonesome Old Town/My First Love Song" (Decca 31952), 1966.

77. *Revista do Radio* 800, 1965, 45, *Diário Carioca*, January 19, 1965, 6.

78. *Revista do Radio* 862, 1966, 36.

79. *Intervalo* 197, 1966, 18.

80. *Manchete*, August 27, 1966, 29.

81. *Correio da Manhã*, March 15, 1966, 10.
82. *Jornal do Brasil*, March 13, 1966, 29; *Tribuna da Imprensa*, April 5, 1966, 11.
83. *O Jornal*, January 15, 1967, 15.
84. Thais Lima Nicodemo, "A Case Study of Brazilian Popular Music and Censorship: Ivan Lins's Music During Dictatorship in Brazil," in *The Oxford Handbook of Music Censorship*, ed. Patricia Hall (Oxford University Press, 2017), 357.
85. Christopher Dunn, *Contracultura: Alternative Arts and Social Transformation in Authoritarian Brazil* (Chapel Hill: University of North Carolina Press, 2016), 23–25. See also Marcos Napolitano, *1964: história do regime militar brasileiro* (São Paulo: Editora Contexto, 2014); and *"Seguindo a canção": Engajamento politico e indústria cultural na MPB (1959–1969)* (São Paulo: Annablume, 2001).
86. *O Jornal*, March 16, 1966, 5.
87. "Eliana: a longa jornada do rádio à sala de concertos." *O Jornal*, October 20, 1967, 17.
88. *Intervalo* 260, 1968, 11.
89. *Revista do Rádio* 775, 1964, 19; *Revista do Rádio* 862, 1966, 19.
90. Some of this information is based on conversations with Eliana Pittman from 2019 and 2022.
91. *Revista do Rádio* 862, 1966, 8.
92. *Revista do Rádio* 749, 1964, 21.
93. *Intervalo*, May 7, 1966, 18.
94. *Intervalo* 199, 1966, cover.
95. *Tribuna da Imprensa*, June 22–23, 1968, 9.
96. *Intervalo* no. 260, 1968, 11.

## CHAPTER EIGHT: THE LONG *ADEUS*

1. While the Bar Castelinho was indeed one of Booker Pittman's favorite haunts in his final years, the remainder of these two paragraphs is mostly speculative, though informed by the author's conversations with Eliana Pittman.
2. *Tribuna da Imprensa*, March 18, 1966, 11.
3. "Eliana Pittman, Songbird with a Past: She's Kin of Booker T. Washington," *Chicago Daily Defender*, May 16, 1966, 11.
4. *TV Guide*, May 1966, 59.
5. *O Jornal*, April 5, 1966, 5.
6. *Correio da Manhã*, March 29, 1966, 10.
7. These descriptions are loosely based on repeated refrains from Booker's memoirs and interviews, as well as the author's conversations with Eliana Pittman.
8. *O Jornal*, June 26, 1966, 15.
9. Fernando Lopes, "Os Pittmans chegam cheios de saudades," *Tribuna da Imprensa*, August 5, 1966, 12.
10. *O Jornal*, August 12, 1966, 11; August 25, 1966, 11.
11. *Diário de Noticias*, October 2, 1966, 33.
12. *O Jornal*, October 9, 1966, 15.

13. *Tribuna da Imprensa*, December 15, 1966, 12.
14. *Diário de Notícias*, December 18, 1966, 39.
15. *Tribuna da Imprensa*, December 23, 1966, 11.
16. From an interview in Porto Alegre, Brazil, recorded in December 1966 and rebroadcast on the show *Mémoria Popular Brasileira*, Rádio Cultura FM 103.3, December 27, 2015. https://cultura.uol.com.br/radio/programas/memoria-popular-brasileira/2022/05/30/24_mestre-do-saxofone.html.
17. *Diário de Notícias*, January 4, 1967, 16; *Jornal dos Sports* January 17, 1967, 10; *Jornal dos Sports*, January 21, 1967, 10; *Tribuna da Imprensa*, January 28, 1967, 12.
18. *Diário de Notícias*, February 14, 1967, 16; Míster Eco, "Eliana no parque," *Jornal dos Sports*, April 9, 1967, 20.
19. Míster Eco, *Jornal dos Sports*, March 16, 1967, 14; *Luta Democrática*, March 19, 1967, 3.
20. "Eliana no parque," *Jornal dos Sports*, April 9, 1967, 20.
21. *Tribuna da Imprensa*, April 28, 1966, 12.
22. O. Pittman, *Por você por mim por nós*, 174.
23. *Diário de Notícias*, May 10, 1967, 16; *Jornal dos Sports*, May 16, 1967, 16; *Jornal do Brasil*, July 13, 1967, 27.
24. Author's interview of Eliana Pittman, 2018.
25. *Diário de Notícias*, December 30, 1967, 10.
26. *Jornal dos Sports*, June 13, 1967, 14.
27. *Tribuna da Imprensa*, June 2, 1967, 10.
28. These semi-speculative descriptions of Booker Pittman's thoughts and routines are based in part on the author's conversations with Eliana Pittman in 2018.
29. Eliana Pittman, *É Preciso Cantar* (Copacabana CLP 11493), 1966.
30. *Jornal do Brasil*, November 26, 1967, 66.
31. *Jornal dos Sports*, November 30, 1966, 10.
32. *Tribuna da Imprensa*, January 17, 1967, 12.
33. *Jornal dos Sports*, April 30, 1967, 16; *Tribuna da Imprensa*, May 9, 1967, 12.
34. *Diário de Notícias*, April 11, 1968, 14.
35. *Tribuna da Imprensa*, August 26–27, 1967, 12.
36. *O Jornal*, May 8, 1968, 15.
37. Diane Lisbona, "Booker faz sax-alto biografia," *Jornal do Brasil*, May 6, 1968, 41.
38. Diane Lisbona, "Booker faz sax-alto biografia," *Jornal do Brasil*, May 6, 1968, 41.
39. "Depoimento para posteridade de Booker Pittman," Museu de Imagem e do Som (MIS), Rio de Janeiro. June 25, 1968. Transcription by Laura Souza.
40. "Depoimento para posteridade de Booker Pittman," *O Jornal*, June 22, 1968, 5 (II).
41. *O Jornal*, June 7, 1969, 16; June 11, 1969, 18.
42. *Tribuna da Imprensa*, July 1, 1969, 9.
43. *Correio da Manhã*, June 10, 1969, 14; June 19, 1969, 16.
44. *Correio da Manhã*, August 16, 1969, 16.
45. *O Jornal*, March 17, 1968, 3.
46. *Tribuna da Imprensa*, July 2, 1969, 9.
47. Based on the author's conversations with Eliana Pittman.
48. Based on the author's conversations with Eliana Pittman.

49. Macksen Luiz, "Booker Pittman: O Fugitivo do Sucesso," *Jornal do Brasil*, October 27, 1969, 66.

50. Keshav Anand, "Through Samba and Painting, Heitor dos Prazeres Centres Afro-Brazilian Narratives," *Something Curated*, January 17, 2024. https://somethingcurated.com/2024/01/17/heitor-dos-prazeres/.

51. Based on the author's conversations with Eliana Pittman.

52. A draft of this letter was included in Booker Pittman's memoirs. It is unclear whether another version was ever sent to his mother.

53. *Jornal do Brasil*, October 14, 1969, 1, 14. Also based on the author's conversations with Eliana Pittman.

54. "Booker Pittman será sepultado junto a instrumentos que amou," *Jornal do Brasil*, October 14, 1969, 14.

55. "Morreu Booker Pittman," *Diário da Noite*, October 14, 1969, 4; *Jornal do Brasil*, October 14, 1969, 1, 14.

56. "Singing Priest from Brazil Gives Recitals in U.S., *Brazilian Bulletin*, March 1, 1964, n.p.; "Booker Pittman recebe no enterro homenagem feita a músicos de jazz dos Estados Unidos," *Jornal do Brasil*, October 15, 1969, 16.

57. *Diario de Notícias*, October 15, 1969, 6; *Jornal do Brasil*, October 15, 1969, 16.

58. "Booker Pittman recebe no enterro homenagem feita a músicos de jazz dos Estados Unidos," *Jornal do Brasil*, October 15, 1969, 16. Other details based on the author's conversations with Eliana Pittman.

## CODA: HOW TO LAY A SAXOPHONE TO REST

1. *Jornal do Brasil*, October 15, 1969, 16.
2. *Jornal do Brasil*, October 16, 1969, 17.
3. *O Jornal*, October 15, 1969, 2.
4. *Tribuna da Imprensa*, October 17, 1969, 9.
5. *Jornal do Brasil*, October 22, 1969, 10.
6. Luiz Gonzaga Larquê, "Eliana Pittman Corre Mundo," *Jornal do Brasil*, April 13, 1970, 64.
7. Eliana Pittman, *Tô chegando, Ja cheguei* (RCA Victor Brazil, 103.0084), 1974.
8. "Eliana Pittman: Carnaval tipo exportação." *Manchete*, April 13, 1974, 94.
9. Ronaldo Bôscoli, "Eliana Pittman: 'Só não sou estrela no Brasil,'" *Manchete*, 1974, 120.
10. *Jornal do Brasil*, June 29, 1970, 25.
11. *Jornal do Brasil*, October 24–25, 1971, B1.
12. Ernani Duarte da Silva, "Booker Pittman, um nome esquecido," *Tribuna da Imprensa*, October 14–15, 1972, 7.
13. Sieiro Netto, "O sucesso de Eliana," *O Jornal*, October 19, 1973, 19.
14. Gilka Serzedello Machado, "Colunão," *Tribuna da Imprensa*, November 24–25, 1973, 7.
15. *Tribuna da Imprensa*, September 19, 1974, 10.
16. *Tribuna da Imprensa*, October 11, 1974, 11.
17. *Tribuna da Imprensa*, December 3, 1975, 10.
18. Antonieta Santos, "Mais uma de Eliana," *Diário de Notícias*, November 13, 1973, 14.

19. *O Jornal*, August 11, 1972, 3.

20. Stewart, *Portia*, 115–27.

21. "DC Visit Reveals Booker T. Washington's Child in Poverty," *Jet*, July 23, 1970, 30–32.

22. In addition to information from the aforementioned *Jet* magazine article, background on Portia Washington Pittman was enhanced by a phone conversation I had with Portia's grand-niece Nettie Washington Douglass in April 2022.

23. Some of this information is based on the author's conversations with Eliana Pittman.

# INDEX

Page numbers in **bold** indicate illustrations.

addiction, 5, 8–9, 12–13, 36–37, 96–97, 102, 106, 112, 116–17, 124, 129–30, 158, 184, 197, 199, 200, 218, 229, 246n59; to alcohol, 5, 8–9, 12–13, 36–37, 74, 96, 102, 108, 116, 118, 124, 129–30, 184, 197, 199, 203, 229, 246n59; to cocaine, 96–97, 102, 184, 200

African Americans. *See* Blackness

Alemán, Oscar, 6, 58–59, 61–62, 95–96, 146

Alf, Johnny, 147, 159

Alves, Francisco, 75–76, 228

Amado, Jorge, 220

Armstrong, Louis, 3–6, 8, 29, 40, 41, 56–57, 125, 128, 140, 154, 171, 174, 184, 186–87, 194, 203, 214, 224, 230; influence on Booker Pittman, 92, 115, 141, 166, 214; in Paris, 56–57, 62; tour of Latin America, 3–6, 132–35, 138, 142

"aural errancy," 7–8, 112, 124, 186, 235n9

Austin, Claude, 6, 109–10, 127, 146–50, 158

authenticity, 7, 54–55, 72–73, 82, 213–14; and nationality, 71–72, 84–85, 176; and race, 72–73, 179

Baker, Josephine, 5, 207; comparison to Eliana Pittman, 228; France and, 5, 57–61, 146–47; Latin America and, 72, 87

Baker Boys, The (band), 58–59, 61

Basie, Count, 33, 36–37, 39–40, 42, 45–46, 52, 93, 125, 146, 154, 168–69, 191, 219, 230

bebop, **39**, **125**, **128**, **164–65**

Bechet, Sidney, 26, 131, 140, 153–55, 170

Beiderbecke, Bix, 29, 125

Belo Horizonte, 158, 173

Benítez, Isidro, viii, 6, 79–80, 82, 88

Bible, Joe, 155–56

Black Stars (band), 82, 88–89, 91

Blackness, 7–8, **53**, **85–86**; in Argentina, 85–87; Black Americans, 7–8, 15, 21–22, 25, 46–47, 52–55, 59, 72–73, 95, 132, 148–49, 180, 236n3, 253n46; Black French, 53; in Brazil, 185–86, 213–14, 253n42; in Uruguay, 99–100

Blanche Calloway and Her Joy Boys (band), 42–43

Blue Moon Chasers (band), 29–30, 33–34

Blue Serenaders (band), 34–35

Booker Pittman's Boys (band), 91–92, 245n30

bossa nova, 152, 159–60, 166, 169, 175–78, 182–83, 190, 208, 227, 233

Bradford Academy, 17–18

Braggs, Jack, 68, 80, 88

Branco, Waltel, 112–13

Briggs, Arthur, 54, 56–57

*Brotherhood Eyes* (newspaper), 33, 149

Brownsville Affair, The, 20, 237n19

Brubeck, Dave, 3, 176, 186

Buarque, Chico, 205, 207

Buenos Aires, vii–ix, 3, 7–9, 13, 58, 78–79, **81–100**, **104–6**, 109, 112, 115, 119, 122, 137, 140, 153, 167, 175, 178, 200, 211, 224, 254n74; Academia Americana, 84, 93; Alvear Palace Hotel, 83–84, **85**;

Bajo Porteño (neighborhood), 81–82, 97; *confiterías* in, 81–84, 92, 104; La Chaumière (nightclub), 97–98; nightlife in, 81–84, 94–95; Odeon Bar, 83, 92, 104; street life in, 81–82, 94
Byrd, Charlie, 175, 178, 183

Calloway, Blanche, 42–44, 49, 55, 158, 203, 230
Calloway, Cab, 43, 49, 52, 110, 128, 194, 203
Cardoso, Elizeth, 150, 157, 166
Carlito's Jazz-Band, 59, 72
Carlos, Roberto, 197–98
Carnegie Hall, 183, 189
carnival, 72–73, 76, 100, 109, 137, 189, 192, 195, 204, 208
Carter, Benny, 41, 44, 52, 55, 57, 63, 146
casinos, 7–8, 13, 60–61, 68, 71, 74–75, 83, 89, 107–10, 116, 146–47
choro (musical style), 59, 62, 71, 117
cinema and films, **46**, 77–78, 80, **84–85**, **125**, **195**, **215**, 220–21, 254n74; *A Revolução de Maio* (Portuguese film), 145–46; *Absolutamente certo* (Brazilian film), 138; *Ídolos de la Radio* (Argentine film), 85; *The Jungle Book* (Disney film), 213–14; *O jovem tataravô* (Brazilian film), 76–78; *The Sandpit Generals* (American film), 220–21; *Tensão em Xangai* (made-for-television Brazilian film), 151–52
Cold War, 3–4, 8, 132, 186
Cole, Cozy, 5, 52
Cole, Louis, 6, 54, 63, 65, 77–78, 109–11, 120–21, 147–48, 158
Cole, Nat King, 137, 157, 159, 163
Coleman, Bill, 43, 50–52, 146, 230
Cooper, Ralph, 43, 49
Corcodel, Philippe, 119–21, 125–30
Cornélio Procópio (Brazilian city), 118–20, 229
Cotton Club Orchestra, 38, 41, 52
Cotton Pickers (band), 41, 104–7
Cravo Albin, Ricardo, 225–26
"critical fabulation," **10–11**

Crosby, Bing, 78, 114, 159
*Cruzeiro, O* (Brazilian magazine), 6, 120, 134–35, 157, 165

Dallas, 5, 13, **20–35**, 37, 38, 62, 74, 95, 111–12, 113–15, 122, 124–25, 126, 140, 148–49, 179, 192, 201, 203, 219, 222, 237n29; Booker T. Washington High School, 28–32, 192; Deep Ellum (neighborhood), 20–21, 24, 66, 113; Grand Lodge of the Colored Knights of Pythias, 20–21, 192; Tip-Top Club, 25–27, 113, 124, 192
Davis, Peter, 40
de Lima, Father João Linhares, 221–22
de Lourdes Pinhel, Maria, 182
de Magalhães, Jordão, 130, 132–34, 138
Dean, Don (Arthur Dean McCluskey), 84–85
Delaunay, Charles, 55, 60–61
Dixie Pals (band), 84, 87
do Nascimento, Abdias, 156
*DownBeat* (US magazine), 95
Driggs, Frank, 169, 171–72
drugs. *See* addiction
Du Bois, W. E. B., 15, 21–22, 237n23
Duprat, Juan, 93–94, 96

*Ebony* (US magazine), 186, 190–91
Ellington, Duke, 3, 41, 43, 44, 56, 58–59, 62, 71, 82, 92, 110, 146, 169, 176, 186
Elpídio, Fats, 66, 127, 139–41, 146, 242n4
expatriates and expatriatism, **5–8**, **50–52**, **55**, **84–86**, **235n10**, **253–54n54**

Fairmont Heights (Maryland), 20
Farney, Dick, 127, 145, 147, 152, 159–61, 164, 224
Fernández, María, 102–4, 108–9, 122, 142, 246n55
Ferreira, Aurino, 222–23
Firzlaff, Frank, 155–56
Fisk Jubilee Singers, 17, 21
Fitzgerald, Ella, 163, 166

INDEX

Fon-Fon (Otaviano Romero Monteiro), 73, 76, 146
Francisco da Silva, Orlando, 135–36, 142–43, 163–64, 214, 220

gambling, 35, 107–8, 113–14, 191
Gershwin, George, 55, 71, 82, 141
Getz, Stan, 175, 178, 182–83
Gillespie, Dizzy, 3, 39, 52, 128–29, 168, 171, 183, 186
Goudie, Frank "Big Boy," 5, 54, 146
Grande Otelo (Sebastião Bernardes de Souza Prata), 78
Grappelli, Stepháne, 56, 146
Great Depression, the, 5, 22, 35, 46, 50–54
Grezzi, Juan Rafael, 90, 98, 100
Guinle, Jorge, 75–76, 109, 111, 139–40, 152, 164, 211

Hamilton, Ken, 84, 91
Harlem. *See* New York City
Hart, Clyde, 38–39, 41–42, 52, 112
Hawkins, Coleman, 39, 42, 52, 56, 146, 175–76, 230
Hodges, Johnny, 41–42, 44–45, 57, 112, 139, 164, 168–69, 170
Holmes, Charlie, 45–46
Horne, Lena, 157, 193, 196
hospitals and hospital stays. *See* Pittman, Booker Taliaferro
Hot Club de France, 54, 56, 61, 146
hot jazz, 34, 41–42, 53–56, 115, 166, 211; revival of, 125–26, 155

Il Conte Grande (ocean liner), 49–50
infra-exile, 8, 116–7, 130
*Intervalo* (Brazilian magazine), 193, 197–98

Jap Allen's Cotton Club Orchestra, 38, 41–42
Jazz Age, The, 7, 50, 72, 87, 125, 207
Jazz-Band Sul Americano, 58, 60
*Jazz-Hot* (book), 57
Jefferson, Blind Lemon, 24, 124, 140, 219
*Jet* (US magazine), 123, 171–72, 186, 231

Jim Crow South, 5, 20–22, 180, 202, 218, 236n3. *See also* segregation, racial
Jobim, Antônio Carlos (Tom), 166, 176, 182
Johnson, Budd, 25, 29–30, 35–36, 230
Johnson, Dink, 26–27
Johnson, Freddie, 5, 51, 54–55, 57, 72, 92, 146, 230
Jones, Jo, 146, 169
Joyce (Booker Pittman's first wife), 46–48, 53, 62–63, 67–70, 217, 242n52

Kansas City, 5, 13, 28, 31, 33–43, 52, 56, 62–63, 68, 95–96, 115, 124, 140–41, 153, 175, 191, 194, 201, 211, 219, 222, 231
Keti, Zé, 187–88, 190, 222
King, Martin Luther, 157, 210
Kubitschek, Juscelino, 135, 148
Kubitschek, Sarah, 148

Lobo, Fernando, 120–21
Londrina (Brazilian city), 112–18, 120, 248n57
Lopes, Fernando, 179, 197–98, 202, 204, 206, 210, 226
Lyra, Carlos, 176, 183

Maia, Tim, 228–29
*Manchete* (Brazilian magazine), 119–22, 191, 193, 228
Manga, Carlos, 179, 213
Mann, Herbie, 176, 183
marijuana, 35, 51, 96
maxixe (musical and dance style), 59, 61–62, 71
McKinney's Cotton Pickers (band), 41–42
memoirs: Booker Pittman, vii, 9–10, 22–23, 25–26, 31, 33, 36–37, 39, 46, 66, 69–70, 74, 78, 96, 104, 111, 120–21, 123, 210, 231, 236n1, 239n94, 242n52, 242n5, 242n9, 243n18, 245n35, 246n48, 246n57, 247–48n32, 248n43, 249n14, 255n7, 257n52; Ofélia Pittman, 123
Menescal, Roberto, 160, 166, 176–77, 183
Meneses, Elton, 189–90
Mezzrow, Mezz, 10, 155

Mickey, Harold, 84–85, 244n10, 254n74
Millinder, Lucky, 49–52, 62
Mingus, Charles, 169–70
minstrelsy, 40, 43, 46, 184–85
Miranda, Bibi, 5, 58, 145–48; Brazil and, 63, 65–68, 72–73, 77–78, 80, 110, 145–47; Paris and, 58–59, 61–63, 146, 182
Miranda, Carmen, 76, 79, 89, 120, 185, 190–92, 196, 227–28
"Míster Eco," 147, 174, 179, 203–7, 209
Monte Carlo, 49–50, 67
Montevideo, viii, 3, 8, 9, 13, 87, **89–91, 98–101**, 108, 112, 132, 159, 167, 178, 246n50; Jazz Club Uruguayo, 90; Rambla Hotel Casino, 89, 99; Restaurant Municipal "El Retiro," 89, 100; Teatro Trocadero, 98
Moore, Paula, 28–29, 30–31
Moten, Bennie, 39, 42, 52
Moura, Paulo, 127, 145, 152, 159, 232

nationalism, 8, 72–73, 107, 175–76
New Orleans, 141, 146
New York City, 16, **43–47**, 53, 55–56, 112, 169, 171, **187–91**, 240n99; Apollo Theater, 43, 49, 169; Carnegie Hall, 183, 189; Great Northern Hotel, 187–90; Harlem (neighborhood), 5, 7, 13, 41, 43–46, 49–50, 52–53, 55–56, 61–62, 63, 68, 71, 73, 82, 95–96, 115, 121, 124, 140, 146, 153, 169, 171, 175, 189, 201, 211, 219, 222; Harlem Opera House, 43, 49; Little Brazil (neighborhood), 189; *New York Times*, 19, 95, 188

Oito Batutas (band), 59, 71, 86–87
Oito Cotubas (band), 71
Oklahoma City, 33–34
Orchestre Brésilienne, 60–61
Ory, Kid, 26–27
Ortiz Oderigo, Néstor, 139–40, 167
Owens, Willie, 28–29, 30

Paar, Jack, ix, 181–88, 190, 194–95, 224, 253n52

painting: art, 9, 215–19, 224; house, 118, 120–23
Panassié, Hugues, 4, 54, 56–57, 90–91, 112, 134, 140, 155, 158
Paraná (Brazilian state), ix, 9, 12–14, 112–25, 129–30, 137, 144, 147, 152, 194, 200, 201, 203, 211, 218, 224, 229, 247–48n32
Paris, viii, 4–7, **49–64, 66–67**, 70–71, 73–74, 79, 81, 92, 95–96, 109, 119, 124, 140–41, 145–47, 153–55, 175, 182, 203–5, 216–17, 224, 226–27, 230–31, 240n17; La Cabane Cubaine (venue), 51; La Salle Pleyel, 4, 54, 56; Le Bal Nègre (venue), 51; Montmartre (neighborhood), 7, 13, 50–51, 53–54, 62, 73, 82, 96, 146, 154; Montparnasse (neighborhood), 51
Parker, Charlie, 28, 39, 52, 57, 164, 168
Paulistania Jazz Band, 125–29, 141, 144
"Pee Wee" (Argentine journalist), 93–94, 105
Pendergast, Tom, 35. *See also* Kansas City
Perón, Juan, 106
Pittman, Booker Taliaferro: attitudes towards marriage, 46–48, 112; birth of, 20; childhood in Dallas, 22–35; conflicts with father, 22–24, 28, 32–33, 34–35, 88, 124–25; death of, 220–21; funeral of, 221–23; hospitals and hospital stays of, 13, 103–4, 108, 119, 130, 131, 201, 207–8, 214–15; to Joyce, 46–48, 63, 69–70, 240n99; to Ofélia Pittman, 10, 136–38, 141–43, 250n25
Pittman, Eliana (Eliana Leite da Silva), vii, ix, 9–10, 70, 135, 142–44, 150, 162–79, 181–200, 202–9, 211–16, 219–23, 224–32, 234, 240n17, 252n1
Pittman, Fannie, 27, 172, 231
Pittman, Ofélia (Ofélia Leite de Barros), 9–10, 70, 123–24, 135–38, 141–44, 150, 152, 155–58, 163–66, 168–70, 172–75, 178–79, 185–87, 191–93, 195–96, 198–206, 208, 213–16, 219–21, 224–29, 231–34, 252n1; *Por você, por mim, por nós*, 9–10, 232
Pittman, Sidney, Jr., 23, 31–32, 231, 238n52

Pittman, William Sidney, 5, 18–24, 27–28, 31–35, 88, 114, 124, 149, 211, 236–37n19, 238n52, 251n51
Poole, Gene, 84, 93
Porter, Cole, 50–51, 71, 82, 154
Porto Alegre, 180, 203
*Por você, por mim, por nós*, 9–10, 232
Pratt, Alfred, 43, 50, 52, 54, 56, 61–63, 65, 67–68, 73, 80, 89, 110
Price, Lovett, 68–69, 80, 88
Price, Sammy, 25, 230

race and racism, 7, 15–16, 20–21, 43, 46–47, 57, 59, 78–79, 85–87, 100, 104, 144, 148–49, 155–56, 178–81, 229–30; marriage and, 46–48, 240n99; "racial democracy," 7, 180; segregation and, 7, 15–16, 20–21, 78, 156, 180
radio and radio stations: in Argentina and Uruguay, 72–75, 79, 83–85, 89, 95–96; in Brazil, 26, 72–75, 109–10, 126–27, 129, 132, 144, 148, 164–66, 193, 212; in the United States, 32, 52, 159
Rangel, Lúcio, 122, 139–40, 149, 211
Ratip, Ahmed "Mike," 84, 104–5, 107–8
recording industry, 43, 195–96, 201
records, LP and EP: *Booker Pittman Plays Again* (LP, 1959), 139–41, 153; *Booker Pittman + Sax Soprano = Sucesso* (Booker Pittman EP, 1965), 190; *Eliana e Booker Pittman* (LP, 1962), 166; *É preciso cantar* (Eliana Pittman, LP, 1966), 176, 208–9; *The Fabulous Booker Pittman* (LP, 1960), 152–55, 158, 172; *Getz/Gilberto* (Stan Getz & João Gilberto LP, 1964), 183; *Jam Session* (B. Pittman and Dick Farney, LP, 1961), 160–61; *News from Brazil—Bossa Nova* (Eliana & Booker Pittman LP, 1963), 176–78; *Tô Chegando, Já Cheguei* (Eliana Pittman LP, 1974), 227
Rehder, Paulo, 179–80
Reinhardt, Django, 56, 58, 146
*Revista do Rádio* (Brazilian magazine), 174, 192

Rímac, Ciro, 145–46
Rio de Janeiro, vii, viii, ix, 3, 7–9, 13, 57, 59, 61–62, 63–64, **65–80, 83–84**, 89, 99, 109–12, 115, 118–20, 122, 127, 138, 144, **146–49, 150–61**, 164–67, **173–81**, 191–93, 195–98, 199, **201–4, 206–14, 221–23, 224–27, 228–29**, 232–34; Botafogo (neighborhood), 151, 222, 233; Bottles Bar, 157, 233; Café Nice, 74, 243n36; Cassino Atlântico, 63, 69–71, 74–76, 78, 80, 107–8, 145, 147, 150, 233; Cemitério São João Batista, 222–23, 228, 233–34; Copacabana (neighborhood), vii, 9, 63, 68–76, 82, 107, 109–11, 127, 141, 146, 150–52, 155–56, 178, 180–81, 194, 199, 213, 215, 224, 232–33; Copacabana Palace, 63, 69, 107, 109–10, 127, 146, 150, 152, 178; Hotel Glória, 147; Ipanema (neighborhood), 182, 199; Lapa (neighborhood), 242n13, 68–69; the Little Club (nightclub), 152, 155, 157, 165, 173, 233; the Manhattan Club, 155–56, 181; Mei Ling (nightclub), 111, 147, 150, 233; Museu da Imagem e do Som, ix, 211–12, 225–26; Porão 73 (nightclub), 193–94, 197; Teatro Municipal, 108, 144–45, 147, 150, 247n9; Vogue (nightclub and hotel), 110–11, 147, 155, 233
Rivera (Uruguayan city), 100–105, 108, 115, 119, 130, 246n50
Roach, Max, 169–70
Rosa, Noel, 71, 74, 76, 109, 145–46
rumors and gossip, 103, 119–21, 147, 178, 197–98
Rushing, Jimmy, 33–34, 169
Russo, Adrián, 88–89, 92

samba, 59, 61–62, 68, 71–72, 74–76, 107, 113, 127–28, 131, 145, 152, 159, 166, 176–78, 182, 187–90, 195–96, 207–8, 211, 215, 227
Salvador (Brazilian city), 66, 152, 174, 220–21
Salvador, Dom Um, 167, 195
Santana do Livramento (Brazilian city), 101–4, 108–9, 203

Santos (Brazilian city), 61, 106–9
São Paulo, 61, 83, 108, 111–13, 115, 117–19, **125–29, 130–45**, 148, 150, 152, 158, 160, 163–64, 175, 178, 180, 197, 201–2, 206, 211, **214–21**; Bosque da Saúde (neighborhood), 143; The Cave (nightclub), 131, 136–38, 141, 147; Congonhas Airport, 3–4, 132–34, 159; Parque Ibirapuera, 4, 126–27; Teatro Paramount, 4–5, 133, 135, 232; Vila Olímpia (neighborhood), 219–21
São Paulo Dixielanders (band), 125–29, 141, 144
segregation, racial, 7, 15, 20–21, 78, 156, 180–81
Silva, Romeu, 58–61, 63, 65–66, 70–72, 74–80, 83, 86, 145–46, 242n4
Silver, Horace, 229
Sims, Trezevent, 29, 31
Sinatra, Frank, 159, 163, 166, 193
*Síncopa y Ritmo* (Argentine magazine), 83, 90–91, 92–94, 105
slavery, 14–15, 133, 211
Smith, Bessie, 24, 42, 66, 193–94
Smith, Buster, 28, 33, 40–41
Smith, Willie "the Lion," 45–46, 170
Soviet Union, the, 132
SS *Siqueira Campos* (ocean liner), 65–66
State Department, United States, 3, 8, 132, 186
Stone, Jesse, 34–35
Stretton, Gordon, 72, 87
swing era, 33–34, 39, 41, 50–53, 71, 73–75, 83, 85, 88–91, 98, 107, 140, 148, 152–54, 158–59, 168, 184, 211–12, 216, 222
Swing Stars, The (band), 88–92, 98

tango, 58, 71, 79, 81, 83, 107–8, 211
Tate, Buddy, 38, 169
television, ix, 9, 127, 143–44, 150–52, 165–66, 175, 176–78, 183–90, 193, 194–97, 201, 202, 204, 205, 213, 226–27, 229, 254n74
television channels, Brazilian: Canal 7 (São Paulo), 127; TV Excelsior (São Paulo), 178–79, 181, 213; TV Globo, 197, 203; TV Record (Rio de Janeiro), 132, 173; TV Rio, 150, 165, 179, 207; TV Tupi (Rio de Janeiro), 138, 151–52, 206
television channels, US: CBS (New York City), 183; NBC (New York City), 181, 183–90, 192
television shows, Brazilian: *Fahrenheit 2000*, 206; *Globo em 2 minutos*, 229; "Musical Carioca," 165
television shows, French: Guitares et Copains, 226–27
television shows, German: *Der Goldene Schub*, 226
television shows, US: *The Ed Sullivan Show*, 183; *The Jack Paar Program*, 183–90; *Merv Griffin Show*, 201; Run for Your Life (NBC fiction series), 192; *The Tonight Show*, 181
territory bands, 33–34, 38–39
theater and theatrical performances, 21, 43–44, 46, 50, 54, 57–58, 78, 81, 86–87, 158, 189, 196, 205–7, 228–29
Tuskegee Institute (university), viii, 15–19, 21, 32, 149, 192, 201, 230, 236n3

Ukon, Masao, 126, 160, 214
*Up from Slavery*, 15, 211

"vagabond internationalism," 7–8
Valle, Marcos, 207–8
Vargas, Getúlio, 72, 107
*Variety* (magazine), 187–88
Veloso, Caetano, 207, 213
Vidossich, Eduardo, 125–29, 141, 160
Villa-Lobos, Heitor, 157–58
violence and abuse, physical, 16, 20, 22, 32, 47, 158–59, 218, 231–32

Wackwitz, Hank, 126
Waller, Fats, 39, 44–45, 125, 128, 140
Walter Page's Blue Devils (band), 33–34
Washington, Booker Taliaferro, ix, 3, 5, 14–25, 28, 32, 47, 163, 171, 173, 186, 189–90, 192, 201–2, 210–11, 219–20,

230–31, 236n3, 236–37n19, 238n52; family legacy and, 163, 171, 173, 186, 189–90, 192, 219–20, 230–31; impact on Booker Pittman, 13–14, 47, 201–2, 210–11; life and death of, 14–18; *Up from Slavery*, 15, 211

Washington, David, 68, 80, 88–89, 91

Webb, Chick, 41, 44, 146

Webster, Ben, 38–42, 52, 111–12, 168–69

Whiteman, Paul, 59, 85, 87

Wooding, Sam, 55, 72, 87

World War I, 24, 45, 65

World War II, 6, 52, 65, 98, 107, 109–10, 126, 132, 159, 230

Wyer, Paul, 6, 87, 89

Young, Lester, 33, 39, 52

Zaccarias, Aristides, 146–47

# ABOUT THE AUTHOR

**Jason Borge** is professor of Latin American Culture and Media at the University of Texas at Austin, where he teaches courses on popular music, film, and literature. Previous publications of his include *Tropical Riffs: Latin America and the Politics of Jazz* (Duke University Press, 2018).